GARDNER

VOL. I
COMMANDOS AND WAR HEROES

COREY GARDNER

GARDNER

GARDNER is the name on my grandfather's tombstone and as I stood there, I said to myself, "That name stands for something." A man's surname is his Y – chromosome. It is passed from father to son, from generation to generation. A man's surname is his mark, his reputation, and his legacy. It is a man's duty to protect the honor of the family name.

It came from your father,
It was all he had to give,
So it's yours to use and cherish
As long as you may live.
If you lose the watch he gave you,
It can always be replaced,
But a black mark on your name, son,
Can never be erased.
It was clean the day you took it
And a worthy name to bear.
When I got it from my father
There was no dishonor there.
So make sure you guard it wisely –
After all is said and done,
You'll be glad the name is spotless
When you give it to your son.

- Anonymous

GARDNER

VOL. I
COMMANDOS AND WAR HEROES

COREY GARDNER

ISBN: 978 – 1 – 7339298 – 0 – 6

Front Cover: Lt. Bill Gardner (Copyright © William E. Gardner)
Back Cover: Col. Alexander Gardner (Public Domain)

Contact information:
GARDNERCA89@aol.com
GARDNERsurname@aol.com
GARDNERbook@gmail.com

Corey Gardner

I dedicate this book to my father, Larry Gardner for giving me his name and to my mother, Jenny Gardner for suggesting I write a book on the "notorious" Gardners. Thank you for always being there for me. Thanks for having my six.

Your son,

Corey Gardner

ACKNOWLEDGEMENTS

Larry Gardner, my father for being my hero, a real man.

Jenny Gardner, my mother for being my hero, always being there.

Leroy Gardner, a distant cousin, author of _GARDNER/BALLARD and ALLIED FAMILIES_, for being a great genealogist who has passed on the torch of becoming the Gardner family historian.

Thomas Edward Gardner, Jr., my great uncle, for family stories on the Gardner family.

Steve Gardner, a distant cousin from Waco, Texas, professor at Baylor for information on my Gardner family in Texas.

Sarah LeBeau Bourque, a friend, for photograph transfers.

Ray Hicks, second cousin, son of Amelia Gardner Hicks Harper, my great aunt, for photographs of the Gardner family.

Frank Cook, a late distant cousin from Hattiesburg, Mississippi, for being a great genealogist and a great friend who always complimented my research.

Brady Cloud, U. S. Marine and U. S. Army soldier, for being a great friend and mentor.

Steve Gardner, a distant cousin from Dallas, Texas, attorney – at – law, for information on my Gardner family in Texas.

Bill Gardner, U. S. Navy SEAL, for being part of this book and helping out so much, along with being a great friend, along with his lovely wife Ann, and their two sons Jon and Owen Gardner.

Bud Gardner, U. S. Navy SEAL, for being part of this book, along with his fellow SEALs for information.

Jason Gardner, U. S. Navy SEAL, for being part of this book and contributing photographs.

GARDNER
Vol. I: Commandos and War Heroes
Corey Gardner

GARDNER Vol. I: Commandos and War Heroes contains over 40 biographies on warriors, mercenaries, knights, commandos, and war heroes surnamed Gardner. They range from Confederate generals to fighter pilots to Navy SEALS, ranging from war heroes of the American Revolution to the Civil War to both of the World Wars, Vietnam, Iraq, and Afghanistan all with the last name Gardner. It lists all the brave men who died in Vietnam and Iraq, biographies on the bravest men who served their country on battlefields all over the world with the proud family surname Gardner.

GARDNER
Vol. I: Commandos and War Heroes
Chapter I: Warriors, Mercenaries, and Knights
Gardner
Sir Osborn Gardner, Knight of Jerusalem
Sir Wyllyam Gardner, the Assassin of King Richard III
Sir Christopher Gardner, Knight of the Holy Sepulchre
Lion Gardner, America's First Hero
Col. Jas. Gardner, the Christian Hero
Admiral Alan Gardner, the 1st Baron Gardner
Col. William Linneaus Gardner, the Cavalry Officer
Col. Alexander Gardner, the Mercenary

Chapter II: Commandos and War Heroes
Col. Thomas Gardner, the Revolutionary War Hero
Carswell Gardner, the Bodyguard of the Washington Family
Capt. Thomas Gardner, the Privateer
Gen. Sir Robert Gardner, the British Artillery Officer
Sgt. Maj. William Gardner, the Scottish Warrior
Colour Sgt. George Gardner, the Irish Warrior
Col. Charles Gardner, the Hero of the War of 1812
Maj. Gen. Franklin Gardner, the Confederate General
Brig. Gen. William Montgomery Gardner, the Southern Gentleman
Lt. Col. Robert D. Gardner, the Confederate Officer
Sgt. Tom Gardner, the Confederate Cavalryman
Pvt. Billy Gardner, the Rebel Sharpshooter
Brig. Gen. John Lane Gardner, the Union Officer
Maj. Asa Gardner, the Yankee Officer
Capt. Joseph Gardner, the Freedom Fighter
Sgt. Barnard Gardner, the Yankee Sniper
Pvt. Peter Gardner, the Yankee Soldier
Commander Frank Gardner, the Sailor
Capt. Cecil Gardner, the Fighter Pilot
Capt. George Gardner, the Flying Ace
Capt. Percy Gardner, the Canadian Warrior

2nd Lt. Cyril Gardner, the World War I Hero
1st Sgt. John H. Gardner, the American Warrior
Col. Larry Gardner, the Aviator
Maj. Madison D. Gardner, U. S. Army Soldier
Capt. Phillip Gardner, the Victoria Cross Recipient
Capt. William A. Gardner, the American Ace
Sgt. Frank Gardner, U. S. Marine
Cpl. Cliff Gardner, the World War II Hero
Alvy Gardner, the UDT Operator
Lt. Russ Gardner, the Canadian Officer
Meredith Knox Gardner, the Cold War Hero
Capt. Alan Gardner, the Green Beret
Capt. Gregory Gardner, U. S. Army Ranger
1st Lt. Jim Gardner, U. S. Army Ranger
Lt. Bill Gardner, U. S. Navy SEAL
Master Chief Bud Gardner, U. S. Navy SEAL
Master Chief Jason Gardner, U. S. Navy SEAL
Vietnam War Heroes, 9/11 Heroes, Iraq War Heroes, and Medal of Honor Recipients

GARDNER
Vol. II: Cowboys and Gunslingers
Corey Gardner

GARDNER Vol. II: Cowboys and Gunslingers contains over 30 biographies on cowboys, gunslingers, outlaws, and lawmen surnamed Gardner. The volume has bad men and good men, who lived on the outside of the law and the men who enforced the law, including a list of fallen heroes who died in the line of duty to serve and protect. They range from mountain men of the Rockies to Indian fighters on the frontier to deadly gunfighters surnamed Gardner.

GARDNER
Vol. II: Cowboys and Gunslingers
Chapter III: Cowboys and Indian Fighters
Johnson Gardner, the Mountain Man
Big Phil Gardner, the Desperado
Thomas Gardner, the Arizona Pioneer
Alfred Gardner, the Texas Ranger
Arizona Bill Gardner, the Army Scout
Col. John H. Gardner, the Cavalryman
Dan Gardner, the Texas Cattleman
John Gardner, the American Cowboy
Joe Gardner, the World Roping Champion
George Gardner, the Wild West Performer
Clem Gardner, the Rodeo Star

Chapter IV: Gunslingers
Lewis Gardner, the Gunfighter
Pliny Gardner, the Pistoleer
Lige Gardner, the Texas Pistolero
Tom Gardner, the Fastest Gun Alive
Charles Gardner, the Colorado Kid
Jeremiah Gardner, the Plainsman
Buck Gardner, the Texas Bad Man
Roll Gardner, the Rifleman
Matt Gardner, the Shootist
The Gardner Gang
Gunslingin' Gardners

Chapter V: Outlaws
Roy Gardner, the Outlaw
Johnny Gardner, the Gangster
Peck Gardner, the Mob Boss of East Chicago
Bud Gardner, the Mobster
Roger Gardner, the Most Wanted Fugitive
Ronnie Lee Gardner, the Convicted Killer
Death Row Inmates

Chapter VI: Lawmen

GARDNER
Vol. III: Athletes and Authors
Corey Gardner

GARDNER Vol. III: Athletes and Authors contains over 20 biographies on prize – fighters, athletes, politicians, authors, and entertainers surnamed Gardner. They range from a British boxing champion to an American wrestling champion to a Hollywood actress to a spy novelist. The volume has all of those who stepped into the spotlight onto a stage or in a ring surnamed Gardner.

GARDNER SURNAME MEANINGS AND ORIGINS

The Gardner surname is derived of various meanings and origins. All family surnames are derived from various meanings and origins, resulting in different families of no relation with the same name. My research will hopefully lead all Gardner families to discover the family patriarch of every Gardner family.

The Gardner surname is most likely derived from the Old French word, 'gardaigne', pronounced 'gar – day – nyuh', meaning a bodyguard, guardian.

Common theory suggests that John the gardener became John Gardner. Although it is stated as fact, it is actually theory with no evidence to present itself. However, if this were true, the Gardner surname would be as common as Smith, Baker, Taylor, Parker, Miller, and other occupational surnames.

The Normans are said to have brought surnames to England after the Norman Conquest of 1066 and most genealogical sites, as well as books, claim without evidence that the Gardner surname derived from the Old Norman French word 'gardin' meaning garden, therefore derived from a gardener. Again, they claim that the word 'gardinier' meaning a gardener was a combination of the Old Norse word 'gard' meaning enclosure and that it is combined with the French word 'jardinier' meaning a gardener. However, it was not until the 17th Century when the word 'gardener' was first used to describe a horticulturist or a landscaper.

The Old Norman French Dictionary by Robert Kelham, states the word 'garden' means lord warden, while the word 'gardior' means guard. This is evidence of a dictionary of words during the 11th to 12th Centuries of the Gardner surname most likely originating from someone who was a deputy constable or a guardsman. For example, many would assume the Farmer surname is derived from John the farmer, but it actually means a tax collector.

People during the Middle Ages spoke a variety of languages and dialects that are extinct, only a handful of words surviving in today's languages. Everything was written in Old Latin. Old French was a common dialect and the Normans brought surnames to England at the same time Old English was still used by the Anglo – Saxons, while the native Gaelic of Scotland and Ireland is still found in the Celtic countries.

The reason for different families is different meanings and origins of the surname. According to the latest census records from 2000, I estimate there are about 300, 000 people surnamed Gardner, Gardiner, and Gardener. The Gardner surname is found in the United States, England, Wales, Scotland, Ireland, Northern Ireland, South Africa, and Australia, as well as all over the world.

GARDNER SURNAME MEANINGS
Old Latin
Gardinis – to guard, to protect

Gardinigus – battle companion

Guardianus – guardian (Medieval Latin)

Gardenarius – gardener

Ortolanus – gardener

Hortolanus – gardener

Old French
Gardaigne – pronounced 'gar – day – nyuh', meaning bodyguard, guardian

Gardeor – guard

Jardinier – gardener

Garden – guardian

Gardenc – guardian (Germanic derived from guarder)

Gardir – guardian

Old Norman French
Garden – lord warden, lord keeper

Gardior – guard

Garder – guardian

Anglo – Norman French
Gardeinrie – guardian; office of warden

Garden – guardian

Gardayne – bodyguard, guardian

Gardiner – garder; gardener; guardian; guardsman

Gardin – guardsman, protector, one who defends

Old English/Old Norse/Anglo – Saxon
Gardene – spearmen

Gardena – spear Danes; warlike Danes

Gar – weapon, spear, javelin

Dyn – sound, noise, alarm

Gardar – stronghold

Gar Danes – spearmen

Old Gaelic (Scotch – Irish Celtic)
Gairden – fortress

Garda – police, enforcer

Middle English
Gardyn – guardian

Garden – guardian

Gardeyn – guardian

Gardian – guardian

A dictionary of the Norman or Old French language; collected from such acts of Parliament, Parliament rolls, journals, acts of state, records, law books, ancient historians, and manuscripts as related to this nation. To which are added the laws of William, the Conqueror, with notes and references by Robert Kelham, 1717-1808; Great Britain. Laws, etc. (William I); Wilkins, David, 1685-1745, states the word 'garden' means lord keeper, lord warden, and 'gardior' means guard while 'garth' means a garden, while 'garner' means to warn, to fortify.

Therefore, a 'gardener' in Old Norman was possibly a deputy constable. Swedish occupation surname expert Bertil Thuresson had found 28 examples of the surname le Gardiner, one in 1308 as William the Gardyner, while there was also a man in 1279 named Robert le Garder, as well as the word 'guardene' in the sense of a guardian.

Sir William de Jardin was said to have led the Norman cavalry in 1066 at the Battle of Hastings during the Norman Conquest of England. He invaded by sea, he and his knights gathering horses. It was at the Battle of Hastings, Sir William de Jardin defeated the Anglo – Saxons in the Norman Conquest of England.

"Since the family-name of Gardiner was first introduced into the British Isles as Des Jardine, it remained unchanged in the areas of heavy Norman population for perhaps a century before it became De Jardine, then Jardine, Gardine, etc. In the areas more heavily populated by the Romans it became De Gardino, D'Gardino, etc. In the areas more heavily populated by the Britons, Danes and Saxons, it appeared in the 12th Century as De Jardin, Jardin, Gardin, etc...Geographical location also played a major role in determining how family names were spelled. In Scotland, for example, Gardiner was known as Gardenkirk. In Wales it was spelled Gardynyr. Across the line in Gloustershire it was slightly altered to read Gardyner..."
– *Gardiner: Generations and Relations* by Thomas Richard Gardiner

There was also a Gardar, meaning "stronghold", or Gardarike, owned by the Rus Vikings along the Baltic.

The Gar Danes, also known as Gardena, were warlike Danes who fought with spears. The Danes were Vikings from Scandinavia. The Old English word 'Gar Danes' or 'Gardena' means warlike Danes who fought with spears.

References:
Gardner & Allied Families by Col. W. L. Gardner, Gateway Press Inc., Baltimore Press, 1979, Library of Congress # 79 – 64274
Gardiner: Generations and Relations by Thomas Richard Gardiner
https://www.wilcuma.org.uk/who-are-the-anglo-saxons/danes-other-tribal-immigrants/ (Beowulf; Gar Danes)

GARDENS AND GUARDS

The "one hundred rolls" in 1273 list the landed gentry as Geoffrey le Gardiner, of Oxfordshire, Ralph le Gardiner, of Huntingdonshire, and William le Gardiner, of Lincolnshire. William le Gardeiner is listed as a land owner in 1273 owning land in Rutland, England. The word 'gardyner' during the Medieval period either means guardian, or perhaps gardeners were not the same entirely as today.

If it does indeed mean a 'gardener', then they were likely yeomen, or middle class, being land owners. The tough gardener of the medieval era was likely a farmer, someone who owned land and sold produce, the office of a 'gardinarus' was an important profession of the Middle Ages. The gardener used a spade along with other tools, and it is likely he was someone of physical strength.

According to *The Medieveal Garden* by Sylvia Landsberg, the Medieval gardener was distinguished from the common laborer. According to *A Little History of British Gardening* by Jenny Uglow, gardening was central to all of the orders, including the Crusaders of the Knights of the Temple of Solomon, better known as the Knights Templar, and the Knights of St. John of Jerusalem, better known as the Knights Hospitallers. Finally, according to *Royal Gardeners* by Alan Titchmarsh, the Royals were involved in gardening and landscapes.

The gardener was likely a strong man of the Middle Ages who was part of the army, along with the miller, the carpenter, as well as other outdoorsmen. As for those who lived in monasteries, they were not gardeners, but only would grow medicinal herbs. It was only Royals who enjoyed ornamental gardens for plants and flowers. The word 'gardener' in the modern sense as far as flowerbeds, lawns, and ornamental gardens arrived in the 16th Century and later.

A gardener could become a knight during the Medieval era, especially if the Knights Templar and Knights Hospitaller practiced gardening within the military orders.

Adam, the first man, was the Gardener of Eden. He was a gardener and shepherd. His son, Cain was a gardener. It is because Cain only offered some of his fruits and vegetables, instead of his best produce to God as a sacrifice, his sacrifice was not accepted while his brother's lamb was accepted, therefore leading him to kill his brother who was the shepherd.

Richard Plantagenet, known to history as King Richard the Lionheart, adopted the Plantagenet surname meaning 'to plant a genista' in Old Latin, from his ancestor, a famous knight named Sir Geoffrey de Bouillon who often wore a genista flower in his helmet.

It is possible the Gardner surname could be a combination of the word 'garde' meaning guard and 'jardinier' meaning gardener. The yeoman were middle class farmers and gardeners who were also expert archers who protected the royalty. It is possible 'Gardinier' was a guardian and a gardener combined.

The Gardner surname seems to have the meaning of a guardian. The word 'gardyner' is found to mean a guardian in the 16th Century in England. Surnames were formed from the 11th Century onward, so the fact the word 'gardyner' was being used in the context of a guardian is evidence.

Essex Wills (England): 1571-1577 - Page 256
https://books.google.com/books?isbn=0880820160
Frederick George Emmison, Essex Record Office, Friends of Historic Essex (Essex, England) - 1982 - Snippet view - More editions
My wife shall be 'gardyner' [guardian] and governor of Robert until he is 23. To her my tenement with 2 gardens called Brettons in Mill Street in Terling, also all my goods. I make John my executor and John Orvice clerk, vicar of Terling, my ...

Essex Wills (England): 1558-1565 - Page 78
https://books.google.com/books?id=DBYrAQAAIAAJ
Frederick George Emmison - 1982 - Snippet view
My wife shall be bound to Richard in such reasonable bond as he and his 'gardyner' [guardian] shall think convenient before she enter on the said farm, to save Richard harmless. She and he shall do with my wethers and rams now on the ...

Elizabethan wills of South-West Essex - Page 18
https://books.google.com/books?id=kaMWAQAAIAAJ
Frederick George Emmison - 1983 - Snippet view
I ordain my overseer John Stoke, which shall be 'gardyner' [guardian] to my child for my goods and lands till she is 21 or marriage. Witnesses: James Gates, Thomas Boyer, John Poore. Proved 5 February 1564/5 [f.24]

The word 'gardyner' was written in quotations, likely the recorder writing the Old Norman French meaning of the word 'gardyner', and the editor from the 20th Century later writing in [guardian] to inform readers of the meaning of the word 'gardyner'.

Sources claim the surname Gardner is derived from the Saxon words 'gar' meaning weapon, 'dyn' meaning sound, noise or alarm, with the termination of 'yr' ending, stating the Gardner surname means warrior.

References:
GARDINER – GARDNER FAMILY HISTORY
www.familysearch.org

CLAN GARDYNE

Scottish Clan Gardyne was from the barony of Gardyne in the parish of Kirkdon in the county of Angus in Scotland. They built a strong tower, Gardyne Castle, which extended to the 17th century. Clan Gardyne men feuded with Clan Guthrie in the 16th Century. Patrick Gardyne was killed in 1578 and in retaliation, Thomas Gairden killed Alexander Guthrie. David Gardyne, the tenth Laird sold the castle and acquired the estate of Lawton.

Clan Gardyne has a boar's head which is associated with the De Gardinis family of lowland Scotland and it is also associated with the Gardner family of Ireland.

CLAN JARDINE

Clan Jardine is a Scottish lowland clan, founded by Sir William du Jardin, a Norman French knight, his name meaning 'of the garden'. Members of Clan Jardine would change the name Jardine to Gardine to Gardner over time, it being a sept of the clan. It is possible the De Gardino family and Clan De Jardine family are connected.

CLAN GORDON

Clan Gordon is a Scottish clan known as the House of Gordon. The first Gordon was Richard of Gordon who was the grandson of a famous knight during the time of King Malcolm III of Scotland. Richard of Gordon was Lord of the Barony of Gordon in the Merse during the 12th Century. His descendant, Sir Adam Gordon was sent with King Louis of France to Palestine and that he later supported Sir William Wallace in 1297 to recapture the Castle of Wigtown from the English. Another member was Bertram de Gordon who wounded King Richard the Lionheart with an arrow.

The Gardner surname is believed to be a sept of these three Scottish clans.

References:
www.wikipedia.com

GARDNER DNA PROJECT

I estimate that there are about 10 to 15 different Gardner families that originated in the British Isles of England, Scotland, Wales, Northern Ireland, and Ireland. A man's Y – chromosome is passed from father to son. The following are labels of where each Y – chromosome originated.

R1b – DF19 originated in Scandinavia, most likely from the Saxons/Vikings:
Daniel Gardner, my 5x Great Grandfather, Virginia to South Carolina
Jas. Gardner, 1790 – 1832, lived in Maryland and Pennsylvania
Charles Justice Gardiner, born about 1830 in Kentucky
Thomas Gardner, born April 1st, 1810
Andrew Gardner, 1793 – 1862, emigrated in 1824 from Northern Ireland

R1b – U152 originated in Italy, Switzerland, Alpine Celtic/Romans:
Isaac Gardiner, 1677 – 1730, listed as R1b – U152, Z46
William Gardner, born about 1791, Sutton, Surrey, England, Z49

R1b – U106 originated in Germany, most likely Frankish/Anglo – Saxons:
Alexander Gardiner, born 1735 Fermanagh, Ireland
William Gardner, born 1790 Lanarkshire, Scotland
Samuel Gardner, born 1787 Virginia, died 1854 Maryland
Thomas Gardiner, born 1695, Ireland
John Gardner/Garner, Shropshire, England
John Gardner, born 1780 North Carolina, died 1850 Tennessee
Luke Gardner, born 1776 Virginia, died 1855 Indiana
George Gardiner, born 1599 England, died 1677 Rhode Island (large family)

R1b – DF27 originated in the Iberian peninsula of Spain, Gaulish/Celtic:
Matthew Gardner, c. 1775, Wishaw, Lanarkshire, Scotland
John Gardner, 1624 – 1682, Isle of Wight, Virginia

R1b – L2 originated in the British Isles, most likely from the Celts:
George Gardner, Edgecombe County, North Carolina
Geo. Gardiner, born about 1690 descended from Niall of Nine Hostages
Percy Willis Gardner, 1894 – 1974
Henry Gardner, born 1820 Hereford, England

I1 originated in Scandinavia, most likely Anglo – Saxons/Vikings:
Lion Gardiner, although some claim he was related to Rhode Island family

I2 originated in Eastern Europe, Slavic, possibly Goths:
John Gardner, born about 1820 County Galway, Ireland
Cleophas Gardner, born about 1852 and died about 1928 Ohio
Thomas Micheal Gardner, born 1786, died 1869 Tennessee

E1b originated in Africa, most likely Romans:
Gardner, emigrated from Germany or Austria

J1 originated in the Middle East:
Gardner, originated from Hungary

J2 originated in the Middle East:
Thomas Gardner, born 1591, Nantucket, Massachusetts (prominent family who also claims to descent along with George Gardiner descendants to Sir Osborn Gardiner)
William Gardner, possibly Guardineer from France, born about 1750 and lived in Northampton County, North Carolina

G2 originated in the Caucasus, most likely Etruscans/Romans:
Gardner, originally Desjardins, emigrated from France

N originated in Russia, most likely Goths/Saxons/Vikings:
Jas. Gardner, born 1779, died 1858 Pennsylvania, emigrated from Northern Ireland

R1a originated in Central Asia, found in eastern Europe, Saxons/Vikings:
Alexander Gardner, born about 1762, Scotland
William Gardner, born about 1750, England

There are 10 to 15 different Gardner families originating in the British Isles, some people often mistaking their lineage, while 15 to 20 different families originated from continental Europe later adopted the surname.

I estimate that there are 15 to 20 different Gardner families who adopted the surname while immigrating from Germany, France, Poland, the Netherlands, Italy and elsewhere with surnames originally being Gaertner, Gartner, Baumgartner, Guardineer, Gardenier, Galareneau, Desjardins, Gargotta, Garton, and many others, along with African – Americans and Native Americans adopting the surname.

We also have to remember that people have been adopted or surnames changed over time, which can lead to confusion.

https://www.familytreedna.com/public/GardnerGarner?iframe=ycolorized

Courtesy to Robert Gardner

Gardner Y – DNA Project is the best way to determine which Gardner families are related.

GARDNER FAMILIES

The Gardner families are derived from the following meanings:

Gardinis meaning to guard, to protect in Old Latin.
Gardayne meaning guardian, bodyguard in Old French.
Gardenarius meaning the office of a gardener in Old Latin.
Gardeinrie meaning the office of a warden in Anglo Norman French.
Gardinier meaning gardener or guardian in Old Norman French.
Gardena meaning warlike Danes in Old English.
Garden meaning lord warden in Old Norman French.
Garden meaning protector in Anglo Norman French.

Families with surnames such as Gaertner, Baumgartner, Galaraneu, Gargotta, Desjardins, Gardenier, Garnier, and a number of other surnames from France, Germany, the Netherlands, Italy, Poland, Austria, Switzerland, and all over changed to Gardner when migrating to the United States or elsewhere.

CONCLUSION ON GARDNER SURNAME MEANING

My conclusion on the meaning of the Gardner surname is that there are a number of meanings and origins. It seems there were about two different types of families. There were the 'Le Gardyner' family and the 'De Gardyner' family.

Those with 'le Gardyner' had the meaning of "the", for either the occupation of a gardener or a guardian or a guardsman.

Those with 'de Gardyner' had the meaning of "of", for a place name or tribe.

I personally believe the Gardner surname is derived from the Old French word 'gardayne' meaning bodyguard, guardian, or the Old English word 'Gardena' meaning warlike Danes who fought with spears.

Chapter I: Warriors, Mercenaries, and Knights

"Just at that moment, when the crowd were rushing on us, their swords high in the air, I managed to fire the two guns, and literally blew them into the air." – Col. Alexander Gardner

GARDNER

The first man named Gardner by many accounts was a knight named Sir Osborn Gardner. His name was read as Sir Osbern le Gardyner. However, the first man by most family histories list Sir Roger de Gardiano as the Patriarch.

Sir Roger de Gardiano, Knight, also spelled Roger de Gardino, was most likely the Patriarch of the first Gardner family.

Sir William de Gardino, Knight, also spelled William de Gardinis, died around 1263 in England.

Sir William de Gardinis, Knight, (c. 1234 – c. 1289) was Lord of Langley, Salop and Ixening, Suffolk, England and married Alexandra de la Haye.

Sir Thomas de Gardinis, known as Sir Thomas de Gardyn, known as Sir Thomas de Gardinor, Knight, (c. 1260 – c. 1328) was a Knight of Ixning Co., Suffolk, England, Lord of lands at Leysdon in the Isle of Sheppey and at Fringford, Cogges and Somerton, Oxfordshire.

It is from 1287 to 1302, he is listed as Sheriff of Gloucester and it is from 1299 to 1300 he is listed as Sheriff of Cambridge and Huntingdon, in 1298 listed as Sir Thomas de Gardinor.

Citations

1. [S1844] G. Andrews Moriarty Jr., "Genealogical Research in England: Gifford-Sargent," *The New England Historical and Genealogical Register* 73 (Jul - Oct 1920): 231-237, 267-274; 74 (Jan-Apr 1921): 57-63, 129-142: 130, further cited as Moriarty, "Gifford-Sargent."

It is from 1180 to 1195, names William, Osmond, Gervase, Umfrey, and Richard de Gardino, of Normandy appear. Sir Bertrand de Gardannes was a Knight Templar in 1195 as a commander in Rou, France. It is in 1202 that William Le Gardenier possessed estates in Rutland.

http://waughfamily.ca/Jardine/Jardine%20Clan%e2%80%94Mountain%20St ates%20Branch.pdf

It is in 1215 Sir William de Gardino is witness to King Robert the Bruce of Scotland. The Ragman Rolls recorded in 1304 William du Gerdyne owning land around Kendal, the name spreading to England. It is said some of Jardine clansmen became known as the Gardine family of Applegirth. Sir William de Gardine received a grant of lands and the barony of Hertishyde in Lanarkshire from King David II during the 14th Century for his loyalty and service.

A History of the Castles, Mansions, and Manors of Western Sussex by Dudley George Elwes states:

"Of Boley or Bogheley, Dallaway states that it was a very ancient manor farm, held in the time of King John by William de Gardinis by the tenure of knight's service, and that his posterity, known by the name of Jarden or Jordan, retained it for several centuries."

Antiquities of Shropshire, Volume 6 by Robert William Eyton states:

"On October 16, 1251, the King granted the land of William Burnell, the Outlaw to William de Gardinis all that pertained to the King, of all manner of debts of the said William Burnel."

Calendar of the Close Rolls Preserved in the Public Record Office by England Court of Chancery states:

Oct. 27, 1328, Salisbury,

"John de Gardinis, executor of the will of Thomas de Gardinis, knight, puts in his place Thomas de Clif and Edmund de Herethorp, clerks, to prosecute the execution of a recognizance for 140 marks made in chancery to Thomas de Guy son of Robert le fitz Wyth."

Knights of Edward I by Charles Moor (1929) states:

GARDINO, Sir Arnulph de, Kt., A Kt. Of Flanders and envoy of John, C., of Namur, to K., sent by Ghent, Bruges, Ypres, Lille, and Douay. Safe conduct for him, returning to Flanders with household, horses, and baggage, 9 Ap. 1303 (P. R.).

GARDINIS, Sir William de, Kt., (Gardyn, Gardino). Sealed, 1266. Two bars. A label of 5 points (Birch). Aged 30, s. h. of Wm. De. G.

Knights

Sir Roger de Gardiano, Knight
Sir Theobald de Gardinis, Knight
Sir Humphrey de Gardino, Knight
Sir Patrick de Gardinus, Knight
Sir William de Gardino, Knight, fought at Battle of Falkirk, Scotland
Sir William de Gardinis, Knight, 1200s, Lord of Langley, Suffolk, England
Sir Thomas de Gardinor, Knight, Sheriff of Cambridge, Oxford, England
Sir Osbern le Gardyner, Knight Hospitaller, 1128 to 1191, Crusader
Sir Theobald Gardyner, Knight
Sir Anthony Gardyner, Knight, 1200s, Otley, England
Sir Richard Gardyner, Knight, Sheriff, Lord Mayor of London
Sir Wyllyam Gardynyr, Knight, 1485 allegedly killed King Richard III
Sir Thomas Gardiner, Knight

Most of the medieval soldiers named Gardiner and Gardyner were archers during the Hundred Years' War according to https://www.medievalsoldier.org/

Walter Gardiner, archer
John Gardiner, archer
Batkyn Gardiner, archer
John Gardiner, archer
John Gardiner, Man – at – Arms
Nicholas le Gardiner
William Gardiner, archer
William Gardiner archer
Robert Gardiner, Holborn, Middlesex
Thomas Gardiner, Esquire, Man – at – Arms, Gissing
Roger Gardiner, archer
Matthew Gardiner, archer, Lancashire
John Gardiner, archer
John Gardiner, archer
Richard Gardiner, Man – at – Arms
John Gardiner, archer
John Gardiner, archer
John Gardiner, archer
John Gardiner, archer
John Gardiner, archer (foot)
John Gardiner, archer
Robert Gardiner, archer
Robert Gardiner, archer
John Gardiner, archer
John Gardiner, archer
John Gardiner, archer
John Gardiner, archer
Henry Gardiner, archer
Simon Gardiner, archer
Smehy Gardiner, archer
Robert Gardiner, archer (foot)
Robert Gardiner, archer (foot)
Robert Gardiner, archer
Robert Gardiner, archer
William Gardiner, archer
William Gardiner, archer
Robert Gardiner, Man – at – Arms
William Gardiner, archer

John Gardyner, archer
John Gardyner, archer
John Gardyner, archer
John Gardyner, archer
John Gardyner, archer
John Gardyner, archer

John Gardyner
John Gardyner

William Gardyner, Esquire, Man – at – Arms
William Gardyner, archer
William Gardyner, archer

Thomas Gardyner, Man – at – Arms, standing force, Scotland
Thomas Gardyner, archer, Lancashire
Thomas Gardyner, Jr.
Thomas Gardyner
Walter Gardyner, archer
Walter Gardyner, archer
Roger Gardyner, archer
Richard Gardyner, archer

John Gardin, archer
John atte Gardyn, archer
Perrin du Gardyn, archer

John Gardener, archer
John Gardener, archer
John Gardener, archer
John Gardener, archer
John Gardener, archer
John Gardener, archer
John Gardener, archer

John de Gardener, archer, Cheshire

Thomas Gardener, Esquire, Man – at – Arms
Thomas Gardener, Esquire, Man – at – Arms
Thomas Gardener, archer

Robert Gardener, Man – at – Arms
Robert Gardener, archer
Robert Gardener, archer
Robert Gardener, junior, archer

Henry Gardener, archer (mounted)
Henry Gardener, archer
Henry Gardener, archer
Henry de la Gardener, archer

Richard Gardener, archer
Roger Gardener, archer

List of People Surnamed Gardner

Anger Gardiner, 1166, London
William le Gardinier, 1199, owned land in Rutland
William le Gardenier, 1199, Lancashire
William Gardin, 1218, Huntingdon
John ate Gardyne, 1296, Sussex
Walter le Gardiner, 1292, London
Robert le Garder, 1273, Oxford
John le Gard, 1273, Cambridge
William del Gardin, 1273, Oxford
Thomas del Gardin
Geoffrey le Gardiner, 1273, Oxford
Richard le Gardiner, Cambridge
Ralph le Gardener
William le Gardiner
William Gardinar
Nicholas Gardener, 1329, Peebles, Scotland first name recorded
Gilbert Garthener, 1327 to 1377, Freeman of York
Gilbert de Iikelely, garthener, Edward III
Thomas Garchiner, 1379
Thomas Gardiner

Knights of England surnamed Gardner

Sir Thomas Gardner
Sir Thomas Gardner
Sir Thomas Gardner
Sir Thomas Gardner
Sir William Gardner
Sir William Gardner
Sir William Gardner
Sir Edmund Gardner
Sir Robert Gardiner
Sir John Gardiner
Sir Thomas de Gardino
Sir Arnulph de Gardino
Sir William de Gardinis

References:

https://www.medievalsoldier.org/dbsearch/
Proceedings of the Newcastle – upon – Tyne Conference, 1985 edited by Peter R. Coss, Simon D. Lloyd
Knights of King Edward I by Charles Moor
The Knights of England: A Complete Record from the Earliest Time..., Volume 1 by William Arthur Shaw

GARDNER COAT OF ARMS

Gardner

GARDINIS

CLAN GARDYN

GARDNER

Gardner Coat of Arms is listed as "Sable on a chevron or, two lions combatant with an engorged boar's head". It is said this Gardner Coat of Arms belonged to a Gardner in Ireland, perhaps Northern Ireland. It is possible the Gardner family was descended from Clan Gardyne of Forfar, Scotland, descended from knights surnamed de Gardinis and de Gardino of Normandy.

GARDNER

This shield design was utilized by many Gardners who made changes in the colorations and crest. The following are some of the variations of this design: (1) arms of Gardner, or Gardener of Willingham and Bishop's Norton, both located within the West Lindsey District of Lincolnshire has a differing crest that shows a red Saracen's head full faced, erased at the neck, and wearing a golden cap; (2) a Gardener of Calais; (3) a Gardener of Northall, Lincolnshire had the same arms with a crest showing a Turk's head topped with a gold and blue turban; (4) the Gardiner Baronetage at Roche Court, near Farnham, Hampshire has similar arms with a silver shield. The crest is also a Saracen's head; and (5) arms belonging to a Gardiner of Wigan, Lancashire.

GARDNER

These arms were granted 24 April, 1680 to a Gardner of Berwick-on-Tweed in Northumberland, England. The black shield is described as containing an ermine chevron between three white bugle-horns with gold strings. The crest, *(not shown)*, features a golden clasped book and a falcon in full flight. Similar arms were granted to a Gardner of Middlesex, England. These arms feature a silver reindeer's head as the crest. A Gardner of Kirton, Lincolnshire has a blue shield with a chevron between three white bugle-horns.

GARDNER

Armorial bearings similar to this coat of arms were bestowed upon Gardiner of Berkshire and neighboring Buckinghamshire. These arms feature a red shield containing an embattled chief of gold and a chevron between white three griffins' heads. The crest is a blue griffin's head charged with three yellow bends.

GARDNER

This coat-of-arms belongs to a Gardner of Torwoodhead, located in Stirlingshire, Scotland. The silver shield contains a fret of four red pieces with four blue hearts and in every interstice a rose. The crest, *(not shown)*, is a griffin's head. The motto is "In virtute et fortuna." Similar arms were granted in 1789 to a Lord Gardiner of Madras, India. The silver shield with a blue border featured a red fret with a rose in every interstice of the second between four gold hearts. The crest contains a golden crown and seven battle axes. The motto of this Gardiner is "Omnia supcrat virtus".

GARDNER

This coat-of-arms belongs to a Gardner of Torwoodhead, located in Stirlingshire, Scotland. The silver shield contains a fret of four red pieces with four blue hearts and in every interstice a rose. The crest, *(not shown)*, is a griffin's head. The motto is "In virtute et fortuna." Similar arms were granted in 1789 to a Lord Gardiner of Madras, India. The silver shield with a blue border featured a red fret with a rose in every interstice of the second between four gold hearts. The crest contains a golden crown and seven battle axes. The motto of this Gardiner is "Omnia supcrat virtus".

GARDNER

These armorial bearings have been attributed to a Gardner of Scotland. The distinctive and intricate shield is red and contains continuous white fretting holding four blue hearts. Between the fretting are eleven white roses. The crest shows a red griffin's head with gold ears.

GARDNER

These armorial bearings were granted in 1683 by Sir Richard Carney, Ulster King of Arms, to William Gardiner, a merchant, of Dublin, Ireland. The gold shield features a blue griffin with wings expanded. In the black chief are three silver pheons, (*head of a dart*), the points down. The crest, as shown, features a gold griffin's head, with a green collar, between two blue wings. The motto that accompanies these arms is, "Honor rewards industry".

GARDNER
Clan Badge

Special thanks and courtesy to Fred Siler for the artwork on the Coats of Arms

Note: According to *The British Herald; Or, Cabinet of Armorial Bearings of the Nobility* by Thomas Robson, there are 60 different Coats of Arms belonging to the Gardner families from the spellings of Gardyn, Gardinis, Gardener, Gardiner, and Gardner.

References:
Burke's General Armorie
Reitstap's Armorial General

SIR OSBORN GARDNER

Gardner Coat of Arms: "Arms: Or, on a chevron, gules between three griffins' heads erased, azure, two lions counter – passant of the field, or. Crest: On a wreath, a Saracen's head, couped at the shoulders, full faced proper; on a head a cap turned up gules and azure, and bearded sable. Motto: *Praestro pro patria*" – The Herald's College

Sir Osborn Gardner, Knight of Jerusalem, was a Crusader. He was a Knight Hospitaller, known as the Knights of St. John, the Knights of Jerusalem. Gardner was deadly, feared, respected, and a warrior of God.

The Coat of Arms is said to date back to 1150 after the Second Crusades and in 1484, King Richard III established the Heraldry of Arms which mentions the Gardner Coat of Arms.

Surnames have a variety of meanings and origins. The Gardner surname derived from the Old French word "gardaigne", pronounched 'gar – day – nyuh', meaning "bodyguard". It possibly derived from the Anglo – French word "gardien" with the suffix "er", meaning "gardien – er". The Old Norman French word, "garden" means "lord warden". The Anglo – Norman word 'gardiner' means gardener or guardsman. The Anglo – Norman word 'gardienirie' means warden. The Anglo – Saxon word "gar" means weapon; "dyn" means sound; and "yr" means ending; therefore "Gardynyr" means 'one who clashes with arms' in Old English.

It is possible he was a gardener before he was knighted for bravery, his name possibly being 'le Jardinier' meaning "the Gardener", later mispronounced over time with a "G". There was a Norman knight named Sir William de Jardin, whose name means "of the garden". There was also a knight named Sir William le Carpentier, his name in French meaning "the Carpenter", due to his strength in battle. Perhaps, Sir Osbern le Gardynyr, if his name had the meaning of "the Gardener", it was due to his strength in battle.

"The race of the Gardiners is traced from the reign of Henry I, and comes of Anglo – Saxon stock." – *Baltimore: Biography, page 296*

Sir Osbern le Gardynyr was born in 1128 by most accounts in Wallonia, Belgium, north of France.

"The Gardiner family has been prominent in Great Britain as far back as the First Crusades." – Asa Bird Gardiner

Sir Osborn Gardner was said to be a Knight Hospitaller, known as the Knights of Jerusalem, the Knights of St. John. The Knights Templars were loyal to the Pope, while the Knights Hospitallers were loyal to King Baldwin. The Hospitallers were stationed in Acre, Israel.

It is said a document was found which stated **'O. Gardyner'** was the **'Personal Protector'** of King Baldwin of Jerusalem. It is possible he was a 'gardayne' meaning bodyguard in Old French. However, it is also said Sir Osbern Le Jardin (meaning the Garden) in French, was part of the bodyguard of King Baldwin and it was known that the military orders such as Templars as well as the Hospitallers practiced gardening.

Legend states Gardner killed a Saracen or chopped through the shoulder of a Saracen who was bearing down on King Richard the Lionheart in 1191 at the Battle of Acre. The Siege of Acre was the deadliest event of the whole period of the Crusades for the Christian ruling class of the east, but it was a key victory for the Crusaders and a serious defeat for Saladin, of the Muslims. It was from August of 1189 to July of 1191 that the bloodiest fighting of the Crusades occurred.

It is said Sir Osborn Gardner was described as being **"disliked by the English courts due to his strong French accent, but he was feared and respected."**

Afterwards, he was granted land in England for his heroic actions and retired to his manor in Wigan, England, it being stated: **"Sir Osborn Gardiner, Knight, Lord of the Manor of Horul (Oral) on Douglas River in Wigan Parish, West Derby Hundred, County of Lancaster, and Lancashire, England."**

Courtesy to Joel Gardner for the drawing of the Coat of Arms
Courtesy to David Gardner for anecdotal information

References:
Baltimore: Biography edited by Clayton Colmon Hall
http://tedgardner.org/gardname.htm

SIR WILLIAM GARDNER

"Richard's horse was trapped in the marsh where he was slain by one of Rhys Thomas' men, a commoner named Wyllyam Gardynyr." – Alleged Welsh account of the Battle of Bosworth.

Sir William Gardner, the Assassin of King Richard III, was the man who by many accounts killed the last English monarch to be slain on the battlefield. It was his one action which led to the Reformation. On August 22nd, 1485 at the Battle of Bosworth, Gardner ended the Medieval Era with the swing of his battle axe.

"Rhys ap Thomas troops found Richard's crown in the hands of William Gardyner and brought it to Henry. Henry knighted William Gardyner, Gilbert Talbot, Humphrey Stanley and Rhys ap Thomas on the battlefield as well as a number of his captains. It is to be noted that neither Thomas nor William Stanley were honoured. All present cried 'God save King Henry'. He was then crowned with Richard's crown – that is, the coronet from Richard's helmet – by Thomas Stanley. Traditionally, he is said to have been crowned on the hill now known as Crown Hill, on the slopes of which the Stanley's were probably stationed. The when Richard was finally struck down. The hawthorn was to feature in heraldry for Henry Tudor from the beginnings of his reign." – *Jasper Tudor: The Man Who Made the Tudor Dynasty* by Terry Breverton

Wyllyam Gardynyr was born in either 1432, 1446, 1451, or 1455 by various accounts in Beaconsfield, South Bucks District, Buckinghamshire, England. Accounts give his father's name as Sir Thomas Gardner, Knight, and his mother was Anna De La Grove Gardner. However, his father also may have been John Gardyner of Exning in Suffolk.

It is believed his brother or cousin was Sir Richard Gardyner, Knight, Sheriff, Alderman, Auditor, and Lord Mayor of London while accounts state his father was John Gardyner of Exning in Suffolk. Sir Richard Garydner was one of the wealthiest men in England. He was a member of the Mercers' Company of London, serving as a longtime Warden and Master of the Worshipful Company of Mercers. Sir Richard Gardyner was also Master of the House of "Hospital of St. Thomas de Acon", the headquarters of the Knights of St. Thomas of Acre. Gardyner also served as Merchant Staple of Calais.

Conspiracy theories suggest the Gardner brothers (or cousins) were forming an army to defeat King Richard III, siding with King Henry VII of Wales. The Gardner family were cloth barons. Sir Richard Gardyner also had possession of the Crown jewels. It was in October of 1470, Lord Warwick marched on London, Sir Richard Gardyner stated:

"Few words, my lord, and I have done," said Richard Gardyner — "there is no fighting without men. The troops at the Tower are not to be counted on. The populace are all with Lord Warwick, even though he brought the devil at his back. If you hold out, look to rape and plunder before sunset to-morrow. If ye yield, go forth in a body, and the earl is not the man to suffer one Englishman to be injured in life or health who once trusts to his good faith. My say is said." – *The Last of the Barons, Volume 20* by Edward Bulwer-Lytton

It was during the War of the Roses, King Richard III of England fought against King Henry VII of Wales.

On August 22nd, 1485, Wyllyam Gardner killed King Richard III with a halberd axe. He was the man with King Richard III's crown. Afterwards, he was knighted on the battlefield.

Gardner married Helen Tudor (sometimes referred to as Ellen Tudor or Eleanor Tudor), the illegitimate daughter of Jasper Tudor, brother to King Henry VII. Some suggest he married her before and that he was no common skinner, but others suggest they were married after the battle. There are a number of different accounts of who his children may have been as well as various accounts of his death.

Children of Sir Wyllyam Gardyner and Helen Tudor:
Richard Gardyner (c. 1485 – c. 1548) Sergeant of Arms to King Henry VIII.
William Gardyner (c. 1486 – c. 1549) married Elizabeth Mitchell; he died in The Grange, Bermondsy, Surrey, England.
Thomas Gardyner (c. 1487 – c. 1542) Chaplain to King Henry VIII.
Stephen Gardyner (c. 1490 – c. 1555) was Bishop of Winchester and Lord Chancellor of England; his last words were allegedly, "Erravi cum Petro, sed non flevi cum Petro (Like Peter, I have erred, unlike Peter, I have not wept.)

Accounts suggest Wyllyam Gardynyr died in the fall of 1485, as he was closing one of his shops, he was murdered by supporters of King Richard III.

However, record states Sir William Gardner died in 1506 and was buried at St. Mary Churchyard in Bury St. Edmunds, St. Edmundsbury Borough, Suffolk, England.

"William Gardiner actually signed his name 'William Gardynyr' which may indicate that he was of Welch origin. Why William Gardiner was allowed to marry into the Royal family remains unclear, but historians have hinted that it was because of his aid to Henry VIII, then Earl of Richmond, in defeating Richard III, in the Battle of Bosworth Field, near Leicester on 22 August 1485. Jean Molinet, a Chronicler from Burgundy, covering the battle, described the scene in this manner.

(Taken from the book 'The Making of the Tudor Dynasty, by Roger Thomas)

"During the vigorous hand-to-hand fighting with axe, sword and pike, both Richard III and Henry Tudor, each surrounded by a vanguard, watched from the side lines, a safe distance apart. Richard, so confident of victory that he was wearing his crown, could observe from a higher level along the hillside, that his own personal vanguard was superior to Henry's and decided to end the battle quickly by slaying Henry Tudor. Sir William Stanley was standing by with an uncommitted force of 3,000 men, ready to rout the losing side. Richard III spurred his horse and in quick time, with his vanguard, engaged Henry in combat.

As Richard went for Henry to deliver his mortal blow, one of Henry's men, a Welsh halberdier, intervened, knocking off Richard's Crown, then giving one mighty swing, smashed Richard's helmet into his skull. Seeing that their leader was slain, his vanguard began to withdraw and immediately Sir William Stanley ordered his men after Richard's fleeing troops, thus ending the Battle in Henry's favor'. Richard's Crown was recovered from a thorn bush and later placed on the head of Henry Tudor who then proclaimed himself King of England.

This act of slaying Henry's adversary in an otherwise losing situation was the most important single effort in the making of the Tudor dynasty, and thus allowed the marriage of William Gardiner, believed to be the Welsh halberdier, to Helen Tudor a few months later.

There has been some dispute as to how a person from the English Midlands could be described as a Welshman by the Burgundy writer, Jean Molinet, but the solution to the mystery is found in the book itself concerning the number of Sir William Stanley's warriors who, in their eagerness to give support to Henry, then Earl of Richmond, pressed ahead to join forces with Henry as his forces moved through Wales, on their way to engage Richard III's army. Jean Molinet may have had no way of knowing from where the halberdier hailed. Although much information on him is lacking, this William Gardiner remains as the earliest member of our Gardiner line from whom I can trace our ancestry on a generational basis, with a great degree of certainty.

William Gardiner and his wife, Helen Tudor, resided on the south bank of the Thames River just across from the walled city of London, prior to the establishment of any town, in an area that was then known simply as "The Bank". His magnificent home was located somewhere between the more recent towns of Bermondey and Southwalk in the county of Surrey. He also retained many of his holding in the Midlands near Oxon Ford, now known as Oxford.

"Wyllyam Gardynyr, son of (father unknown) and of (mother unknown), born in 1450 in Midlands, Oxfordshire, England; died 1495 in The Bank, Surrey, England. He married in 1485, in London, England to Helen Tudor, daughter of Jasper Tudor. William Gardiner, who was born circa 1450, married Helen Tudor, first cousin to Henry VII, as found on Betham's Genealogical Table DCX in Guildhall Library, London, England. William Gardiner and his wife, Helen Tudor, resided on the south bank of the Thames River just accross from the walled city of London, prior to the establishment of any town, in an area that was then known simply as "The Bank". His magnificent home was located somewhere between the more recent towns of Bermondey and Southwalk in the county of Surrey. He also retained many of his holdings in the Midlands near Oxon Ford, now known as Oxford." – *Gardiner Generations & Relations, Vol. I* by Thomas Richard Gardiner

Photograph is public domain, retrieved on April 2nd, 2019 at https://en.wikipedia.org/wiki/Battle_of_Bosworth_Field#/media/File:Battle_of _Bosworth_by_Philip_James_de_Loutherbourg.jpg

References:
Gardiner: Generations and Relations by Thomas Richard Gardiner, in 1991, self-published

SIR CHRISTOPHER GARDNER

"There is in the early history of New England no more singular episode than that of Sir Christopher Gardiner. Who the man was, and why or whence he came, or whither he subsequently went, are mysteries unlikely now to be ever wholly solved; but he none the less stands out in picturesque in congruity against the monotonous background in colonial life. It is somewhat as if one were suddenly to come across the portrait of a Cavalier by Vandyck in the vestibule of a New England village church." - *Harper's New Monthly Magazine, Volume 66*, edited by Henry Mills Alden

Sir Christopher Gardner, Knight of the Holy Sepulchre, was America's first outlaw. It is likely he was America's first playboy, a bigamist with wives in England, France, and a mistress in the New World. Gardner was a knight – errant.

He arrived in Massachusetts Bay Colony in 1630 in Boston and was known by William Bradford, governor of the Plymouth Colony. He had servants with him along with Mary Grove, a young woman, whom he called his cousin, but according to Bradford, she was his mistress. It is said that how he arrived was something of a mystery as no ships had sailed for New England that would account for his presence.

It is believed Sir Christopher Gardner was a secret agent for Robert Gorges, who owned a charter for the land. The Puritans had a truce with Gardner, but then learned he had two wives in Europe. The first Lady Gardyner in London wanted him to return to England. The second Lady Gardyner in Paris wanted him dead.

The magistrates in March 1631 ordered the knight – errant to be returned to England on the *Lyon*. However, Gardner fled into the woods with his sword, gun, and dagger. William Bradford hired the Pakanoke Indian tribe hunt the knight – errant and capture him.

The Pokanokets waited and caught Gardner separated from his gun and sword, then confronted him. He drew his knife, but was overpowered by the tribesmen. Afterwards, he was handed over to Bradford and the Puritans, being returned to Boston.

Gardner traveled back to England in 1632 and later joined in a case against the Puritans trying to force them to yield their claims in New England to Robert Gorges. His story has been retold and fictionalized in Henry Wadsworth Longfellow's poem, *The Rhyme of Sir Christopher*, stating:

"It was Sir Christopher Gardiner,
Knight of the Holy Sepulchre,
From Merry England over the sea,
Who stepped upon this continent
As if his august presence lent
A glory to the colony.

You should have seen him in the street
Of the little Boston of Winthrop's time,
His rapier dangling at his feet
Doublet and hose and boots complete,
Prince Rupert hat with ostrich plume,
Gloves that exhaled a faint perfume,
Luxuriant curls and air sublime,
And superior manners now obsolete!

He had a way of saying things
That made one think of courts and kings,
And lords and ladies of high degree;
So that not having been at court
Seemed something very little short
Of treason or lese-majesty,
Such an accomplished knight was he."

Photograph courtesy to the New England Historical Society
References:
The New England Historical Society

LION GARDNER

Lion Gardner, America's First Hero, was a soldier and settler in the New World. He founded the first English settlement on Long Island. His legacy is Gardiners Island.

He stood 6' 2, with a broad forehead, and a strong jawline.

Lion Gardner was born in 1599 in England. He was a military engineer in the service of the Prince of Orange in the Netherlands. Gardner was hired by the Connecticut Company in 1635 to oversee construction fortifications in the new colony.

It was in July of 1635, he left the Netherlands with his wife Mary Willemsen Deurcant, who was Dutch, on the ship *Batcheler*, and arriving in November of that year landing in Boston. On November 28th, Governor John Winthrop noted: **"Here arrived a small Norsey bark of twenty-five tons sent by Lords Say, etc, with one Gardiner, an expert engineer or work base, and provisions of all sorts, to begin a fort at the mouth of the Connecticut. She came through many great tempests; yet, through the Lord's great providence, her passengers, twelve men, two women, and all goods, all safe."**

Gardner commanded the Saybrook Fort during the Pequot War from 1636 to 1637, which he took part in leading the English militia.

Lion Gardiner in the Pequot War by Charles Stanley Reinhart, painted on February 22nd, 1637, displayed at the Manor House on Gardiners Island from a July 2007 exhibit by the East Hampton Historical Society on Gardiners Island. (Public Domain)

He purchased an island from the Montaukett tribe located between North Fork and South Fork in Suffolk County, New York. The grant made Gardner the owner of the plantation and was no way connected with New England and New York. Gardner called it the Isle of Wight and it has since become known as Gardiners Island.

Lion Gardiner fathered three children named David, Mary, and Elizabeth, his son being the first white child born on the Isle of Wight. It was in 1660 he wrote his account titled *Relation of the Pequot Warres* which was lost, but in 1809 rediscovered and published in 1833, years later. Lion Gardner died in 1663 in East Hampton, New York in the South End Cemetery by Town Pond.

Photograph of Statue by the East Hampton Historical Society

References:
https://en.wikipedia.org/wiki/Lion_Gardiner
Relation of the Pequot Warres by Lion Gardiner

COL. JAS. GARDNER

Col. Jas. Gardner, the Christian Hero, was a Scotsman in the British Army. He was a sinner who found Christianity. Gardner was one of the **"bravest and most gallantest men in Britain."**

"In personal appearance, colonel Gardiner was tall, well proportioned, and strongly built, his eyes of a dark grey, and not very large; his forehead pretty high; his nose of a length and height no way remarkable, but very well suited to his other features; his cheeks not very prominent, his mouth moderately large, and his chin rather a little inclining to be peaked. He had a strong voice, and lively accent; with an air very intrepid, yet attempered with much gentleness: and there was something in his manner of address most perfectly easy and obliging, which was in a great measure the result of the great candour and benevolence of his natural temper; and which, no doubt, was much improved by the deep humility which divine grace had wrought into his heart; as well as his having been accustomed from his early youth, to the company of persons of distinguished rank and polite behaviour."

"It is extracted from a journal of the historian Wodrow, where it appears under date May 1725, as having just been taken down from the mouths of various informants:

"From him and others, I have a very pleasant account of major Gardiner, formerly master of horse to the earl of Stair, and now lately on the death of Craig, made major of Stair's grey horse. He seems to be one of the most remarkable instances of free grace that has been in our times. He is one of the bravest and gallantest men in Britain, and understands military affairs exactly well. He was a lieutenant or a captain many years ago in Glasgow, where he was extremely vicious."

James Gardner was born on January 11th, 1688 in Carriden near Edinburgh, Scotland and was educated at Linlithgow, Scotland. He was the son of Captain Patrick Gardner from Torwood – head. Captain Gardner died abroad from fatigue with the British forces in Germany after the Battle of Hochstet.

His brother, Robert Gardner, died at age 16 in 1695 at the Siege of Namur.

It was his mother, Mrs. Gardner who was a strong Christian woman. As a lad, James Gardner had fought in three duels and suffered from a scar on his right cheek when he was just eight years old. It was at 14 years old he received an ensign's commission in a Scots regiment in the Dutch service in 1702, and it was then he began his military career.

On May 23rd, 1706, as a young officer, Gardner fought against the French at the Battle of Ramillies where he was shot in the mouth, it exiting through his neck, surviving the wound. He immediately believed God had preserved him by miracle. The next morning he was captured by the French and nursed back to health by a group of women who attempted to persuade him to acknowledge the Catholic Faith, but he still chose no religion.

Gardner served with distinction under the Duke of Marlborough and in 1706 was made lieutenant, earning a cornet's commission in the Scots Greys, commanded by the Earl of Stair. On January 31st, 1714, he was made captain – lieutenant in Colonel Ker's Regiment of Dragoons. They took Preston in Lancashire in 1715 where Gardner led the action. He then was made an aid – de – camp and accompanied the Earl of Stair on his celebrated embassy to Paris, France.

Capt. Gardner was his master of the horse and on July 22nd, 1715, received a commission as a captain. He became a captain in June of 1724, and then in July of that year earned the rank of major. Then in 1729, he earned the rank of lieutenant – colonel and by April of 1743, he was commissioned as a colonel.

Col. Gardner, a tall, handsome officer, took advantage of the lewdness of the Parisian court, distinguishing himself in the court of the regent Orleans and it was here he was known as "the happy rake" for his conduct of vice.

It was in the middle of July of 1719, then Capt. Gardner had a religious awakening. He was about to meet a married woman to have an affair. And while he was waiting, he came across a book.

He began reading a book that his mother had slipped into his baggage. It was titled _The Christian Soldier_ by the Puritan Thomas Watson. As he read he saw a bright light fall upon the book.

"He thought he saw an unusual blaze of light fall on the book while he was reading, which he at first imagined might happen by some accident in the candle. But lifting up his eyes, he apprehended, to his extreme amazement, that there was before him, as it were suspended in the air, a visible representation of the Lord Jesus Christ upon the cross, surrounded on all sides with a glory".

Gardner raised his eyes and gazed at a vision of the Lord Jesus Christ upon the cross and the vision surrounded on all sides. The voice seemed to say, **'O sinner, did I suffer all this for thee, and are these the returns?'**

He felt guilt that he deserved eternal damnation, but instead Jesus Christ had died for his sins.

Two months later, he was assured with the words of Scripture:
"Christ Jesus: whom God hath set forth to be a propitiation through faith in his blood, to declare his righteousness for the remission of sins."
(Romans 3:25 – 26).

Gardner spent from 4 to 6 a. m. in the morning reading the Bible and refrained from swearing. This was even while he was on active military service. He also mixed with high society, such as with the Prince and Princess of Wales.

On July 11th, 1726, Maj. Jas. Gardner married Lady Frances Erskine, daughter to the fourth Earl of Buchan, having thirteen children, five surviving, two sons and three daughters. It was during his time as a family man he either lived at his villa of Bankton in East Lothian or moved around through the country with his regiment. It was in 1742, he embarked for Flanders and his regiment spent time at Ghent.

On September 21st, 1745, Colonel Gardner fought at the Battle of Prestonpans, the first major conflict of the Jacobite Rising. It was between the Jacobite army loyal to the Roman Catholic Charles Stuart versus the government forces, the British Army led by Sir John Cope, loyal to Hanoverian George II.

The Highland charge of the Jacobites broke through the British troops. It was in the final skirmish, Col. Gardner, a senior royal commander, was wounded by a bullet in the left breast and fought on, then being shot in the right thigh, bringing down the insurgents around him. The tall, gallant officer rode toward a party of his men in need, commanding them to **"Fire on, my lads, and fear nothing."**

A highlander advanced towards him with a scythe on a long pole and gave the officer a deep wound on his right arm, causing him to drop his sword. A number of others dragged him from his horse. Another highlander hit him on the back of the head with an axe.

One of his servants ran towards Col. Gardner who waved and stated: **"Take care of yourself."** It was the last words the gallant officer spoke. The servant fled to the mill, being saved.

The Jacobites stripped the fallen officer of his watch, shirt, and boots. Although he was still breathing, he was unable to speak and his men brought him to The Manse of Tranent where he died in the arms of the minister's daughter during the night on his own land. On September 24th, 1745, he was buried and honored.

English writer Phillip Doddridge wrote a biography on him, detailing his life and career. The play *Colonel Gardiner: Vice and Virtue*, written by playwright Andrew Dallmeyer was performed as part of Prestonpans' 2009 Homecoming celebrations. Colonel Gardner is believed to be mentioned as a "tall, handsome and active, though somewhat advanced in years", by a character in the novel titled _Waverly_ by Walter Scott. It was in 1853 a memorial was dedicated to him at the Bankton House approximately where he fell.

It was at his funeral, Phillip Doddridge, his biographer, quoted the Scripture stating: **'Be thou faithful unto death, and I will give thee a crown of life'.** (Revelation 2: 10).

References:
https://www.electricscotland.com/history/other/gardiner_james.htm
https://en.wikipedia.org/wiki/James_Gardiner_(British_Army_officer)
Bare – Arsed Banditti: Men of the '45 by Maggie Craig

ADMIRAL ALAN GARDNER

Admiral Alan Gardner, 1st Baron Gardner, was one of the most dashing officers of the Royal Navy. He was one of most daring captains of the Georgian era and a Major – General of Marines. Capt. George Vancouver, a fellow British Royal Navy officer, named Gardner Canal in British Columbia, Canada, Mount Gardner in Australia, and Port Gardner in Washington State in his honor.

The British naval officer was described as having heavy black eyebrows and a strong jaw, and known to a drinker, like all sailors.

Alan Gardner was born on April 12th, 1742 in Uttoxeter, England, the third surviving son of Lieutenant Colonel William Gardner of the 11th Regiment of the Dragoon Guards, while his mother was Elizabeth Farrington. His older brother was Maj. Valentine Gardner, a British Army officer. The Gardner family originated in Colerain, Northern Ireland, Alan's grandfather being William Gardner who defended the Protestant city of Londonderry during a legendary 105 – day siege in 1689, the family originating with Theophilus Gardner.

On May 1st, 1755, Alan Gardner joined the *Medway 60* attached to the Western Squadron. Then in January of 1758 he moved to the *Dorsetshire 70* and fought at the Battle of Quiberon against the French on November 20th, 1759 in one of history's greatest naval battles, being commissioned in March of 1760 as a lieutenant. He joined the *Bellona 74* which was part of Admiral Sir Edward Hawke's fleet and took part in the capture of the *Courageux 74* in August of 1761 after Captain Robert Faulknor succeeded to the command.

On his 20th birthday, April 12th, 1762, he was promoted to commander of the sloop HMS *Raven 10* and was posted captain in May of 1766, joining the *Preston 50* which he took out to the West Indies in August of that year.

On May 20th, 1769, Gardner married a Jamaican heiress named Susannah Hyde Gale, daughter of a plantation owner named Francis Gale and his wife Susanna Hall. The couple were married in Kingston, Jamaica and had ten children. They had nine sons and one daughter.

His son Lord Alan Hyde Gardner, 2nd Baron Gardner, was a Vice – Admiral; his son William Henry Gardner was a Major – General; and his son Francis Farrington Gardner was a Rear – Admiral.

After his marriage, he commanded the frigate *Levant 28* and after paying her off, he returned to England the next year. It was in January of 1774 he was appointed to the *Maidstone 28* and took her out to Jamaica three months later, leaving that station in April of 1777 with a convoy for England. He was sent back across the Atlantic with another convoy for New York.

On March 27th, 1778, the *Maidstone* drove the American rebel privateer *Columbus 16* ashore off Point Judith, Rhode Island where the ship was burned by boats from Gardner's squadron. It was in the summertime the frigate cruised off Virginia to look out for the *Comte d' Estaing's Toulon* fleet, preparing for the defense of New York.

Captain Gardner commanded a number of warships during the American Revolution including the *Maidstone* which in April of 1778 captured rebel privateers *Greenwich*. Then in September, he captured the large French private ship the *Lyon 40* in November of 1778 off Cape Henry, being wounded. He sailed to Antigua and remained in the Leeward Islands.

On July 6th, 1779, Capt. Gardner commanded the *Sultan 74* at the Battle of Grenada with great distinction, being one of three ships exposed to the fire of the whole French fleet, sustaining 16 men killed and 39 wounded.

He commanded the 98 – gun HMS *Duke* at the end of 1781 which he sailed out to the Leeward Islands and on April 12th, 1782, his 40th birthday, Captain Gardner fought at the Battle of the Saintes in the West Indies, a decisive victory for the British against the French during the Revolutionary War.

He later voyaged to North America and then returned to Jamaica, the *Sultan* sailing to England in 1783 being paid off. Afterwards, in 1786 he served as Commodore of the Jamaica Station and suppressed smuggling in the Gulf of Mexico. He also ordered detailed hydrographic surveys of the Caribbean locations for the interest of the Royal Navy and it was during this time he commanded and mentored future famous officers such as George Vancouver, Peter Puget, and Joseph Whidbey.

He became a Member of Parliament in 1790 and later for Westminster. He was appointed to the Board of Admiralty that year and was commander – in – chief of the Leeward Islands Station in 1793, then being promoted to Rear Admiral later that year. It is also noted that he demanded lemons for his sailors in order to prevent scurvy. It is said Gardner was the first to demand having lemon juice onboard which proved to minimize outbreaks.

On June 1st, 1794, Gardner commanded the second division of the central squadron at the Battle of the Glorious against the French Navy. It was for this action he was created a baronet and the same year he was appointed a Major – General of Marines. Gardner was promoted to colonel two years before and vice – admiral in the Royal Navy.

He was promoted to full Admiral in 1795 and commanded a squadron during the Mutiny at Spithead in 1797 where he was brought forth to negotiate with the mutineers due to his experience. However, he lost his temper, seized a mutineer by the throat and threatened to hang them all. It is said at one point, they surrounded him, he broke through the melee, sprang onto the hammock nettings, he threw a noose around his neck and dared them to hang him, ending the mutiny, it being said, with the mutineers cheering his bravery.

Admiral Gardner became Commander – in – Chief of the Cork Station in 1800 and that year he was created Baron Gardner, of Uttoxeter, in the Peerage of Ireland. On November 27th, 1806 the title of Baron Gardner in the Peerage of the United Kingdom was created, entering the House of Lords. Along with having a quick temper, Lady Hamilton had written a letter in May of 1803 to Lord Nelson, describing Admiral Gardner as a drinker.

Then in 1807 he was made Commander – in – Chief of the Channel Fleet and due to ill health resigned from his post the next year.

On New Year's Day, January 1st, 1809, Admiral Alan Gardner died at age 66 from an illness in Bath, England. The seamen knew him as 'Old Junk' due to him keeping his ships at sea until they were on salt junk. His peers described him as zealous, forceful, exceedingly brave, excitable, nervous, and bellicose.

An East Indiaman was named after Admiral Gardner and it was wrecked on the Goodwin Sands on January 24th, 1809, carrying copper coins minted by the East India Company.

References:
Heart of Oak: Letters from Admiral Gardner (1742–1809), edited Francis Day
The Conquest of Scurvy in the Royal Navy 1793 – 1800: a Challenge to Current Orthodoxy by Brian Vale
The Great Mutiny by Jas. Dugan
The Interwoven Lives of George Vancouver, Archibald Menzies, Joseph Whidbey and Peter Puget: The Vancouver Voyage of 1791 – 1795 by John Naish

COL. WILLIAM LINNAEUS GARDNER

Col. William Linnaeus Gardner, the Cavalry Officer, was something out of a Romance novel. He was described as **"a gentleman in every sense of the word."** Gardner was a skilled swordsman, officer and gentleman who founded the Indian cavalry regiment known as Gardner's Horse.

"He was a specimen of British gentleman of high type, handsome, tall, and brave." – H. G. Keene

"A gentleman and a soldier of pleasing address and uncommon abilities. His figure was tall and commanding, and his handsome countenance and military air rendered his appearance very striking." – Lewis Ferdinand Smith

"Gardner, a skilled rider and swordsman in his prime, is described in later years as a tall, soldier like old man, of very courteous and dignified manners, and very kind to his ailing wife." – Sir Leslie Stephen, _The Dictionary of National Biography_

"A very fine corps of men, called Gardner's Horse, was raised by him; single handed. Nothing can resist them such masters are they of their horses and weapons." – Fanny Parkes

Col. William Linnaeus Gardner stated:
"My father Valentine was born in Uttoxeter, Staffordshire, England. His father Colonel Gardner of the 11th Dragoons had a house there which is situated in the Kirby and which had to descend to me and will go to my male heir. My mother was the daughter of Governor Livingston of New York. My father was a Captain in the army when he married her and I was born June 19, 1771 at Brunswick in New Jersey, in a country house which was the property of my mother and was nearly opposite New York. At an early stage of infancy the occurrence of war obliged my parents to leave Brunswick, and I was taken to Livingston Manor and brought up by my grandfather till I was six years of age when my mother took me away in 1777."

His father, Maj. Valentine Gardner was a British officer in the 16th Foot. He was an officer of the Crown under the command of Lord Cornwallis, part of Gen. George Howe's force. Maj. Gardner invaded Philadelphia by the sea route beating the Americans at the Battle of Brandywine.

He had married Alida Livingston of a wealthy American Patriot family. However, he remained a Loyalist. Maj. Valentine Gardner was a friend of Lord Cornwallis and served right up until Yorktown.

The Gardners were from Colerain, Northern Ireland, headed by Theophilus Gardner. His son was William Gardner who defended the Protestant city of Londonderry during its legendary 105 – day siege in 1689, dying with the rest of his 8,000 men. Queen Anne bestowed his son a Cornet's Commission.

Col. William Gardner of the 11th Dragoons settled in Uttoxeter, Staffordshire, England, being the father of Maj. Valentine Gardner and Admiral Alan Gardner.

William Linnaeus Gardner wrote: **"I was with my father who commanded the Light Infantry Corps at the taking of Savannah. It was till 1779 that I stayed with my father."**

He later wrote: **"My father upon the end of the war was embarked on a ship for England but was after a running fight taken by a frigate and carried into Boston. My father from his activities and success deserving his military operations had become particularly obstructive to the Americans who determined on putting him to death from which he was only saved by interest my mother had formally held in the American Congress at the peace in 1781."**

The Gardner family immigrated to Great Britain after the war. His father bought him a commission in the 89th Regiment of Foot and he was sent for a superior education in the town of Evian, France. Gardner stated: **"We all came to England in 1784 and I was sent to a school in France to get the French language."**

"The three years he spent at Evian helped him develop a smattering command of the French language that he retained all his life along with a strongly Francophile attitude that he displayed in social and cultural matters." – Narindar Saroop

When he was 16 years old he moved to the University of Gottingen, Germany for two years and returned to England, exchanged his commission into the 74th Highlanders, stationed in the Madras and first made his way as an Ensign in the 52nd (Oxfordshire) Regiment of Foot, being promoted at age 18 to Lieutenant while in India. Gardner participated in the "Third Mysore War" under Lord Cornwallis fighting against the rule of Tipu Sultan. Due to fever, he was evacuated to Bangalore.

Afterwards, he set off to England and after the death of his mother, he returned to America for a time. Afterwards, he bought a commission in the 30th (Cambridgeshire) Regiment of Foot. Gardner was part of the Marine force sent to Corisca by King George III, and survived a massive explosion that blew up the ship he was aboard.

He gained a position in the staff of Maj. Gen. Lord Moira and in June of 1795 he took part in the Quiberon expedition to aid Royalists in the revolution against French Republicans.

He returned to England at age 24, and in August of 1796 he left and never returned, beginning his career as a soldier of fortune in India. As a captain, Gardner accompanied Captain Moor in 1797 in Poona and served with Joshua Uhthoff. Afterwards, he traveled to the south of India, and while negotiating a treaty with one of the native Princes of Cambay, he met his wife.

Gardner stated:

"When a young man, I was entrusted to negotiate a treaty with one of the native Princes of Cambay. Darbars (hall with an audience) and consultations were continually held; during one of the former, at which I was present, a parda (native curtain) near me was gently moved aside, and I saw, as I thought, the most beautiful black eyes in the world. It was impossible to think of the treaty; those bright and piercing glances, those beautiful dark eyes, completely bewildered me.

I felt flattered that a creature so lovely as she of those deep black, loving eyes must be, should venture to gaze upon me; to what danger might not the veiled beauty be exposed, should the movement of the purda be seen by any of those at the Darbar! On quitting the assembly I discovered that the bright – eyed beauty was the daughter of the Prince. At the next Darbar, my agitation and anxiety were extreme again to behold the bright eyes that had haunted my dreams by night, and my thoughts by day! The parda again was gently moved, and my fate was decided.

I demanded the Princess in marriage; her relations were at first indignant, and positively refused my proposal; however, on mature deliberation, the ambassador was considered to influential a person to have a request denied, and the hand of the young Princess was promised. The preparations for the marriage were carried forward; 'Remember,' said I, 'it will be useless to attempt to deceive me; I shall know those eyes again, nor will I marry any other'.

On the day of the marriage I raised the veil from the countenance of the bride, and in the mirror that was placed between us beheld the bright eyes that had bewildered me; I smiled, - the young Begum smiled also."

His wife was bestowed the title of "Her Highness Furzund Azeza Zubdehtul Arrakeen Nawab Maha Manzil – ul – Nissa Begum Dehlami."

Col. Gardner became a freelancer for Mahadji Rao Scindia and his wife was once captured by his enemy Ghatge. The tall English soldier faced him, but was captured himself, being strapped to a cannon at the fortress of Ahmednagar. However, he scaled over the fort wall, jumped onto the Maratha horse line below, and cut the horses loose before galloping away on one of them. As he was chased by guards, Gardner made his way to the rival camp of Yeshwant Rao Holkar.

It was with his help Gardner rescued his wife and began his career as a freelancer for Yeshwant Rao Holkar. It was in 1801 that Gardner raised and trained a regiment. Then in July of that year, he fought at the battle of Ujjain.

Holkar sent him to meet with Lord Lake, and suspecting treachery, insulted him on his return. Gardner stated: **"I drew my sword instantly and endeavored to cut His Highness down, but was prevented by those around him; and before they had recovered from the amazement and the confusion caused by the attempt, I rushed from the camp, sprang upon my horse, and was soon beyond the reach of recall."**

However, he was captured in 1804 by Amrit Rao during his flight and was strapped to a gun ready for execution, but as soon as he was unbound and marched off, Gardner made his escape and jumped off a 50 – foot cliff into a stream below, swam downstream, disguised himself as a grass – cutter and made his way to a British camp.

On May 12th, 1809, "Lt. Col. Gardner's Corps of Irregular Horse" was officially raised at Farrukhabad and Mainpuri.

General Lake hired Colonel Gardner as the leader of an irregular cavalry regiment which became known as "Gardner's Horse", "Gardner's Corps", and the "2nd Lancers". He was in the service of the East India Company in January of 1819 and was stationed at Kasganj that year; Sagar in 1821; Bareilly until 1823; and Arracan in 1825, returning to Kasganj.

Colonel Gardner served during the Gurkha War from 1814 to 1816, and with 621 men under his command, he fought in the Arracan War from 1824 to 1826, and on April 1st, 1825, captured the city.

Brig. Gen. Morrison reported:
"If ever instances of mental energy triumphing over bodily infirmity were exemplified, they have been displayed by Col. Gardner of the 2nd Local Horse, who on each occasion when there was a probability of the cavalry being engaged, caused himself to be removed from his palanquin to be placed on his horse, though so weakened by long sickness, as to be unable to be for any length of time to prolong the exertion."

Col. Gardner and his men traveled 2,000 miles back from Arracan in November of 1825 and on April 11th, 1826, the regiment was authorized to bear "ARRACAN" on its Standards as a Battle Honour.

He retired and relinquished his command in 1828 at age 57, ending his military career. It was during retirement he met, perhaps his greatest admirer, a woman named Fanny Parkes. She stated:

"He must have been, and is, very handsome; such a high caste man! How he came to marry the begum I know not. What a romance his love must have been! I wish I had his portrait, just as he appears, so dignified and interesting. His partiality flatters me greatly."

She stated: "I was delighted to sit by my dear Colonel Gardner, and to hear his explanations. In conversation he was most interesting, a man of great intelligence, and in mind playful as a child. I often begged him to write his life, or to allow me to write his dictation. The description of such varied scenes as those which he had passed would have been delightful; and he wrote so beautifully, the work would have been invaluable."

Colonel Gardner had three children, a daughter and two sons, one named Alan who died at age 29, and another son named James Gardner; Fanny Parkes, in March of 1835, wrote:

"Mr. James Gardner, whom I had never met before, received us with much pleasure; his countenance reminded me of his father, whom, in manner, he greatly resembled; he was dressed in handsome native attire, a costume he usually wore... Mr. Gardner has a fine estate at Kutchowra with an indigo plantation: his establishment is very large and completely native."

"He reads and writes Persian fluently as a native. He is very hospitable, expert in all manly exercises, a fine horseman, an excellent swordsman, skilled in the lance exercise, and admirable shot with the bow and arrow. James Gardner is most perfectly suited to the life he leads: The power of the sun does not affect him as much as it does other people: he rides about his estate and farms all day: he has a great number of villages of his own, of which he is lord and master, and is able to conduct his affairs and turn his indigo and farming into profit."

Fanny Parkes stated:
"Colonel Gardner's name is William Linnaeus, so called after his godfather, the great botanist; he is himself an excellent botanist, and pursues the study with so much ardour. His garden at Khasgunge is very extensive and a most delightful one, full of find trees and rare plants, beautiful flowers and shrubs, with fruit in abundance and perfection; no expense is spared to embellish the garden."

Colonel William Linnaeus Gardner died from an illness at age 64 on July 29th, 1835 in the village of Chhaoni in India, far from New York and Staffordshire. He had stated, "I shall not last long; the poor Begum, she will not survive me long; mark my words." His wife did not eat and speak to anyone, dying a month later from grief.

William Linnaeus Gardner.

He was so well known by the British and Indians, a friend once wrote to Fanny Parkes from England, **"I shall always regret having left India without seeing Colonel Gardner and the Taj."**

Fanny Parkes stated: **"In the evening our party set off for Khasgunge: we walked into the garden, and visited the tomb. Major Sutherland spoke of Colonel Gardner as a most gallant officer, and recorded several most dashing actions in which he had distinguished himself in many parts of the country; gallantry that had not met the recompense due to it from the Government; - the value of a spirit such as Colonel Gardner's had not been properly appreciated by the rulers of the land."**

Courtesy to Frank Gardner for his information and advice as well as for his excellent book on Colonel William Linnaeus Gardner.

References:
Life and Legacy of Col. William Linnaeus Gardner by Frank Gardner
North Indian Notes and Queries, Volume 5
Wanderings of a Pilgrim by Fanny Parkes

COL. ALEXANDER GARDNER

Col. Alexander Gardner, the Mercenary, was a warrior who had killed hundreds of men in battle. He was one of the most extraordinary explorers and a soldier of fortune, a master of warfare. Gardner was the deadliest warrior and one of the deadliest men in history.

"Just at that moment, when the crowd were rushing on us, their swords high in the air, I managed to fire the two guns, and literally blew them into the air." – Col. Alexander Gardner

"The old colonel, while on the verge of his eightieth year, had a gait as sturdy and a stride as firm as a man of fifty. Some six feet in height, he usually wore a tartan – plaid suit, purchased apparently from the quartermaster's stores of one of the Highland regiments serving in India. In consequence of a severe wound in the neck, received in battle many years before, the old commandant had long been unable to eat solid food; he had, moreover, lost from age nearly all of his teeth. The photograph while indicating the outline of his countenance, gives but a dim idea of the vivacity of expression, the play of feature, the humour of the mouth, and the energy of character portrayed by the whole aspect of the man as he described the arduous and terrible incidents of a long life of romance and vicissitude. The English he spoke was quaint graphic, and wonderfully good considering his fifty years of residence among Asiatics."
– Mr. Frederick Cooper

"I can perfectly recollect my first interview with him. He walked into Cooper's reception – room one morning, a most peculiar and striking appearance, clothed from head to foot in the 79th tartan, but fashioned by a native tailor. Even his pagri was of tartan, and it was adorned with the egret's plume, only allowed to persons of high rank. I imagine he lived entirely in native fashion: he was said to be wealthy, and the owner of many villages." – Captain Seagraves

"Faithful to his standard, whatever it was, obeying without questioning military orders, he presented and presents, perhaps, one of the finest specimens ever known of the soldier of fortune." – Sir Henry Durand

"Gardner actually traversed the Gilgit valley from the Indus to the Snowy Mountains, and finally crossed into Chitral, being, in fact, the only Englishman up to the present time (1872) who has ever performed the journey throughout." – Sir Henry Rawlinson

"Gardner seems to have been indebted for life, and that many a time over, to his cool audacity, which never failed him for a moment, be the strait what it might." – Sir Henry Durand

"The travels and adventures of Colonel Gardner are of such an extraordinary character that, had they ever been placed in a readable form before the public, he would long ago have enjoyed a world – wide reputation." – Sir Henry Yule, introduction to the book titled, _Journey to the Sources of the River Oxus_

"Gardner finished off many a foe...no telling how many." – Mike Leahan

"Gardner was a gunfighter and swordfighter." – Dave Hardy

Alexander Haughton Campbell Gardner was born in 1785 on the shores of Lake Superior in America. His grandfather was a Scotsman who emigrated and his father was a surgeon who had served during the American Revolution as well as being an adventurer himself. His mother was of English and Spanish heritage, whom he described as "in all respects a well – educated and accomplished woman, of a rare sweetness and strength of character."

The Gardner family migrated to the town of St. Xavier in Mexico along the mouth of the Colorado River. As a student at Jesuit school, Gardner obtained a book about travels among the American Indians. He stated: **"From this early period of life the notion of being a traveller and adventurer, and of somehow and somewhere carving out a career for myself, was the maggot of my brain."**

After the death of his mother in 1809, Gardner traveled to Ireland to begin his maritime career, where it is believed he learned the science of gunnery. He returned to America in 1812, landing in New Orleans, Louisiana, but finding that his father had died, he left for Philadelphia where his uncle was living and then never returned, traveling to Astrakhan, Russia, where his brother was working as an engineer. However, on December 14th, 1817, his brother died later after falling from his horse and on January 19th, 1819, at age 34, Alexander Gardner began his career as a soldier of fortune.

He traveled Central Asia through the deserts of Turkestan, and traveled with another European known as Aga Beg. They had stolen their horses back from the Kipchaks and he wrote: **"Three horsemen of the Ura – tube chief suddenly over took us to halt and yield in the name of the Government. On our refusal they threatened to fire, and in self – defense we slew them and fled on, taking their arms and horses, through the tracks most remote from habitations."** Gardner killed three armed men near Kunduz before he reached the Oxus, stating: **"Food, we obtained by levying contributions from every one we could master, but we did not slaughter unless in self – defense."**

He was recruited as a mercenary in 1823 for Afghan rebel Habib – ulla Khan, fighting against Dost Muhammad Khan. Habib – ulla Khan was an outlawed Afghan prince. It was during this time, Alexander Gardner became the first American to fight in Afghanistan **"for a good cause of right against wrong."**

Gardner stated: **"Being, like Habib – ullah Khan, of a sanguine disposition, and, moreover, being favourably impressed by his appearance and manner, I proffered the services of myself and my followers, which were readily accepted, and I was engaged as commandant of 180 picked horse to be employed in forays into the enemy's country, and in levying contributions on all caravans, especially seizing every morsel of baggage and property that was intended for Dost Muhammad Khan."**

"From this date for a period of two and a half years I led a life in the saddle, one of active warfare and continual forays: so successful were we that we had our advanced posts within twenty miles of Kabul, and the Dost dared not show his nose in the whole mountain region."

Gardner later wrote: **"We lived, as I have said, in the saddle, and fed in common, for the good cause of right against wrong which we had espoused."**

During a raid, he stated:
"In the course of the running fight to our stronghold I was enabled to see the beautiful face of a young girl who accompanied the princess. I rode for a considerable time beside her, pretending that my respect for the elder lady made me choose that side of her camel on which her attendant was carried.

On the following morning Habib – ulla Khan richly rewarded all his followers, for he was generous to a fault; but I refused my share of the gold, and begged for this girl to be given me in marriage as the only reward I desired. She was of royal birth on the mother's side, being the daughter (as was at once discovered) of one of Habib – ulla Khan's nearest relatives. He, however, freely and willingly gave her to me, and established me as commandant of a fort near his own adobe. There I was very happy for about two years, in the course of which time my wife made me the father of a noble boy."

Gardner made himself a home in 1825 which he called the "*Castello*", but his happiness was short lived.

It was in March of 1826, Dost Muhammad Khan's forces had employed 12, 000 troops and he wrote: **"They hemmed us in on the west, south, and east, and for a period of from two to three months there was a series of bloody and desperate fights."**

"I had reached Habib – ullah Khan about half – way between Parwan and my home, and found him fighting desperately with twelve of his men about him. Cutting my way through the enemy, I reached him, and found that he was badly wounded in the arm. I myself had previously received a ball in my knee."

His mountain home was overrun by Dost Muhammad's forces while he was fighting the enemy in caves in Afghanistan. He had been shot in the knee, along with having his throat cut, and came back to his home to find it in ruins. Although all of the intruders had been killed in battle, his wife and child were murdered, along with others.

He stated:

"I had left them all thoughtless and happy but five days before. The bodies had been decently covered up by the faithful mullah (priest), but the right hand of the hapless young mother could be seen, and clenched in it the reeking katar with which she had stabbed herself to the heart after handing over the child to the priest for protection. Her room had been broken open, and mortally self wounded as she was, the assassins nearly severed her head from her body with their long Afghan knives and sabres."

"The boy seized and barbarously murdered. There he lay by the side of his mother. I sank on my knees and involuntarily offered up a prayer for vengeance to the Most High God."

It is said that Alexander Gardner was unable to tell without tears the sad story of his Afghan wife and child. Afterwards, he became an outlaw, drifting throughout Afghanistan, as well as Kafiristan where the Kafirs promised him 20, 000 troops. He and his Sowars faced 50 of Kunduz chief Mir Ali Murad's forces in a cut – and – thrust affair, in which several of his men died. And it was during this time that he acquired a slave, a faithful servant whom he called Therbah. It was sometime during his travels, Gardner shot and killed a bandit in a gunfight.

Gardner stated:

"I covered them with my weapon, when they dropped the clothes. We speedily recrossed the ford, not knowing how many more marauders might be about, when "bang" went a matchlock, and a ball struck the ground at our feet. A second shot went through the Syad's pirpank (a high, conical, black lambskin cap), a third took off the top joint of the second finger of my poor Therbah's left hand. The ball struck him while waving his arm to me to fire. Feeling that there was no help for it, I took steady aim, fired, and rolled over the elder robber, who fell down the khad (declivity)."

It was later discovered Gardner killed the chief of a gang of robbers and murderers that had terrorized the Jerm district for 3 years, the survivors being captured and sold into slavery.

Alexander Gardner was the leader of a band of Khyberi outlaws who had him released from a dungeon when he was imprisoned for nine months in 1829 by the Kandahar brothers. It was in 1830, 'Prince' Gardner rode ahead of an army of forty troopers, being hired as a mercenary for Mir Alam Khan and Syed Ahad. After eight years of fighting in Afghanistan as a rogue and renegade, he left because **"there were too many Afghans whose fathers and brothers had met him in battle to make a residence in a country where blood – feuds were a sacred duty even moderately safe from treachery and violence."**

Gardner was hired as Chief of Artillery for the governor of Peshawar, Sultan Mohamed Khan and in the spring of 1832, the Maharaja Ranjit Singh sent him a letter desiring his services.

He stated:
"On the day of my presentation to the Maharaja, and while I was waiting outside the Shalimar Gardens, an incident occurred which is described in the work called 'Adventures of an Officer," by the great and good Sir Henry Lawrence (afterwards my well known and honoured friend).

"A certain Nand Singh, an officer in the Maharaja's cavalry, rode his horse intentionally against me and endeavoured to jostle me into the ditch, which was deep and filled with running water. I touched the rein of my good steed, gave him half a turn, pressed him with my sword – hand the veriest trifle on the loins, and in an instant Nand Singh and his horse were rolling on the ground. I calmly expressed a hope that the fallen man was not hurt, and was treated with much civility during the remaining time that I was kept waiting."

It was the Maharaja's goal to turn his Sikh army into a professional fighting force, one that could stand against the European armies. The Maharaja recruited such European officers as General Ventura, General Allard, and even a few American officers. After displaying his marksmanship, Gardner was hired as Colonel of Artillery.

He stated: **"I took a few soldiers in hand, and in a few days' time all this was done with a degree of success unexpected even by myself, the shells bursting exactly as required at 600, 800, 1000, and 1200 yards."**

Colonel Alexander Gardner was known by the Sikhs as "Gordana Sahib".

On January 15th, 1841 at the Hazuri Bagh, Gardner killed over 300 Akali warriors, for Gulab Singh against Sher Singh at the Siege of Lahore, Pakistan.

Gardner stated:
"The little fort was surrounded by a sea of human heads. Gulab Singh made contemptuous replies, and roared out to Sher Singh, demanding that he should surrender. There was a brief but breathless pause, and I had not time to warn my artillerymen to clear out of the way when down came the gates over our party, torn to shreds by the simultaneous discharge of all the fourteen guns.

Seventeen of my party were blown to pieces, parts of the bodies flying over me. When I had wiped the blood and brains from my face, and could recover a moment, I saw only one little trembling Klasi. I hurriedly asked him for a port – fire, having lost mine in the fall of the ruins.

He had just time to hand it to me, and I had crept under my two guns, when with a wild yell some 300 Akalis swept up the Hazuri Bagh and crowded into the gate. They were packed as close as fish, and could hardly move over the heaps of wood and stone, the rubbish and carts, with which the gateway was blocked.

Just at that moment, when the crowd were rushing on us, their swords high in the air, I managed to fire the two guns, and literally blew them into the air.

In the pause that followed I loaded the guns with the aid of the three of my artillerymen who survived, and our next discharge swept away the hostile artillerymen who were at the fourteen guns outside, who had remained standing perfectly paralysed by the destruction of the Akalis. Then Sher Singh fled, and grievous carnage commenced."

Gulab Singh stated that he had **"a high opinion of Gardanah as a thorough – going friend, and ... [one who] always stuck by him when ... others deserted him."** Although, Gardner was looked upon as a hero, he was involved in assassinations. After the death of Dhyan Singh, his wife vowed to have the heads of her husband's assassins, Lehna Singh and Ajit Singh. Gardner stated: **"I myself laid their heads at the feet of Dhyan Singh's corpse that evening."**

It was under Jowlahir Singh, Gardner was described as a **"great desperado"** and was hired to cut off the nose, fingers, and ears of disgraced official Jodha Ram. Afterwards, under the reign of Tej Singh, he was let go from the Sikh service in 1846 for his mutilation of Jodha Ram. Later, Colonel Gardner wrote that he was forced to perform the deed, the lives of his men depended on him.

Afterwards, Gulab Singh, the last surviving of the Dogra brothers, had become Maharaja of Jammu and he hired Colonel Alexander Gardner as his commandant of artillery. It was during this time in the 1850s that he also ran a saltpetre business called 'A. Gardner and Company'. Colonel Gardner gained celebrity status among the British military officers entering the region.

It was in 1864 that East India Company British civil servant Frederick Cooper met Colonel Gardner at age 79, and the famous photograph of him was taken by Samuel Bourne and printed by Charles Shepherd.

"Colonel Gardner, a soldier of fortune, ninety years of age, was born on the shores of Lake Superior, and had wandered into Central Asia at an early period. It was something almost appalling to hear this ancient warrior discourse of what have now become almost prehistoric times, and relate his experiences in the service of Ranjit Singh and other kings and chiefs less known to fame." – Andrew Wilson, _The Adobe of Snow_

Gardner wrote his autobiography titled _Soldier and Traveller: Memoirs of Alexander Gardner_, edited by Maj. Hugh Pearse, and these papers were not published until years after his death. His "good and honoured friend", Sir Henry Lawrence based a character known as Bellasis on him. Rudyard Kipling published a book titled _The Man Who Would Be King_, in which he seems to have taken information from Gardner's travels throughout Kafiristan.

It was said he had fourteen wounds from his many battles and a gaping wound in his throat forced him to have a steel collar metal contraption, so whenever he raised his glass to drink, he "clutched his neck with an iron pincer".

Gardner killed over 300 men by his own account and suffered from 14 wounds. It is said, **"Gardner finished off many a foe…no telling how many."**

On January 22nd, 1877, the legendary Alexander Gardner died at age 91 in Srinagar, Jammu and Kashmir, Pakistan and was buried in a British military cemetery, among Christians. Major Hugh Pearse published Gardner's _Memoirs_ and on July 9th, 1898, _The New York Times_ reported: **"A Strange Career. Alexander Gardner. Born on the Shore of Lake Superior, Who Served Ranjit Singh."** His book was a success and his daughter Helena Gardner Gerl Botha tried to search for her father's fortune.

On August 9th, 1933, Barcelona's _La Vanguardia_ stated Helena Gardner's mother was a Sheikh's daughter named Kali from Turkestan, whose tribe carried out raids on Kashmir until it was exterminated by Colonel Gardner, her father. She stated only four women remained alive and the most beautiful one was Kali, her mother who was taken to Gardner's harem. She died two years later after giving birth and Helena was raised by her father's second favorite. Colonel Gardner had four wives, his daughter Helena being born about 1866 in Kashmir, and eventually she died in 1947 in Dublin, Ireland.

On June 20th, 1898, pg. 4 of the _Standard_ stated, aside from his mutilation of a Brahmin official, described Colonel Gardner as a **"remarkable man in many ways."** On July 17th, 1898, pg. 12 of the _New York Tribune_ stated, he was **"an extraordinary man"** and **"fearless, romantic vagrancy."** On October 5th, 1898, pg. 21 of _The Guardian_ stated, Gardner was **"an adventurer of the good old cut – and – thrust kind who may fairly take his place alongside Ivanhoe, D' Artagnan, and Amyas Leigh"**.

The Tartan Turban: In Search of Alexander Gardner by John Keay stated:
    "As a hired gun transposed from the American West to the Asian East, for over a decade he had quartered the forbidden lands between what are now Turkmenistan and Chinese Xinjiang. He had survived arrest in Khiva, fled retribution in Samarkand, repeatedly forded the Oxus River (Amu Darya), and wintered in the unknown tundra of the Pamirs."

Like the travels of Marco Polo, those of Alexander Gardner clip the white line between credible adventure and creative invention. Either this Scots-American is the nineteenth century's most intrepid traveller or its most egregious fantasist, or a bit of both. Contemporaries generally believed him; posterity became more sceptical. And as with Polo, the investigation of Gardner's story enlarged man's understanding of the world and upped the pace of scientific and political exploration. Before more reputable explorers notched up their own discoveries in innermost Asia, this lone traveller had roamed the deserts of Turkestan, ridden round the world's most fearsome knot of mountains and fought, as the first American in Afghanistan, 'for the good cause of right against wrong'.

From the Caspian to Tibet and from Kandahar to Kashgar, Gardner had seen it all. At the time, the 1820s, no other outsider had managed anything remotely comparable. When word of his feats filtered out, geographers were agog. Historians were more intrigued by what followed. After thirteen years as a white-man-gone-native in Central Asia, Gardner re-emerged as a colonel of artillery in the employ of India's last great native empire. He witnessed the death throes of that Sikh Empire at close quarters and, sparing no gruesome detail, recorded his own part in the bloodshed (the very same featuring as the exploits of 'Alick' Gardner in the 'Flashman' series).

Fame finally caught up with him during his long retirement in Kashmir. Dressed in tartan yet still living as a native, he mystified visiting dignitaries and found a ready audience for the tales of his adventurous past. But one mystery he certainly took to the grave: the whereabouts of his accumulated fortune has still to be discovered."

"There appears to me to be good internal evidence that, as regards the main routes he professes to have travelled, Gardner's story is truthful." – Ney Elias

"Of all the many Europeans who lived and travelled in South and Central Asia in the 19th century, none is more mysterious than Alexander Gardner. Doubts and uncertainties are attached to everything about him." – Schuyler "Skye" Jones, professor of ethnology, Oxford University

"Though far from the Victorian ideal of the detached scholar – explorer who took scientific readings throughout his travels, Gardner is now shown to be a crucial, if erratic and sometimes criminal, pioneer of Himalayan exploration; one of the most extraordinary, eccentric and remarkable figures in the history of travel and exploration." – William Dalrymple

"The hero of one of the most remarkable romances of real life." – _The Geographical Journal, Volume 12, Royal Geographical Society (1898) Great Britain_

Alexander Gardner. Albumen print, Kashmir, c. 1870. Collection of Gursharan S. and Elvira Sidhu.

Courtesy to Parmjit Singh, Mike Leahan, and Dave Hardy for information.

Life of a Soldier of the Olden Time: An unwritten Page of History
By: Sir Henry Durand

"Even in outline the story is of great interest, - a life drama indeed, as full of incident and adventure as drama can well be. The story of Dugald Dalgetty is nothing to this, as it will be seen by the light of times to come.

To take the two ends of the long tangled line is something wonderful, - one end bright and sunny on the banks of Lake Superior in the Far West; the other end approaching, where the chapter will close, in lands watered by the Indus. And then the schooling in Ireland, and the teaching in Lahore; the parting from home for ever for a life from end to end of perils such as very few men have ever imagined, still less known.

It is difficult perhaps to comprehend all the career, but much may be understood. There is no mistake about the high heart, the undaunted courage, the unflagging will. Colonel Gardner's personal influence, too, must have been great – what is called magnetic; for how else could he have bound to himself for nine months, and he all the time a prisoner, men who seemed to have an interest in separating from him as far as possible? And how else could he have drawn to himself those Sowars and others whom he led to Kabul and elsewhere?

That such a man has been so little mentioned in the history of the times is a marvel. But we must remember that he was a man without a country, though England or any country might be proud to claim him.

Faithful to his standard, whatever it was, obeying without questioning military orders, he presented and presents, perhaps, one of the finest specimens ever known of the soldier of fortune.

He must have been a man, too, who did not care to force himself into notice so long as he could obtain employment; and the fact that he secured the respect and confidence of so many persons, of characters so widely different, is enough to show that besides being a bold soldier, he was possessed of rare tact and skill, of qualities indeed which, if the love of adventure had been urged on by anything like an equal share of ambition, would have gone far to gather together the turbulent elements among which he lived, and make of them a more devastating flame than even Gardner himself ever saw."

References:
Soldier and Traveller: Memoirs of Alexander Gardner edited by Major Hugh Pearse, Edinburgh and London: William Blackwood & Sons. 1898
Journey to the Sources of the River Oxus by Sir Henry Yule
The Tartan Turban: In Search of Alexander Gardner by John Keay

Photograph is public domain, retrieved on April 2nd, 2019 at
https://en.wikipedia.org/wiki/Alexander_Gardner_(soldier)#/media/File:Colon
el_Gardner_of_Cashmere.jpg
Famous public domain portrait of legendary mercenary Alexander Gardner

Chapter II: Commandos and War Heroes

"Listen only to yourself, not someone else." – Lt. Bill Gardner

COL. THOMAS GARDNER

Col. Thomas Gardner, the Revolutionary War Hero, was an American patriot. He was the leader of Gardner's Regiment in the Continental Army. The City of Gardner, Massachusetts is named in his honor.

"Colonel Gardner is to be buried tomorrow, at three o' clock, P. M. with military honors due to so brave and gallant an officer, who fought, bled, and died in the cause of his country and mankind." – Gen. George Washington, July 4th, 1775, General Orders

If he had not died at the Battle of Bunker Hill, he most likely would have been one of the great generals of the American Revolution.

Thomas Gardner was born in 1724 in Cambridge, Massachusetts. He was a descendant of Thomas Gardner of Roxbury, a planter, who has numerous descendants throughout the country. Gardner married Joanna Sparhawk in 1755, her family being one of Brighton's founding families.

He was a political figure in Massachusetts before the Revolution and was at the forefront of resistance to the King's dissolution of the General Court in 1774, following the Boston Tea Party. Gardner was chosen to represent Cambridge in the Middlesex County Convention and in May of 1775, he was elected to the Revolutionary Council of Safety. He was commissioned in the spring of 1775 as a Colonel of a regiment he had organized mostly at his own expense.

Col. Gardner was mortally wounded at the Battle of Bunker Hill in June of 1775 and lingered until his valiant death on July 3rd, 1775, being the second – highest ranking American officer killed at Bunker Hill.

Gen. George Washington, afterwards President of the United States, attended the funeral of the Revolutionary War hero Col. Thomas Gardner.

The City of Gardner, Massachusetts is named for him in his honor, as well as the Gardner Pilot Academy School, and Gardner Street in Boston, Massachusetts.

References:
Thomas Gardner Planter and Some of his Descendants, Essex Institute, Salem, MA (1907) by Frank Gardner
History of Bunker Hill Battle, With a Plan, Second Edition, Munroe and Francis, Boston (1826) by S. Swett

CARSWELL GARDNER

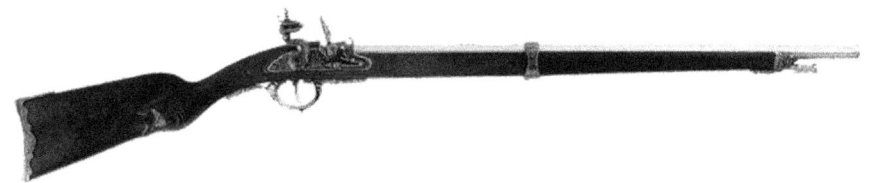

Carswell Gardner, the Bodyguard of the Washington Family, was an American patriot. He had the honor of guarding General George Washington. Gardner fought in some of the major battles of the American Revolution.

His brother was William Gardner, a private in the British Army during the French and Indian War. It was in 1754 at Fort Necessity, family legend tells of Gardner shooting an enemy sniper who was aiming at then Colonel George Washington. As Gardner was wounded by another enemy sniper, he took the musket of another soldier, and fired killing the sniper. Record shows Private William Gardner, but no evidence other than family legend presents itself.

Carswell Gardner was born in 1756 in Virginia Colony. He enlisted in the Continental Army in 1776 under Col. Ward, then being taken prisoner by the British on Dorchester Neck and was carried to Boston. After he was confined on board a transport – ship in Boston Harbor for six weeks, he escaped in one of the cutters.

Afterwards, Gardner was appointed sergeant of the foot – guard of General Washington. He fought at the battles of Long Island, White Plains, and Princeton. It was at the Battle of Trenton, Gardner took part in defeating the Hessians and after his term expired, Gen. Washington made Gardner his horse – guard due to his skills with horses.

He was at the historic Valley Forge and it was at the Battle of Germantown, he was the bearer of the flag of true. Gardner also fought at the Battle of Brandywine in 1777, as well as the Battle of Monmouth. He served as a member of the horse – guards until Gen. Washington made his way to West Point in 1779 and was then transferred. Gardner served in a regiment of light dragoons under Col. William Washington. Afterwards, in 1780 he received an honorable discharge from Col. Washington and served as a recruiting – officer.

After the War for American Independence had been won, Carswell Gardner engaged in agricultural pursuits and he died at age 86 in 1842 in New London, Chester County, Pennsylvania.

Courtesy to David Gardner

CAPT. THOMAS GARDNER

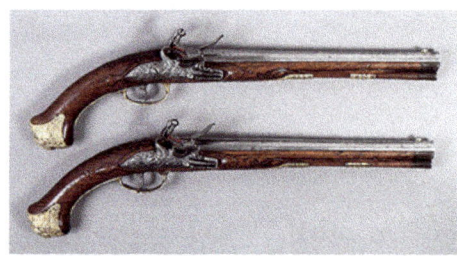

Capt. Thomas Gardner, the Privateer, was my 6th great uncle, possibly my 5th great grandfather. He was a Continental soldier during the Revolutionary War. Gardner was an American patriot.

Thomas Gardner was born around the year 1750 in Virginia Colony. He lived in Spotsylvania and Orange Counties where he was a farmer. His brother was Daniel Gardner, also a patriot during the American Revolution.

On June 25th, 1776, Thomas Gardner enlisted in the 5th South Carolina Regiment in the Continental Army during the Revolutionary War.

Family legend states that a British ship anchored somewhere off the coast and his regiment captured ship and men. Gardner was elected as Captain of the former British vessel that had been commandeered. It is said Capt. Gardner used the ship's guns on other British warships approaching, acting as a privateer.

It is said Capt. Thomas Gardner carried a pair of steel flintlock pistols.

His slave, known as Uncle George, who lived until he was almost 100 years old during the Civil War era, told of this story to Thomas' son Reuben Gardner who told it to his son, Thomas Washington Gardner, who then told the story to a distant cousin named Meredith Knox Gardner.

Journal of the Commissioners of the Navy of South Carolina page 144 states:
"At a meeting of the Commissioners on 12 March 1778, an order was drawn on the State Treasury in favour of Thos. Gardner - - wages due on board the Brigg Defence."

It appears Gardner and his men had commandeered the *Defence*.

Thomas Gardner later removed to Kershaw County, South Carolina where he was a farmer, slave owner, and served as justice of the peace. He married Eliza Kennard and they had about ten children. Thomas Gardner died in 1815 from an illness in South Carolina.

GEN. SIR ROBERT GARDNER

Gen. Sir Robert Gardner, the British Artillery Officer, was the Master Gunner at St. Jas. Park. He was a veteran of the Battle of Waterloo. Gardner was the most senior Ceremonial Post in the Royal Artillery after the Sovereign.

Robert William Gardner was born on May 2nd, 1781 in England. His father was Captain John Gardner of the 3rd Buffs. His brother was Lieutenant – General Sir John Gardner, Colonel – in – Chief of the 61st Foot.

He was educated at the Royal Military Academy, Woolwich and was commissioned into the Royal Artillery in April of 1797, being sent to Gibraltar.

Afterwards in 1798, he was the Capture of Minorca.

He was appointed to the staff on the island's Mosquito Fort and was later aide – de – camp to General Henry Fox. Then in 1802 he returned to England and was promoted second – captain in 1804 commanding 12 guns in an advance corps as part of Cathcart and Count Tolstoy's campaign in North Germany. The British troops advanced as far as Hanover before the Battle of Austerliz.

Gardner joined the Marquis of Wellington's Army in 1812 and commanded a Field Battery at the Battle of Salamanca, the Capture of Madrid, and the Siege of Burgos. Then in 1813 he took company of the E Troop Royal Horse Artillery and fought at the Battle of Vitoria, the Battle of Orthez, and the Battle of Toulouse. It was in 1815 during the Corn Law Riots in London, he and his men helped to restore order.

He then traveled to the Southern Netherlands and at Quatre Bras he and his troop covered the left of the army and Gardner then fought at the Battle of Waterloo.

Afterwards, he married Caroline Mary McLeod and became Principal Equerry to Prince Leopold of Sax – Coburg – Saalfeld in 1816 until the 1830s, later serving as aide – de – camp to monarchs George IV, William IV, and Queen Victoria. Later, in 1848 he was appointed Governor of Gibraltar.

General Sir Robert William Gardner died on June 26th, 1864 in Esher, Surrey, England.

References:
www.oxforddnb.com
www.wikipedia.com

SERGEANT MAJOR WILLIAM GARDNER

Sgt. Maj. William Gardner, the Scottish Warrior, earned the Victoria Cross for his gallantry in battle. He was a Scotsman in the British Army. Gardner fought and distinguished himself during the Crimean War and the Indian Mutiny advancing the British Empire.

William Gardner was born on March 3rd, 1821 in Nemphlar, Lanarkshire, Scotland. He served in the British Army in the 42nd Regiment of Foot (later The Black Watch Royal Highlanders) during the Crimean War against the Russian Empire, at age 37 earning the rank of colour – sergeant.

On May 5th, 1858 at Bareilly, India, during the Indian Mutiny, Colour – Sergeant Gardner was awarded the Victoria Cross, the highest and most prestigious award for gallantry in the face of the enemy that can be awarded to British and Commonwealth forces.

A letter from Captain MacPherson, 42nd Regiment, to Lieutenant – Colonel Cameron, Commanding that Regiment, states:

Indian Mutiny
Bareilly, 5th May 1858
Citation: "For his conspicuous and arid gallant conduct on the morning of the 5th May, in having saved the life of Lieutenant-Colonel Cameron, his commanding officer, who, during the action of Bareilly, on that day had been knocked from his horse, when three Fanatics rushed upon him. Colour-Sergeant Gardner ran out, and in a moment bayoneted two of them, and was in the act of attacking the third, when he was shot down by another soldier of the regiment." – *The Black Watch Medal Roll, 1801-1911,* John Stewart (Ed.), p 290; August 23rd, 1858, *London Gazette*

Gardner later achieved the rank of sergeant – major and earned the Distinguished Conduct Medal along with his Victoria Cross. His medal was sold by one of his descendants to raise money for charity. His VC is on display in the Lord Ashcroft Gallery at the Imperial War Museum in London, England.

He married Margaret Watson and they had two children, David W. Gardner, born in 1870 and Annie Gardner born in 1871 in Scotland.

William Gardner died on October 24th, 1897 at age 76 in Bothwell, Lanarkshire, Scotland, being buried at the Bothwell Park Cemetery.

As a decorated Scottish warrior, Sergeant – Major William Gardner earned the Victoria Cross, the Distinguished Conduct Medal (DCM), the Crimea Medal (1854 – 1856) 1 clasp: "Sebastopol", the Turkish Crimea Medal (1855 – 1856), the Indian Mutiny Medal (1857 – 1858) 1 clasp: "Lucknow", and the Army Long Service and Good Conduct Medal.

References:
The London Gazette
Scotland's Forgotten Valour by Graham Ross
Monuments to Courage by David Harvey

Courtesy to the Black Watch Castle and Museum for photographs of Scotsman William Gardner

SERGEANT MAJOR GEORGE GARDNER

Sgt. Maj. George Gardner, the Irish Warrior, earned the Victoria Cross for his gallantry in battle. He was from Northern Ireland and served in the British Army. Gardner fought and distinguished himself during the Crimean War.

George Gardner was born on July 18th, 1821 in Warrenpoint, County Down, Northern Ireland. He enlisted in the 57th Regiment of Foot (later the Middlesex Regiment) and was posted in 1846 to Lifford Barracks. Gardner married Elizabeth Courtney in 1848, fathering four children, none of whom survived adulthood.

His son George Gardiner died at sea on November 22nd, 1854 at 5 years old. His son Arthur Trafalgar Gardiner died in Trafalgar Bay on November 29th, 1854 at 2 years old. His daughter Elizabeth Jane Gardiner died on April 7th, 1869 at 12 years old. And his son Richard Gardiner died on April 14th, 1869 at 3 years old.

Gardner and his regiment traveled in 1854 to Crimea. On March 22nd, 1855 while at Sebastopol he rallied his men in regaining the trenches from the Russians. And on June 18th, 1855, he encouraged his men to remain behind in the holes made by the explosions of the shells, and continue firing on the enemy forces.

His Victoria Cross Citation reads: **"On the 22nd March, 1855, at Sebastopol, Crimea, Sergeant Gardiner acted with great gallantry upon the occasion of a sortie by the enemy, in having rallied the covering parties which had been driven in by the Russians, thus regaining the trenches.
On the 18th June, during the attack on the Redan, he himself remained and encouraged others to remain in the holes made by the explosions of the shells, and whence they were able to keep up a continuous fire until their ammunition was exhausted, and the enemy cleared away from the parapet."**

Gardner was discharged from the Regiment in 1861 and reposted as Sergeant Major to the permanent staff of the Prince of Wales Own Donegal Militia based at Lifford. On November 17th, 1891, he died at age 70 and was buried in Clonleigh Churchyard in Lifford, County Donegal, Ireland. His medals are held by the Princess of Wales' Royal Regiment RHQ, in Dover Castle, England.

References:
The Register of the Victoria Cross (1981, 1988 and 1997)
Irish Sword. XVI
Monuments of Courage by David Harvey
Irish Winners of the Victoria Cross by Richard Doherty and David Truesdale

COL. CHARLES GARDNER

Col. Charles Gardner, the Hero of the War of 1812, was a distinguished American soldier and military author. He achieved the status of war hero when he carried the severely wounded General Winfield Scott off the battlefield at Niagara. Gardner was described as an **"amiable and courteous gentleman"**.

"No matter what happened, Colonel Gardner was on top, or near it". – "A History of the City Post Office" by Madison Davis, Columbia Historical Society, Vol. 6

Charles Kitchell Gardner was born on February 27th, 1787 in Morristown, New Jersey. His father was Thomas Gardner, a Revolutionary War hero, who was descended from John Gardner, an immigrant from England according to record. The Gardner family was prominent along the Hudson River.

He studied medicine, and then accepted a commission as an ensign in the 6th U. S. Infantry in 1808, serving as brigade inspector, earning the rank of Captain of the 3rd Artillery during the War of 1812 where he distinguished himself in the 25th Infantry. Afterwards, he was Adjutant – General of the Division of the North under General Jacob Brown. Gardner fought in several battles including Chrysler's Field, Chippewa, and Niagara, as well as the Siege of Fort Erie.

It was at the Battle of Niagara, Capt. Gardner carried General Winfield Scott off the field after being severely wounded. As a major in the 3rd U. S. Infantry he was the first to suggest the practice of using letters of the alphabet to indicate companies in a regiment in 1816, the U. S. Infantry in 1875 later adopting the crossed rifles insignia. Gardner was promoted to Lieutenant Colonel in February of 1815 for distinguished service.

He served as First Assistant Postmaster – General during both terms of President Andrew Jackson and from 1836 to 1841 served as Auditor of the Treasury in the Post Office Department under President Martin Van Buren. It was during the administration of President Polk from 1845 to 1849 he was Postmaster of the City of Washington. Gardner later was transferred in 1850, serving as surveyor – general of Oregon from 1853 to 1857, then as clerk to the U. S. Treasury Department where he remained until his retirement.

Col. Gardner authored _A Dictionary of Commissioned Officers Who Have Served in the Army of the United States from 1789 to 1853_, _A Compendium of Military Tactics_, and _A Permanent Designation of Company Books, by the First Letters of the Alphabet_ as well as a number of other military reference works, being a noted military author.

He was a Republican who supported the Union. His son Maj. Charles Gardner served as an officer in the Union Army while his son Maj. Gen. Franklin Gardner served as an officer in the Confederate Army. It was said Col. Charles Gardner was present as his son and his Rebels soldiers entered New York City, shaking the hands of the brave men who fought under his son's command at the Siege of Port Hudson, Louisiana.

Col. Charles K. Gardner died on November 1st, 1869 at age 82 in Washington, D. C.

References:
A History of the City Post Office by Madison Davis, Columbia Historical Society, Vol. 6
Dictionary of American Biography

MAJ. GEN. FRANK GARDNER

"He was every inch a soldier, gallant and true, and the idol of his men."

Maj. Gen. Frank Gardner, the Confederate General, was one of the finest battlefield generals during the American Civil War. He was tall, handsome, charming and witty. General Gardner was one of the hardest fighting generals in the War Between the States and he was the Rebel commander at the Battle of Port Hudson, Louisiana, the longest siege in American military history.

"Gardner's first appearance at Port Hudson impressed the men favorably, and he was at once popular. Part of his appeal was his looks. He was a tall man, with a fine military bearing and slightly receding hairline, hazel eyes that crinkled at the corners when he smiled – which was often – and a full brown beard that he stroked incessantly."
"At age forty Major General Franklin Kitchell Gardner was something of an enigma. Like Banks, he was charming, handsome, and witty, but unlike Banks, he was 'every inch a soldier, gallant and true, and the idol of his men.' He was also guilty of two counts of apostasy, which, in any other man, or in any other country, might have earned him a reputation of perpetual notoriety, if not a hangman's noose." – Lt. Wright, *Port Hudson: Its History From An Interior Point of View*

Franklin Kitchell Gardner was born on January 29th, 1823 in New York City, New York. His father was Col. Charles Gardner, a hero of the War of 1812, a noted military author, and a prominent man in Tammany Hall politics. His grandfather, Capt. Thomas Gardner, was a Revolutionary War hero, who served as a volunteer brigade wagon master. His brother would serve as an officer in the Union Army, while he served as an officer in the Confederate Army.

Gardner was educated at West Point Military Academy, in New York, being appointed by the State of Iowa, which he entered on July 1st, 1839 and as the top Drawing student during the whole time, he received several demerits and he graduated on July 1st, 1843 as number 17 in a class of 39, ranking higher than fellow classmate and future president at number 21, Ulysses S. Grant.

As a respected engineer, he was a Brevet Second Lieutenant and served in the 7th Infantry. He was on garrison duty at Pensacola Harbor, Florida in 1844 as a scout during the time of the Seminole Indian Wars. Afterwards, he served in the military occupation of Texas and on September 12th, 1845, he was promoted to full Second Lieutenant.

Gardner fought in the Mexican War and was noted for courage under fire, earning two brevets for gallantry. He participated in the Defense of Fort Brown, the Battle of Monterey, the Siege of Vera Cruz, the Battle of Cerro Gordo, the Battle of Contreras, the Battle of Churubusco, the Battle of Molino Del Rey, and operations before and the capture of Mexico City. It was at the Battle of Monterey and the Battle of Cerro Gordo, he proved himself as a warrior.

On September 23rd, 1846, Gardner was promoted to Brevet First Lieutenant for **"Gallant and Meritorious Conduct in the Several Conflicts at Monterey, Mex."**

On April 18th, 1847, Gardner was promoted to Brevet Captain for **"Gallant and Meritorious Conduct in the Battle of Cerro Gordo, Mex."**

"Lieut. Gardner became engaged with the enemy, but, he gallantly maintained his position against fearful odds..." – Col. William S. Harney

He was promoted to full First Lieutenant of the 7th Infantry on September 13th, 1847, and mustered out troops in New York in 1848, later being involved in the Florida hostilities from 1849 to 1850, being Acting Assistant Adjutant – General of the Eastern District of Florida. Afterwards, he was on frontier duty at Fort Gibson, Indian Territory. Later, he was on recruiting duty.

On July 9th, 1850, he married Matilde Mouton, daughter of Alexandre Mouton, former Governor of Louisiana. The former governor had married his sister, Emma Gardner. Thus, Frank Gardner was brother – in – law and son – in – law to Alexandre Mouton.

"Most men are changed by love and marriage, but rarely does such a transformation as Gardner's occur. From the day of his wedding until the end of his life, Franklin Gardner was Southern, heart and soul, temperment and behavior, politics and association. The rough and tumble world of Tammany Hall politics paled into insignificance by comparison with his new connections." – Lt. Howard Wright, _Port Hudson: Its History From An Interior Point of View_

On March 3rd, 1855, Gardner was promoted to Captain of the old 10th U. S. Infantry. He was on frontier duty at Fort Crawford, Wisconsin and Fort Snelling, Minnesota in 1856, and led an expedition to Red River of the North. Afterwards, he fought in the "Utah War", or the Mormon Expedition.

Captain Gardner was the commander at Fort Bridger, Utah, but on April 6th, 1861, he resigned his post as an officer in the U. S. Army, it being mentioned in the _Daily Dispatch_ and the _Alexandria Gazette_. However, on May 7th, 1861, he was listed as having dropped from rolls, being a deserter. It was likely some of his fellow Northerners acted as if he had not resigned.

Gardner was commissioned as Lieutenant Colonel in the Confederate Army and was reassigned Captain and Adjutant – General to Brig. Gen. Early. Then in March of 1862, he was assigned with a brigade of cavalry in the Army of Mississippi while at Corinth. Gardner led a brigade of cavalry in April of 1862 at the Battle of Shiloh and was a volunteer aide on the staff of General Bragg during the Kentucky invasion.

"The general commanding avails himself of this occasion to return his thanks to General Gardner for his services in the reorganization of the cavalry of this army." – General Pierre Beauregard

(M. D. Jones Collection)

On April 11th, 1862, Gardner was promoted to Brigadier General and was named Chief of Cavalry, fighting at the Battle of Perryville. Afterwards, he commanded an infantry brigade of Alabamians in Withers' division of Polk's Corps. Then on December 13th, 1862, he was promoted to Major General and was assigned command of fortifications at Port Hudson, Louisiana, north of Baton Rouge, replacing General William N. R. Beall.

Lt. Howard C. Wright noted General Gardner as **"a man of keen observation, a quick and practiced eye, frank and outspoken in all his comments, of a rapid delivery, always talking practically and directly to the point, and more than all, an able military engineer."**

General Gardner had 16, 000 forces strong, but most of the troops were ordered to Vicksburg. He was left with 7, 000 soldiers and on May 22nd, 1863, General Johnston gave orders to leave Port Hudson for Jackson, Mississippi. However, Union forces surrounded the fort from all sides.

General Nathaniel Banks, former governor of Massachusetts, had 40, 000
troops along with Admiral David Farragut of the Union Navy on the river.

On May 27th, 1863, General Banks ordered the first assault. It was a failure. It
demonstrated the brilliant military strategy of General Gardner.
The Union troops suffered 293 killed and 1, 545 wounded, while the
Confederate troops suffered 235 killed and wounded.

On June 14th, 1863, General Banks ordered another assault, which was
repelled by General Gardner and his Rebels.
The Union troops suffered 203 killed, 1, 401 wounded, and 188 missing, while
the Confederate troops suffered 22 killed and 25 wounded.

(Tulane University/Louisiana Research Collection)

The Confederate soldiers at Port Hudson, Louisiana idolized General Gardner,
and nicknamed him, "Daddy Long Legs". However, the Confederate forces
began suffering due to starvation and began deserting. The Rebel soldiers were
forced to eat their horses and mules; the Confederates also ran low on
ammunition.

General Gardner ordered 15 pounds of mule meat to his own mess.

On July 4th, 1863, General Pemberton surrendered to General Ulysses S. Grant at the Siege of Vicksburg; General Gardner, commander of the last Rebel stronghold on the Mississippi River, wrote a letter, stating:

HEADQUARTERS,
Port Hudson, La., July 7, 1863.
Maj. Gen. N. P. BANKS,
Comdg. U. S. Forces, near Port Hudson, La.:
GENERAL: Having received information from your troops that Vicksburg has been surrendered, I make this communication to ask you to give me the official assurance whether this is true or not; and, if true, I ask for a cessation of hostilities, with a view to consider terms for surrendering this position.
I remain, general, very respectfully, your obedient servant,
FRANK. GARDNER,
Major-general, Commanding C. S. Forces.

HDQRS. DEPT. OF THE GULF, NINETEENTH ARMY CORPS,
Before Port Hudson, La., July 8, 1863--1.15 a.m.
Maj. Gen. FRANK. GARDNER,
Comdg. C. S. Forces, Port Hudson, La.:
GENERAL: In reply to your communication, dated the 7th instant, by flag of truce, received a few moments since, I have the honor to inform you that I received yesterday morning, July 7, at 10.45 o'clock, by the gunboat General Price, an official dispatch from Maj. Gen. Ulysses S. Grant, U. S. Army, whereof the following is a true extract:
HEADQUARTERS DEPARTMENT OF THE TENNESSEE,
Near Vicksburg, Miss.; July 4, 1863.

On July 9th, after 48 days, the Siege of Port Hudson ended. The Confederates surrendered. General Gardner offered his sword to General George L. Andrews, but it was refused. The Siege of Port Hudson became known as the "Forty Days and Nights in the Wilderness of Death".

On December 3rd, 1892, *The Opelousas Courier* stated that after the prisoners of war were transferred from New Orleans to New York City, Col. Charles Gardner shook the hands of the brave men under his son's command.

"Gardner had defended Port Hudson to the utmost of his ability. After more than forty days of merciless pounding from the [Union] fleet and land batteries, his men were exhausted and dispirited. Improperly clothed, sheltered, and fed, they sickened, and there was no medicine for them. Hope that Johnston would send relief grew fainter as each day of the siege progressed. As Gardner's meager supply of ammunition was nearly exhausted, many of his guns were wrecked, and his food stock was dangerously low, the news of the surrender of Vicksburg decided the fate of Port Hudson." – John D. Winters, *The Civil War in Louisiana* (1963)

General Gardner in December of 1863 on Royal Street in New Orleans
(Louisiana State Museum)

General Gardner was forever known as the "Hero of Port Hudson". The Union forces had 708 men killed, 3, 336 wounded, and 319 captured or missing. The Confederate forces had an estimated 176 to 250 killed, 447 wounded, while about 200 died from disease and about 250 deserted.

Gardner earned fame as a great fighter for his defense at the Siege of Port Hudson. He built extensive fortifications at the important garrison at its peak. The conflicting orders of his superiors found him surrounded, besieged, and greatly outnumbered.

His achievement at holding out for 48 days, from May 22nd, 1863 to July 9th, 1863, and his ability to inflict severe losses on the enemy before surrendering has been praised by military historians.

As a war hero to the South, he was a prisoner of war to the North. It was in July of 1864, he was one of the "Immortal Six Hundred" placed within range of Confederate batteries during the Federal assault at Charleston. Once again proving his toughness, he made it out alive and refused to take the Oath of Allegiance.

It was in August of 1864, he was exchanged and in 1865 he commanded an infantry division under General Richard Taylor in Mississippi, serving in the Department of East Louisiana, Mississippi, and Alabama, his last engagement on December 28th, 1864 at the Battle of Egypt Station, Mississippi.

As the war ended in 1865, General Gardner, a great warrior, excellent soldier, and brilliant commander, retired as a farmer with his wife and children, but had first moved to New Orleans where he was a draftsman, newspaper reporter, and appointed surveyor of Lafayette Parish, Louisiana. His father was a defender of the Republican faith, and his brother Charles Gardner was an officer in the Union Army. However, Franklin Gardner, a true Rebel lived the rest of his life as a Southerner.

(Public Domain)

After the war, he lived peacefully as a planter on the banks of Bayou Vermilion. On Tuesday, April 29th, 1873, at 9 p. m., he died at age 50 in Vermilionville (now Lafayette), Louisiana, ten years after he had earned fame as the Confederate commander of the longest siege in American history. General Gardner was buried near his young daughter Ann Emma Gardner, and years later his son Alfred Mouton Gardner in 1892, and his wife Matilde Mouton Gardner in 1915, at St. John Cemetery.

On May 3rd, 1873, Page 2, Col. 5, of the *Lafayette Advertiser* stated:
> **"He was every inch a soldier, gallant and true, and the idol of his men; and the announcement of his death will be received with universal regret throughout the South."**

Entered according to act of Congress, in the Clerk's office of the U. S D. C., Eastern District of Louisiana, by T. Lilienthal, 15th September, 1863.

(Louisiana State Museum)

(Library of Congress)

References:
Port Hudson: Its History from an Interior Point of View by Howard C. Wright
Generals in Gray by Ezra Warner
Major General Franklin Gardner: Hero of the Siege of Port Hudson by Michael Dan Jones
www.la-cemeteries.com

Courtesy to my parents; my father, Larry Gardner told me we were related to General Gardner, and my mother, Jenny Gardner helped me research the life story of General Gardner, beginning my passion of reading and writing biographies of those with the last name Gardner.

BRIG. GEN. WILLIAM MONTGOMERY GARDNER

Brigadier General William Montgomery Gardner, the Southern Gentleman, was a Confederate general in the American Civil War. He was a native of Georgia and a man of the Old South. Gardner was a valuable Rebel officer.

William Montgomery Gardner was born on June 8th, 1824 on the Sand Hills near Augusta, Georgia. His father was James Gardner, the son of a Scotsman, and he married Elizabeth McKinnie, of Newburn, North Carolina, and settled in Augusta, Georgia. James Gardner was an attorney and editor of the *"Constitutionalist"*, the leading newspaper in Georgia.

The elder Gardner had the reputation of being a duelist, and he was described as **"one of the bravest of the brave"** and **"no man wrote with more logical force, polish, and brilliancy than did James Gardner."** – *Georgia: Comprising Sketches of Counties, Towns, Events, Institutions, and...* by Allen David Chandler.

As a young man, William Montgomery Gardner began his education at Georgetown College, D. C., but his interest in the military led him to the United States Military Academy. He graduated from West Point in 1846 in the same class as Thomas "Stonewall" Jackson. Afterwards, he served in the 2nd United States Infantry.

Brevet Second Lieutenant Gardner fought in the Mexican War and arrived at noon to join his regiment, the 1st U. S. Infantry at the Battle of Monterey. He was promoted to full Second Lieutenant in the 2nd U. S. Infantry at the Siege of Vera Cruz. Gardner charged a battery of 12 – pound cannons successfully taking the guns at the Battle of Contreras and was wounded in the groin but refused to report to a doctor.

Gardner was wounded at the Battle of Churubusco in the breast. He staggered back in a corn field as the Mexican soldiers murdered the wounded American soldiers. It was stated: **"The surgeons feared to probe for the bullet, which had lodged somewhere in his lung, and he carried that Mexican bullet with him to his dying day. The extreme severity of this wound incapacitated him for duty for several months."**

After the Siege of Mexico City, the war ended and he was appointed by General Riley on his personal staff and accompanied him on his march to Vera Cruz, being promoted to First Lieutenant due to gallantry. They left for New Orleans and then had orders to march to California.

Gardner fought Indians on the Plains while on scouting expeditions and he married Helen Maria Long in 1852 while in the 2nd U. S. Infantry with her brother John Long, and afterwards led a pioneer march to the Red River of the North, completing the maps for the War Department.

On March 3rd, 1855, he was promoted to Captain in the U. S. Army, and after the State of Georgia seceded from the Union, Captain Gardner resigned in January of 1861 after 15 years in the U. S. Army. He was promoted to Major in the Confederate Army and Assistant Adjutant General for the Defenses of Savannah, Georgia.

Gardner was promoted to Lieutenant Colonel of the 8th Georgia Regiment and on July 21st, 1861, he fought at the First Battle of Bull Run (First Manassas). He was severely wounded in the leg with a mini cannon ball, and it was thought to be a mortal wound. General Beauregard stated: **"Heavy losses had now been sustained on our side, both in numbers and in the personal worth of the slain. The Eighth Georgia regiment had suffered heavily, being exposed, as it took and maintained its position, to a fire from the enemy, already posted within a hundred yards of their front and right, sheltered by fences and other cover. It was at this time that Lieutenant Colonel Gardner was severely wounded, as also several other valuable officers."**

On November 14th, 1861, he was commissioned Brigadier General and was in command of the District of Middle Florida. General Gardner fought at the Battle of Olustee in 1864, it being a decisive Confederate victory. Afterwards, in July of that year he was assigned to the command of military prisons.

Brigadier General William M. Gardner commanded the post at Salisbury, North Carolina and from January to April of 1865, he commanded the post at Richmond, Virginia.

There has been no record of his parole found.

After the war, he lived in Rome, Georgia, with his wife Helen, and their children: James Gardner (1860 – 1934), Marion Gardner (1861 – 1947), John Long Gardner (1862 – 1929), Alexander Gardner (1864 – 1866), Sarah Gardner (1865 – 1866), and Helen Gardner (1870 – 1870), three surviving to adulthood.

On June 16th, 1901, he died at age 77 from malaria at his son's home in Memphis, Tennessee, and he was buried at the Elmwood Cemetery.

Elizabeth McKinnie Gardner edited a book titled, *The Memoirs of Brigadier General William Montgomery Gardner*.

On Junc 17th, 1901, *The New York Times* reported:

"Gen. William Montgomery GARDNER, a veteran of the Mexican and Civil Wars, died at Memphis, Tenn., last night. He was a native of Augusta, Ga., seventy – eight years old, and was graduated from the Military Academy at West Point in the class of '46. In the battle of Contreras, in Mexico, Aug. 26, 1847, young Gardner, then a Lieutenant, stormed a battery of twelve – pounders, casemated, with a single platoon of American soldiers, taking the guns. At Churubusco a few days later Gen. Gardner was severely wounded. At the outbreak of the war of the rebellion Gen. Gardner became Colonel of the Eighth Georgia Regiment."

Photograph of William M. Gardner retrieved on April 2nd, 2019 at
https://en.wikipedia.org/wiki/William_M._Gardner#/media/File:William_Montgomery_Gardner.jpg
https://de.wikipedia.org/wiki/William_Montgomery_Gardner#/media/File:William_Montgomery_Gardner.jpg

Photographs of General William M. Gardner are public domain

References:
Confederate Military History, Volume IV
Thirty-Second Annual Reunion of the Association of the Graduates of the United States Military Academy

LT. COL. ROBERT D. GARDNER

Lt. Col. Robert D. Gardner, the Confederate Officer, fought at the Battle of Antietam. He was a proud Southerner. Gardner was a warrior of the South.

Robert Davison Gardner was born on December 27th, 1830 in Montgomery County, Virginia. He served in the First Virginia Regiment during the Mexican War. Afterwards, he moved to Pulaski County and worked as a carpenter.

On April 17th, 1861 he enlisted in the 4th Virginia Infantry, Company C, and was elected First Lieutenant. Then on July 25th, 1862 he was elected Captain and on April 22nd, 1863, he was elected Lieutenant Colonel of the Regiment. As he was in command of the Regiment on the Maryland Campaign, he took over the brigade after Colonel Grigsby was mortally wounded while at the Battle of Antietam.

Lt. Col. Gardner was badly wounded in the jaw at the Battle of Fredericksburg on December 13th, 1862 and returned home to recover, being resigned from field service and took the post as Commander of the depot at Dublin, Virginia.

After the war he was elected clerk of the County and Circuit of Courts of Pulaski in 1870 and served until 1889, and on July 12th, 1906 he died in Dublin, Virginia and was buried in Newbern, Pulaski County, Virginia.

References:
Hardesty's Historical and Geographical Encyclopedia, Special Virginia Edition by R. A. Brock
4th Virginia Infantry by Jas. I. Robertson

SGT. TOM GARDNER

Sgt. Tom Gardner, the Confederate Cavalryman, was a Rebel warrior. He was a Southern gentleman. Gardner was a warrior for Southern Independence.

Meredith Thomas Gardner was born on June 12th, 1833 in Reform, Pickens County, Alabama. His parents were Daniel B. Gardner and Elizabeth Taylor Gardner. The Gardner family removed to Chickasaw County, Mississippi and on December 20th, 1859, Tom Gardner married Flora Isabella Buchanan, the couple having ten children.

Tom Gardner enlisted in the Confederate Army during the American Civil War. He served in Company C, 8th (Wade's) Confederate Cavalry as a private. Gardner earned the rank of ordinance sergeant at the end of the war.

After the war he removed to Lee County, Mississippi, then back to Chickasaw County by 1880 and by 1900 he was living in Blue Mountain, Tippah County, Mississippi where he died on July 9th, 1911, being buried at the Blue Mountain Cemetery.

Courtesy to the late Jack Hanun Gardner and Tom Garner for photograph

PVT. BILLY GARDNER

"I am the man who captured and took prisoner R. B. Hayes at this battle."
– W. G. "Billy" Gardner

Confederate Pension Application stated:
"Mr. W. G. Gardner, the faithful old soldier and very worthy applicant did on 6th day of April 1863 capture his highness ex – president Hays then a General in the U. S. A. and one orderly by himself having to shoot off his majesty's forefinger before he would surrender, bringing him into camp and turning him over to the provo guard, said capture was made to the left of the old plank road near Chancellorsville in the wilderness in old Va. He is also burdened with an afflicted wife and has been for twenty years and prays that you may accept this application for a small pension. Very truly, W. P. Wright, M. D."

Pvt. Billy Gardner, the Rebel Sharpshooter, claimed he shot and captured General Rutherford B. Hayes, afterwards President of the United States. The claim has not been confirmed or denied. Gardner was a warrior of the South who had been wounded five times in four of the bloodiest battles during the War Between the States, earning the Southern Cross of Honor.

William Gayden Gardner was born on November 30th, 1832 in South Carolina. His parents were James Gardner and Catherine Elizabeth Thompson Gardner, and the Gardner family removed to Monroe County, Georgia in the 1830s where his father was a gunsmith and farmer. As a young man he became an expert with firearms.

He was a farmer in Monroe County, Georgia, and he married Sarah Meriwether Littlejohn during the 1850s, producing several children. Billy Gardner was an unlikely hero, standing 5' 5, with light hair, light complexion, and blue eyes, according to his Veterans' papers. The War Between the States came in 1861 and at age 29, Gardner enlisted in Company A, 14th Georgia Infantry Regiment as a private on August 7th, 1862 in Forsyth, Georgia.

According to newspapers, Billy Gardner was a sharpshooter. There is record of a soldier named James Gardner who was in the 1st Georgia Sharpshooters Regiment, which may have been an alternate name he used, it being his father's name. However, it is likely that he was one of the best shooters in the 14th Georgia Infantry, and he was often used as a sniper during battle.

On August 30th, 1862, he was wounded in the head at Second Manassas, Virginia, the Second Battle of Bull Run. Afterwards, he fought at the Battle of Chancellorsville, Virginia, on May 3rd, 1863, being wounded in the left shoulder. It was a major Confederate victory led by General Stonewall Jackson.

Gardner claimed he shot and captured Union officer Rutherford B. Hayes on April 6th, 1863 at Chancellorsville; May 6th, 1863 at Chancellorsville; and on May 6th, 1864 at Wilderness. It is possible the capture took place during a skirmish and why it was unrecorded. The most likely date was at the Battle of Chancellorsville.

It was at either Chancellorsville or Wilderness, Gardner claimed he was looking for a place to shoot a Yankee officer, when he heard a commotion in a tree above his head. He spied Union army officer Rutherford B. Hayes and ordered him to surrender. Hayes replied he would never surrender to a private and raised his saber, Gardner shooting the sword out of his hand, taking off his forefinger, and taking him prisoner.

Rutherford B. Hayes was wounded four times during the Civil War, but never served at Chancellorsville or Wilderness, and was never recorded as being captured.

From Hayes diary: **"Camp White, April 5, 1863: Dearest: The weather is good, our camp dry,.....Camp White, April 9, 1863: Dear Uncle: Yours of the 3rd received........
May 5, 1864: Thursday. From Prince's to Camp Creek....May 6. Friday To Princeton sixteen miles. Very hot and dusty...."**

It is possible that it happened at a skirmish, but the most likely scenario is Billy Gardner shot and captured a different Union army officer named Hayes.

"On May 6th, 1864, received gunshot wounds in forehead and left shoulder which said wound in left shoulder has rendered said left arm essentially and substantially useless to me. I am the man who captured and took prisoner R. B. Hayes at this battle (Wilderness)." – W. G. Gardner's Confederate Pension application

Afterwards, Gardner fought at the Battle of Petersburg and was wounded in the right foot on April 3rd, 1865, his name appearing on a roll of Prisoners of War captured in a hospital in Richmond, Virginia. He was turned over to the Provost Marshall on April 14th, 1865 and was transferred on April 23rd to Libby Prison in Richmond to Newport News, Virginia. Gardner was released on June 26th, 1865 at Newport News, Virginia upon taking the Oath of Allegiance, after being wounded in the head at the Second Battle of Bull Run; the left shoulder at the Battle of Chancellorsville; the head and left shoulder during the Wilderness Campaign; and the right foot at the Battle of Petersburg.

Gardner was now 32 years old and had been wounded five times. He made his way back to Gogginsville, Georgia and resumed his life as a farmer and family man. It is said he also made moonshine whiskey, or "spirits".

It was in the fall of 1876 that a former Union general named Rutherford B. Hayes ran for President of the United States.

The legend of Billy Gardner made it to *The Monroe Advertiser* that year, stating **"Here's a hero!** The South hailed him as a hero, while the Northern press denied his allegations. The alleged date was May 6th, 1864 at Wilderness or Chancellorsville, the newspapers describing him as a **"gentleman and an old Confederate soldier."** Gardner's company commander, Capt. Robert Merritt, confirmed the capture.

However, there is no record of Rutherford B. Hayes being captured or being in the same areas as William G. Gardner during battles. There were six Union officers by the name of Hayes or Hays during the American Civil War. Three Yankee officers by that name were captured.

1st Candidate:
General William Hays was a Union general who was shot and captured on May 3rd or 6th, 1863 at the Battle of Chancellorsville, Virginia, along with all but one of his immediate staff.

2nd Candidate:
General Edwin Hayes was a brevet Union general who was captured in September of 1863 and sent to Libby prison.

3rd Candidate:
General Joseph Hayes had participated at the Battle of Chancellorsville, but was not captured there. It was written that Hayes received a bullet in the skull on May 5th, 1864 at the Battle of Wilderness. General Hayes was captured on August 19th, 1864 at the Siege of Petersburg, where Gardner had participated.

4th Candidate:
General Alexander Hays was shot and killed by a sharpshooter's bullet to the head on May 5th, 1864 at the Battle of Wilderness. Gardner had given the date of May 6th, 1864 at Wilderness as when he shot Hayes. Although General Alexander Hays was killed instead of captured, he had indeed attended West Point Military Academy, as Gardner had stated in an interview.

The 5th Candidate was General Philip C. Hayes, who was never captured or wounded, and was brevetted a general after the war.

It is possible there are more Union officers named Hayes or Hays.

President Rutherford B. Hayes died in 1893 and on January 31st, 1893, the *Columbus Daily Enquirer* stated how the death of the president revived the story of his capture at the Battle of Chancellorsville by William G. Gardner, even stating it was a fact Hayes had been captured despite being denied by the Northern press.

It stated: **"When Mr. Gardner captured General Hayes he led him to the Confederate headquarters. On reaching there the prisoner was warmly greeted by Gen. A. P. Hill, the two having been at West Point together.**

Mr. Gardner tells of this incident with a great deal of pride."

However, Rutherford B. Hayes never attended West Point Military Academy. On the other hand, a Union general named William Hays was an 1840 graduate of West Point, while General A. P. Hill was an 1842 graduate of West Point. Records state General William Hays was shot, wounded, and captured with all but one of his immediate staff on May 3rd, 1863 at the Battle of Chancellorsville.

Report of Maj. Gen. Ambrose P. Hill, C. S. Army, commanding Second Army Corps.

APRIL 27-MAY 6, 1863.--The Chancellorsville Campaign. O.R.-- SERIES I--VOLUME XXV/1 [S# 39]

HEADQUARTERS SECOND ARMY CORPS,
Archer's brigade captured four guns, and Brig. Gen. William Hays was captured by Pender's brigade.

On May 3rd, 1863, Gardner shot and wounded Brigadier General William Hays, taking him prisoner, along with all but one of his immediate staff at the Confederate victory at the Battle of Chancellorsville. This is the most likely scenario. Later in May of 1863, General Hays was exchanged as a prisoner of war.

It is likely in the 19th Century, William G. Gardner had never seen a picture of President Rutherford B. Hayes and if he had, the president's beard would have changed his appearance, as General William Hays only had a mustache in photographs.

General William Hays continued his career as a U. S. Army officer until his death in 1875, a year before the 1876 election when Rutherford B. Hayes ran for the presidency.

William G. Gardner was a brave warrior, described as a gentleman and respected by the people of his county in Georgia.

On December 6th, 1912, the *Monroe Advertiser* stated:

"The many friends of "Uncle Billy" Gardner will be interested in learning that he has been sent to the Confederate Soldiers' Home in Atlanta. Few of the county's veterans are better known than he and he will be missed by his comrades and his friends.

"Uncle Billy" was a sharpshooter. His father had been a gunsmith and the young man grew up accustomed to the handling of a gun and throughout the entire war he served in this branch of the service.

Mr. Gardner is the man who had the honor of capturing Rutherford B. Hayes, afterwards President of the United States. Mr. Gardner was one day seeking an advantageous firing position when he heard a commotion in a tree over his head; looking up he spied Hayes, then an officer, and commanded him to surrender. Hayes replied that he would only surrender to an officer and when Mr. Gardner's further commands were unavailing he fired taking off one of the fingers with which Hayes held his drawn sword."

The saga of Gardner shooting and capturing Hayes was told again and again in the local newspapers.

Gardner was a local hero in Monroe County, Georgia, a living legend. His son, Tom Gardner was principal of the school in Zebulon, Georgia. Later, "Uncle Billy" was sent to the Confederate Soldiers' Home in Atlanta.

On December 23rd, 1912, William G. Gardner died at 80 years old in Atlanta, Georgia and was buried at Shiloh Baptist Church Cemetery in Lamar County, next to his wife.

Gardner was awarded the Southern Cross of Honor in 1933 by Willie Hunt Chapter #49, the United Daughters of the Confederacy.

The Jackson Progress – Argus stated: **"The medal was presented to Juanita Gardner Weaver (Mrs. W. S. Weaver) of Jackson, his only living grandchild recently by a cousin, Leroy Gardner of McDonough. Mr. Gardner said the medal was given to him along with other "keep sakes."**

Courtesy to Leroy Gardner, Van Gardner, and Charlene Weaver

References:
The Monroe Advertiser
Columbus Dailey Enquirer
Barnesville Gazette

Billy Gardner is a distant cousin, a descendant of Daniel Gardner.

BRIG. GEN. JOHN LANE GARDNER

Brig. Gen. John Lane Gardner, the Union Officer, was a brevet brigadier general in the Union Army during the American Civil War. He was a veteran of the War of 1812, the Seminole Indian War, the Mexican War, and the American Civil War. Gardner was perhaps the oldest field officer of the Civil War and served in the U. S. Army for 40 years.

John Lane Gardner was born on August 1st, 1793 in Boston, Massachusetts. He joined the U. S. Army during the War of 1812 and was appointed with the rank of Third Lieutenant on May 20th, 1813 in the 4th Infantry. Gardner was wounded on March 30th, 1814 at the Battle of La Cole Mills serving under Gen. Wilkinson. He fought in the Second Seminole War in Florida from 1835 to 1839, in 1836 fighting at the Battle of Wahoo Swamp, later writing and publishing the book titled *Military Control*.

Gardner earned the rank of major and commanded the 4th Artillery Regiment during the Mexican War under Maj. Gen. Winfield Scott. On April 18th, 1847 he fought at the Battle of Cerro Gordo and was brevetted as a lieutenant colonel **"for Gallant and Meritorious Conduct"**. On August 20th, 1847 he fought at the Battle of Contreras and was brevetted as a colonel **"for Gallant and Meritorious Conduct"**. He then served as Superintendent of Assessment for the Federal District in 1848 during the occupation of northern Mexico.

Col. Gardner was in command of Charleston Harbor in November of 1860, but was replaced by Maj. Robert Anderson, chosen by Secretary of War, John B. Floyd, a Confederate loyalist. On November 1st, 1861, Gardner retired from active service and was involved in recruitment duty for the remainder of the war. He was brevetted to brigadier general **"for long and faithful service"** in 1866 and served on the Board for Retiring Disabled Officers in Philadelphia, Pennsylvania. John Lane Gardner died at age 75 on February 19th, 1869 of pneumonia in Wilmington, Delaware, being buried at Immanuel Episcopal Church on the Green.

Photograph is public domain (Library of Congress)

MAJ. ASA GARDNER

Maj. Asa Gardner, the Yankee Officer, was a controversial Medal of Honor recipient. He earned notoriety as a New York prosecutor and trial attorney. The former Union officer and war hero was Judge Advocate most of his career.

Gardner was notorious for his corruption, stating, **"Reform be damned."**

Asa Bird Gardner was born on September 30th, 1839 in Manhattan, New York, the son of Asa and Rebekah Willard Bentley Gardner. His father worked as a bartender of the Fraunces Tavern. As a young man, Asa Gardner received a BA from City College and in 1860, received his LL. B. from New York University School of Law.

Afterwards, he received his admission to the New York City Bar Association and went into private practice as an attorney.

On May 27th, 1861, Gardner was commissioned as a first lieutenant in Company H, 31st New York Infantry Regiment. However, he resigned on August 7th of that year and on May 31st, 1862, he was commissioned as a captain in the 22nd New York Militia. He mustered out in September, but was again commissioned on June 18th, 1863 as a captain in the same regiment.

Gardner fought at the Battle of Gettysburg and distinguished himself for bravery under fire. He musterered out again in July of 1863 when the regiment's term of service expired. Afterwards, he was commissioned as a first lieutenant in the Veterans Reserve Corps on February 11st, 1865 and served as regimental adjutant until he was honorably mustered out a year later.

On March 13th, 1865, Gardner was brevetted a captain for **"gallant and meritorious service during the war."**

After the war, he married Mary Austen of Baltimore in October of 1865 and they had five children, all sons named Asa Bird Jr., George, Philip, William and Norman.

He was then commissioned as a second lieutenant of the 9th Infantry Regiment of the Regular Army, being promoted on February 14th, 1868 to first lieutenant. He transferred in April of 1869 to the 1st Artillery Regiment. On August 18th, 1873, he earned the rank of major.

On September 23rd, 1872, Gardner was awarded the Medal of Honor for **"distinguished service performed during the war while serving as Captain 22nd New York State Militia"** and **"conspicuous bravery and distinguished conduct during the Gettysburg Campaign, particularly in the action of Sporting Hill...and the defense of Carlisle."** It was noted he was wounded during the fighting near Carlisle and that it was also for his actions at Sporting Hill. His past record also indicated his courage under fire.

His actions were for Sporting Hill on June 30th, 1863 and for the defense of Carlisle on July 1st and 2nd, of the same year.

West Point Military Academy established a Department of Law in 1874 and Secretary of War William W. Belknap appointed Gardner to the post of senior Judge Advocate, becoming the first lawyer to teach law at the Academy. He initiated the entire law curriculum and included the study of the Lieber Code. Gardner also wrote a textbook himself.

He served from July of 1874 to August of 1878 and was commonly known as "Colonel Gardiner", despite actually being a major.

President Ulysses S. Grant chose Maj. Gardner as judge advocate general of a number of legal proceedings in 1875, including the court – martial of Brig. Gen.

Orville Babcock. Later, he reviewed the court – martial of Fitz John Porter and in 1880, reviewed one of the first black West Point cadets, Johnson Chestnut Whittaker. Gardner acted as prosecuter.

Then in 1884, he was selected for another high – profile prosecution of his superior Brig. Gen. David G. Swaim, the Judge Advocate of the Army, resulting in a conviction and suspension from duty.

On July 11th, 1884, he legally changed the spelling of his name from "Gardner" to "Gardiner". According to a letter he wrote to the *New York Times*, conformed to the spelling of the last name of his ancestors. It is believed his ancestors originated in Rhode Island.

Asa Bird Gardner also claimed to have descended from Sir Osborn Gardner, Knight, Lord of the Manor of Horul (Oral) on Douglas River in Wigan Parish, West Derby Hundred, County of Lancaster, and Lancashire, England.

Then in 1887, Asa Bird Gardiner was appointed Acting Assistant Secretary of War and held the position until he retired the next year.

Maj. Asa Gardner, alias Gardiner, served as a Judge Advocate for 15 years until December of 1888 when he retired from the U. S. Army. He practiced private law in New York City. He was then elected on the Democratic ticket as New York County District Attorney in 1897 but was put on trial for corruption. He was aquitted, but was removed from office in 1900 by Governor Theodore Roosevelt for refusing to prosecute the corrupt Tammany Hall bosses of New York City.

Gardiner proclaimed, **"The hell with reform!"** His beneficiaries of his anti – reform attidue included saloon keeper Frank Farrell who opened three hundred pool halls, bringing in a fortune which he would later use to bring the New York Yankees ball team to town.

His wife Mary died in 1900 and he remarried two years later to Harriet Isabelle Lindsay of New York, fathering two sons named John and William.

On September 10th, 1913, he was the orator at the commemoration of the Battle of Lake Erie in Newport, Rhode Island. He wore a Veteran Corps of Artillery uniform and spoke as the Commandant of the Military Society of the War of 1812, being described as a a great orator. Gardiner also belonged to a number of military and hereditary societies, including the Society of the Cincinnati, the Military Order of the Loyal Legion of the United States, the Grand Army of the Republic, the Sons of the Revolution, as well as being Commandant with the rank of colonel in the Military Society of the War of 1812, along with the Veteran Corps of Artillery of the State of New York.

He was also a member of the Union Club, the Metropolitan Club, and the Delta Kappa Epsilon fraternity and like his father, he was Sachem in the Tammany Society.

Asa Bird Gardiner wrote *The Order of the Cincinnati in France*, which was published in 1905 by the Rhode Island Society which contains all of the senior French Army officers that served in America during the revolution.

It was in 1917, his Medal of Honor was revoked after being reviewed by a panel led by Lieutenant General Nelson A. Miles. They found no evidence to support Gardiner deserving the award. However, Gardiner refused to return the medal.

On May 24th, 1919, Asa Bird Gardner, alias Gardiner, died at age 79 from a stroke of apoplexy at his home, Orrell Manor in Suffern, New York, being buried in Brooklyn.

Photograph is public domain created January 1st, 1865, Asa Gardner and retrieved on April 2nd, 2019 at https://en.wikipedia.org/wiki/Asa_Bird_Gardiner#/media/File:Asa_Bird_Gardiner.png

References:
The Brown Book: A Biographical Record of Public Officials of the City of New York by Martin B. Brown
Grant: A Biography by William S. McFeely
History of the Tammny Society: Or Columbian Order by Euphemia Vale Blake
Register of Commissioned Officers of the United States Army, 1889. pp. 350 - 351
Dyer's Compendium of the War of Rebellion

CAPT. JOSEPH GARDNER

Capt. Joseph Gardner, the Freedom Fighter, was a militant abolitionist. He was an officer in the Union Army during the Civil War. Gardner was the victor of one of the last violent battles of the Kansas – Missouri border war.

"He opened the door. Standing upon the broad stone step were two men, revolvers in hand. In less than one second, he shot one of them, dropping him in his tracks." – Theodore Gardner, *The Last Battle of the Border War: A Tragic Incident in the Early History of Douglas County*

He stood 6' 4, with piercing eyes, and a full beard.

Joseph Gardner was born on July 7th, 1820 in Indiana Territory, his family originating in North Carolina, it being said they were of Quaker stock in 1620 from Nantucket Island. His father was William Gardner and his mother was Mary Hollingsworth, both being opposed to slavery.

He lived in Union County, Indiana where he married Eliza Weaver in 1841, the couple having three children, Mary, Theodore, and Eudorus. His wife died in 1848 and in 1849 he remarried to Sarah Maxwell, having three children, Enos, Eva, and Orlando. Then in May of 1855, he removed the family to Kansas where he staked a claim in Douglas County on Washington Creek near Lone Star.

Gardner became involved in the border wars of Kansas and Missouri in 1856, later arranging his affairs back in Indiana, then returning to Kansas in February of 1857, landing in Leavenworth via a steamer.

It was in June of 1859, Joseph Gardner participated in the rescue of abolitionist Dr. John Doy from the St. Joseph jail in Missouri. He became a marked man. The sheriff of Buchanan County, Missouri, offered a $500 Reward on his head, wanted dead or alive.

Aside from being an outlaw, in the fall of 1859, he assisted in the organization of the first Douglas County Agricultural Society and was elected president.

It was in November of 1859, Joseph Gardner was in a party of men to release the infamous John Brown from the Harper's Ferry Jail, but Brown refused to be part of the scheme, being hanged as a martyr for slavery.

The 6' 4 Jayhawker was part of the Kansas underground railroad and in the summer of 1860 he employed two runaway slaves. He knew that pro – slavery bounty hunters would retaliate. Gardner visited his friend George Stearns, asking for additional weapons.

On the night of June 9th, 1860, one of the last violent battles of the Kansas and Missouri border wars happened at his home. The pro – slavery bounty hunters made war upon his home. As one of the bounty hunters approached the door, Gardner fired his Colt Navy revolver into Hard Petrican's chest, wounding him. A gunfight ensued in which one of his runaway slaves named Napoleon Simpson was mortally wounded. The desperadoes attempted to burn down his home, but a light rain poured and the attackers fled.

Joseph Gardner stated: **"Three or more men came to my door demanding admission, and to the question as to their names and business I got only curses with a renewal of the demand to open the door. I then discharged my revolver at the person...This was the signal for hostilities. My shot was answered with promptness and vigor on both sides."**

His runaway slave, Napoleon Simpson had been mortally wounded in the gunfight, Gardner stating: **"While he was weltering in his blood I went to him and asked if I could do anythnig for him, expressing a regret that I still had to watch. His only reply was fight! Fight hard!"**

Joseph Gardner had won the last gun battle of the Kansas – Missouri border war.

He enlisted in July of 1861 at Fort Leavenworth into the Union Army in the Third Kansas Infantry, spending the winter with Lane's Brigade at Camp Defiance on Mine Creek, Linn County, Kansas and he was discharged in the summer of 1862, accepting a commission in the First Kansas Colored Regiment and assisted in recruiting a company at Lawrence.

Capt. Joseph Gardner led his troops in October of 1862 to Island Mound, Missouri where he was wounded, while one other officer was killed, eight enlisted killed, and eleven wounded.

He recovered from his wounds in April of 1863 and rejoined the regiment at Fort Scott, but became ill and died on August 23rd, 1863 while at a field hospital in Fort Gibson, Indian Territory in modern day Oklahoma.

His son, Theodore Gardner later stated: **"On that fateful night of June 9, 1860, when my father opened the door of his domicile in the face of desperadoes, standing upon its threshold with cocked revolvers, bent upon murder, planting the muzzle of his navy against the breast of one of them, and shooting him down, he exhibited a shining example of the indomitable courage of the pioneers of Kansas, who by such deeds of valor saved her virgin soil from the blighting curse of human slavery."**

"He passed on over the divide into the realms of the great mysterious beyond at Fort Gibson, Indian Territory, August 23, 1863, idolized by his family, respected by his neighbors and friends, and cordially hated by his enemies.

If there be records in the great hereafter upon which are registered the names of those who died battling in the cause of freedom and humanity, the name of Joseph Gardner will be inscribed there in letters of shining gold."

Courtesy to the Clinton Lake Historical Society for photograph

References:
A Standard History of Kansas and Kansans by William E. Connelley
The Last Battle of the Border War: A Tragic Incident in the Early History of Douglas County by Theodore Gardner
Proslavery Attack on Gardner Home by Theodore Gardner

SGT. BARNARD GARDNER

Sgt. Barnard Gardner, the Yankee Sniper, was an elite sniper with the 1st U. S. Sharpshooters. They wore green uniforms to distinguish themselves from the other Union soldiers. Gardner was one of Berdan's elite sharpshooters and fought in numerous battles during the American Civil War.

Barnard C. Gardner was born about 1842 in Lenox, New York. He worked as a carpenter and stood 5' 7 with grey eyes and brown hair. On August 24th, 1861, he enlisted at Babylon, New York in Company H, 1st Regiment, U. S. Sharp Shooters.

He was promoted to the rank of corporal and in April to May of 1862 he was at the Siege of Yorktown. Then in May of 1862 he fought at the Battle of Williamsburg and later that month was at the Battle of Hanover Court House. Then in June of that year he was at "Seven days before Richmond", then the Battle of Mechanicsville, and Gaine's Mill.

On July 1st, 1862 he was at Malverin's Hill. Then in August he was at the Battle of Grovton and the Rebel victory at the Second Battle of Bull Run. Later in September he fought at the Battle of South Mountain.

On September 16th, 1862 he was wounded in the left arm at the Battle of Antietam. However he continued to fight at Sharpsburg and on September 29th, 1862, he was promoted to sergeant. Gardner then fought at the Battle of Fredericksburg in December of that year.

Then in January of 1863 he was promoted to Sergeant – Major of the Battalion and was at Falmouth Camp until April of that year.

It was from May 1st to May 5th, 1863 he fought at the Battle of Chancellorsville, a Rebel victory and then in June of that year he was at Plains of Manassas.

Gardner acted as an "irregular" scout in June of 1863 and was captured by Mosby's Rangers, which included a Confederate Partisan Ranger named Private L. M. Gardner. As Sgt. Barnard Gardner was about to be hanged, he was saved by the 69th New York Regiment. He camped near Emmitsburg and was present for muster in July of that year.

On July 2nd, 1863, Sergeant Barnard Gardner fought at the Battle of Gettysburg, a Union victory, and was wounded in the shoulder. He was in the hospital from July to August of that year. Colonel Berda assigned him as a recruiter for the Union Army.

It was from September to October of 1863 he was a recruiter on Rikers Island, New York and then later that year he was on duty in Brooklyn, New York. Afterwards, from January to June of 1864 he was on recruiting service on Rikers Island, New York. Then in May of that year he was on hospital muster roll for an illness due to contracting tuberculosis in Alexandria, Virginia, later being discharged.

After the war, he married in March of 1866 in Albany, New York. He lived in Schenectady and Amsterdam, New York where he worked in the furniture business. Later, he settled in Addison, New York where he continued to work in the construction business with his father and brothers.

Gardner fathered five children and was a member of the Adams Center Baptist Church. He joined the local West Angle GAR post and the Addison Lodge of the Odd Fellows, also forming a drill team for boys and worked with the youth of Addison for Memorial Day celebrations. Gardner was an honorary member of the Pennsylvania Bucktails who fought side by side his 1st U. S. Sharpshooters Regiment and he was post commander of GAR Post #372 when he was 60 years old in May of 1902 and continued to help orphans and widows of the war.

On June 7th, 1910, Barnard C. Gardner died at age 68 following a fall from a construction project in Addison, New York and was buried in Addison Rural Cemetery.

References:
http://www.correctionhistory.org/civilwar/units/gardner/meetsgtgardner2.html
http://suvcw.org/past/bcgardner.htm

PVT. PETER GARDNER

Pvt. Peter Gardner, the Yankee Soldier, served in the Ohio Militia as one of the famous "Squirrel Hunters" Division. He was a handsome 6' 4 soldier. Gardner served his country in the War Between the States.

Peter Powell Gardner was born on September 17th, 1843 in Fulton, Morrow County, Ohio to James Gardner and Mary Frances Kaufman Gardner. His grandfather was Andrew Gardner who immigrated in 1824 from County Down, Northern Ireland. It was being raised on a farm that he learned marksmanship.

He enlisted in the militia, 39th Ohio Infantry and was part of a special unit known as the "Squirrel Hunters" which blocked Rebels from marching past Ohio. His uncle, William Gardner served in the Black Horse Battalion of Indiana and died at age 36 in July of 1863 at the Battle of Gettysburg. After the war, Peter Gardner married Nancy Fickell and they had six children.

Gardner raised high quality horses imported from Europe and owned a farm in Fulton, Ohio where he died at age 62 on January 4th, 1906, being buried at the Fulton Cemetery.

Photograph from www.findagrave.com courtesy to Steve Peters

COMMANDER FRANK GARDNER

Commander Frank Gardner, the Sailor, had a full life on the high seas. His career took him from serving in the Royal Navy in Crimea to the battlefields of Sebastabol to taking the Taku forts during the Second Opium War in China to gunrunning for the Confederate States of America. Commander Gardner lived out his days as an Australian Naval officer.

"No one was prouder than he to see the beautiful statue. He had seen a little war himself in his younger days, he hoped that on the anniversary of that ceremony peace would have been declared. In handing the statue over to the mayor for the people, he thanked them all for having sung that 'he was a jolly good fellow." – *Newcastle Herald*

Francis "Frank" Gardner was born on December 17th, 1841, at Bell's Inn, Church Street, Tewkesbury, in Gloucestershire, England. His parents were George and Mary Lewis Gardner and Frank was the youngest of six brothers, also having three sisters. As a boy, he was educated at Shothonger House Academy.

Afterwards, at age 14, he was sent to sea with the Royal Navy in 1855 aboard the new troopship *Earl of Eglinton* and engaged in transporting troops to the Crimea. Gardner assisted in the evacuation of British troops in the Crimea in 1856 towards the end of the war. Then in May of 1858, Gardner fought in the Second Opium War in China and lost part of a finger on one of his hands.

The sailor returned to England and left the Royal Navy in 1860, joining the mercanitle service where he journeyed to Savannah, Georgia in the United States. Gardner joined the Confederate forces and was present when the Rebels burned Northern vessels on the Savannah River. After six weeks of service at Fort Palaski, he was drafted to Charleston and joined the steamer *Sir Charles Napier*.

Gardner spent time blockade running making two trips from Liverpool to Savannah with cotton turpentine and tobacco cargoes, as well as iron for railroad track, medicine, and coffee. It is said he also did a bit of gun – running. Then in 1862, Gardner was a second mate on *The Lightning*, one of the fastest clipper ships, and it was on this voyage he first came to Australia.

The vessel first arrived at Melbourne, then New Zealand to Sydney. After he was paid, Gardner stayed in Australia. He gained employment on a station in Namoi in New South Wales where he assisted taking a flock of sheep to Queensland.

Gardner arrived in Newcastle in 1862 and associated himself with W. K. Lockhead, setting up a business in the School of Arts building. He opened a free store on Bolton Street, yet it burned down. Gardner established a general agency, insurance and auctioneering business at 97 Scott Street which he maintained until his death.

He took part in the first sale of land at Tighes Hill and helped lay out Adamstown. On April 30th, 1868, Frank Gardner married Jane "Jenny" Berwick from Lincolnshire, England and they settled on Church Street. However, his wife died in June of 1883 at only 32 years old.

As a lieutenant in 1886, Frank Gardner traveled to England and the Government appointed him one of the Commissioners at the Indian and Colonial Exhibition in London. It was here he was presented to Queen Victoria and other members of the Royal family. It is said the Queen questioned Lt.

Frank Gardner about the Australian troops volunteering for active service in the Soudan of northern Africa.

He traveled back to Australia where he was devoted to Newcastle Cathedral which he gave the marble alter of the Warriors Chapel. Gardner made several funds during the Great War and he presented the City of Newcastle with the Anzac memorial monument and statue in 1916 placed outside the Newcastle Post office. It is known as the Gardner Memorial.

Frank Gardner had joined the Newcastle Naval Brigade in 1863 and was promoted to Second Lieutenant in 1879, Lieutenant in 1886, Lieutenant Commander in 1893, and finally in 1902 he was promoted to Commander. He retained his post until 1913 after 40 years of service, he retired from the newly formed Royal Australian Naval Reserve. On the day of his retirement he was one of the oldest officers in the Australian Naval Reserves and had been a member of the Naval and Military Association since the beginning.

Along with H. Contis, he was founder of the Newcastle Sailors Home and was also involved in the formation of the Shipwreck Relief Society. Gardner served with the volunteer fire service as an honorary superitendant of the Newcastle brigades from 1882 until his retirement. He was also one of the founders of the Newcastle School of Arts and was a prominent Mason, being treasurer of the Hunter River Lodge.

Commander Gardner was described as an excellent marksman with a rifle and a good fisherman. He was nicknamed "The Father of Bowls" due to his skill at bowling in the northern district, being president of the Northern District Bowling Association. Gardner was also a good "draw shot" and "driving" player.

His hobbies included gardening, fishing, shooting, painting, and bowling.

On November 2nd, 1926, Commander Frank Gardner died at age 84 from natural causes. The *Newcastle Morning Herald*, Nov. 3rd, 1926, p8 c9, stated: **"He was also a lover of music and in his earlier days possessed a tenor voice of good quality. His home bears evidence of his prowess in sport in many cups and other trophies, and also of the esteem bore him in handsome gifts. The late Commander Gardner was of a quiet disposition, and was extremely liberal in cases of need. During his long and useful life he had made many true and lasting friends."**

Courtesy to Dr. Richard Walding of Brisbane, Australia for photographs and information

CAPT. CECIL GARDNER

"This officer is keen, dashing, and absolutely without fear." – E. R.
Pretyman, Major, Commanding No. 19 Squadron, Royal Air Force

Capt. Cecil Gardner, the Fighter Pilot, was a flying ace of the Great War. He
was an aerial assassin with ten notches. Gardner shot four planes down out of
control and destroyed six of the enemy in dogfights to the death.

Distinguished Flying Cross (DFC)
Lieut. (T. /Capt.) Cecil Vernon Gardner
**"A bold and skillful leader, who has carried out many offensive patrols,
proving himself at all times to be a brilliant fighting pilot. During recent
operations he has accounted for eight enemy machines."** - *FLIGHT*
Magazine (November 7th, 1918)

Cecil Vernon Gardner was born on September 14th, 1889 in Banbury,
Oxfordshire, England, the son of Jas. and Hannah Elizabeth Gardner. He was
raised at Grovehill Farm in Tingewick Parish near Buckingham and was
educated at the Royal Latin School. Gardner enlisted in December of 1915 into
the British Army.

He was a Second Class Air Mechanic before he was transferred into the Royal
Flying Corps in March of 1917 and in July of that year he was commissioned,
and began his training as an officer and pilot. Gardner was assigned to 19
Squadron Royal Flying Corps in January of 1918 to fly a Sopwith Dolphin.
Then on April 1st, 1918, the Royal Flying Corps and the Royal Naval Air Service
merged forming the Royal Air Force.

Fighter pilots were the gunslingers of the sky and Gardner had ten notches on his gun during his career, and he rode a steel horse called the Sopwith Dolphin in all of his escapades.

As a lieutenant in the Royal Air Force, Gardner attacked massed troops on Bapaume Roads on March 26th, 1918, firing 15 long bursts and dropped 4 bombs among the enemy as they ran in complete disorder. The next day he fired 110 rounds on German infantrymen. On March 30th, 1918, Gardner fired 360 rounds and dropped bombs on targets east of Albert with fellow pilots Hardman and Aldridge.

On June 6th, 1918, Gardner shot down his first enemy plane along with other British fighter pilots, Gordon Budd Irving, Finlay McQuistan, and John De Pencier at Vieux Berquin. On June 9th, 1918, he shot down a German pilot at Neuf Berquin. On June 28th, his engine cut out at 2, 000 feet near Ablain St. Nazaire and crashed. Then, in July of that year, four enemy planes fell before Gardner in duels to the death.

Capt. Gardner standing in his Sopwith Dolphin (*Fighter Squadron* by Derek Palmer)

On July 1st, 1918, Gardner shot down a Pfalz D.III over Fleurbaix and then on July 4th, he shot down another Pfalz D.III over Esterelles.

On July 13th (some reports suggest the 15th), the aerial assassin shot down a Fokker D.VII, destroying the enemy, over Bois du Biez, adding a fifth notch, making Gardner a flying ace.

On July 31st, Gardner shot down and destroyed an enemy flying a Pfalz D.III in a dogfight.

On August 11th, 1918, Gardner shot down two enemy planes in one afternoon. His seventh notch was a Pfalz D. III at 1700 hours which was shot down over Estrées, the pilot parachuting out. Gardner's eighth notch was at 1755 hours, in which he completely destroyed the enemy flying a Fokker D. VII over Brie.

He shared his ninth aerial victory on September 16th, 1918 with Capt. Hardman. Afterwards, he was promoted to temporary captain in the Royal Air Force. Capt. Gardner led the Dolphins on patrols that month.

On September 27th, 1918, Capt. Gardner destroyed a Fokker D. VII over Haynecourt, his tenth victory. However, on that same day he was shot down out of control by a German ace of Royal Prussian Jagdstaffel 1, being fatally injured over Bourlon Wood. And like many fighter pilots, he died as he had lived.

On September 30th, 1918, three days later, the 29 – year old fighter ace died from his wounds and was buried at Grevilliers British Cemetery, Pas de Calais, near Bapaume.

Gardner's name is recorded on the War Memorial at the Parish Church of St. Peter & Paul in Buckingham along with his older brother, Percy Gardner, who was killed on the Western Front in May of 1917 while serving as a private in the London Regiment known as the "Artists Rifles".

On November 2nd, 1918, fighter ace Capt. Cecil Gardner was awarded the Distinguished Flying Cross.

To
Headquarters
10th Wing R. A. F.

I wish to bring the name of LIEUT. CECIL VERNON GARDNER R. A. F. (Pilot) before you for IMMEDIATE AWARD for gallantry in the Field when attacking enemy aircraft and for continuous good service.
This officer was posted to this Squadron on 22nd January 1917 and carried out much steady and very valuable work during the months following.
During the last few weeks however he has shown unusual determination to attack and destroy E/A, and his enthusiasm has met with considerable success. He has accounted for the undermentioned E/A:

6 – 6 – 18 One Two – seater Out of Control VIEUX Berquin
9 – 6 – 18 One D. F. W. Destroyed (Seen to crash to ground) Neuf Berquin

1 – 7 – 18 One Pfalz Scout. Destroyed Fleurbaix
4 – 7 – 18 One Pfalz Scout. Out of Control. Esterelles
13 – 7 – 18 One Fokker Biplane Destroyed (in flames -) Bois de Biez

This officer is keen, "dashing" and absolutely without fear. He sets the right example and his zeal is altogether most praiseworthy. He is good in all branches of his work and I feel that I can recommend him most strongly for IMMEDIATE AWARD.

E. R. Pretyman,
Major,
Commanding No. 19 Squadron,
Royal Air Force

In the Field

Fighter ace Capt. Cecil Gardner

	Date	Time	Unit	Aircraft	Opponent	Location
				Victories		
1	06 Jun 1918	1715	19	Sopwith Dolphin (C4129)	DFW C.V (OOC) [1]	Vieux Berquin
2	09 Jun 1918	0945	19	Sopwith Dolphin (C4057)	DFW C.V (DES)	Neuf Berquin
3	01 Jul 1918	1755	19	Sopwith Dolphin (D5236)	Pfalz D.III (OOC)	Fleurbaix
4	04 Jul 1918	1700	19	Sopwith Dolphin (C3788)	Pfalz D.III (OOC)	Esterelles
5	15 Jul 1918	2005	19	Sopwith Dolphin (C3792)	Fokker D.VII (DESF)	Bois du Biez
6	31 Jul 1918	1950	19	Sopwith Dolphin (D5236)	Pfalz D.III (DES)	S of Douai
7	11 Aug 1918	1700	19	Sopwith Dolphin (D5236)	Pfalz D.III (DESF)	Estrées
8	11 Aug 1918	1755	19	Sopwith Dolphin (D5236)	Fokker D.VII (DES)	Brie
9	16 Sep 1918	0940	19	Sopwith Dolphin (C3818)	Fokker D.VII (OOC) [2]	Lille
10	27 Sep 1918	0730	19	Sopwith Dolphin (E4501)	Fokker D.VII (DES)	Haynecourt

References:
Fighter Squadron XIX by Derek Palmer
Dolphin and Snipe Aces of World War I by Norman Franks
http://en.wikipedia.org/wiki/Cecil_Gardner
http://www.theaerodrome.com/aces/england/gardner.php

GROUP CAPT. GEORGE C. GARDNER

Group Capt. George C. Gardner, the Flying Ace, was a long time fighter pilot and flight instructor. He served in the British Army and the Royal Air Force. Gardner was a veteran of World War I, the Iraqi Revolt, and World War II.

George Cecil Gardner was born on March 28th, 1892 in Poona, India. His father was Colour Sergeant Charles Gardiner of the Worcestershire Regiment. His mother was Beatrice Delahay Gardiner.

He attended the Duke of York's Royal Military School in Dover, Kent, England from 1901 to 1906, joining the British Army in the Royal Irish Regiment. Gardner served as a corporal in the 16th (The Queen's) Lancers during World War I and in 1915 he was commissioned a second lieutenant for his service in the field. Then in May of 1916 he was with the Machine Gun Corps and in October he was transferred to the Royal Flying Corps, being appointed a flying officer (observer) in December of that year.

Afterwards he served with No. 14 Squadron RFC in the Middle East before training as a pilot. It was in July of 1917 he was promoted to lieutenant and was assigned to No. 47 Squadron RFC, serving on the Macedonian Front. Gardner gained his first aerial victory on October 1st, 1917 while flying a B. E. 12, driving down an Albatros C down out of control.

On April 1st, 1918, the Army Royal Flying Corps and the Royal Naval Air Service merged, forming the Royal Air Force, Gardner transferring to No. 150 Squadron RAF based at Salonika, Greece.

On June 3rd, 1918, in the King's birthday honours list, Gardner was awarded the Distinguished Flying Cross and on June 6th, 1918, while flying a Sopwith Camel, he destroyed an Albatros D. III over Mravinca. Then on June 12th, 1918 he destroyed an Albatros D. V near Pardovica. This was his fourth aerial victory.

On June 25th, 1918, Gardner became an ace with a victory over another Albatros C east of Cestovo.

On June 28th, 1918, he was promoted to acting captain, gaining his sixth and final victory on September 3rd, 1918 destroying another Albatros D. V west of Cerniste.

Capt. Gardner remained in the Royal Air Force and was made a *Chevalier* of Legion d'honneur receiving the Croix de guerre from France. He served in the Iraqi Revolt and was promoted to flying officer to flight lieutenant in January of 1922 while serving with No. 48 Squadron in Iraq. Gardner returned to the

United Kingdom and was assigned to No. 2 Flying Training School at RAF Duxford in 1924 and then in 1927 he was assigned to the Air Ministry, later in Estonia.

He was promoted to squadron leader in May of 1930 and the next year posted to No. 55 Squadron based at RAF Hinaidi in Iraq.

On June 23rd, 1931, he was awarded the Distinguished Service Order for his gallant and distinguished service in Iraq.

He served as Chief Flying Instructor in 1934 to No. 4 Flying Training School in Egypt and later in 1937 he was promoted to Wing Commander and Commander of No. 216 (Bomber Transport) Squadron based at Heliopolis, a suburb outside of Cairo, Egypt.

It is noted in the 216 Squadron Operational Record Book AIR27/13333, he flew General Wavell around his command.

On March 1st, 1940, Gardner was promoted to group captain during World War II but died on July 30th, 1940 at age 48 while on active service at the Helmieh Hospital while serving as station commander at RAF Helwan. He was buried at the Cairo War Memorial Cemetery. Gardner was survived by his wife Kathleen August Lyle Gardiner of Tiverton, Devon, England.

It was during his career, Group Captain George Cecil Gardner earned the Distinguished Service Order, the Distinguished Flying Cross with palm, the Legion d'honeur, the Croix de Chevalier, and the Croix de Guerre.

References:
The Aerodrome
1940 George Cecil Gardiner DSO, DFC Duke of York's School
Gardiner, George Cecil Commonwealth War Graves Commission
The London Gazette

The Battle of Britain Fighter Pilots Named GARDNER

Sgt. Eric Cecil Gardiner trained as an Air Gunner and served with 219 Squadron at Catterick in June of 1940, and later died in October of 1940 when his plane crashed.

F/O Frederick Thomas Gardiner joined No. 610 Squadron in July of 1940 and he was wounded in the arm on July 25th, 1940 by a Bf 109 over the Channel at 15: 20 but he managed to land safely. On the August 25th, 1940 he bailed out of his Spitfire I (K9931) after combat with a Bf 109 over Dover at 19: 20 hours and was slightly wounded. It was during the Battle of Britain he shot down a Bf 110 and in March of 1944, Gardiner was awarded the Distinguished Flying Cross.

Sgt. William Nairn Gardiner was born in 1921 in Perth, Scotland, joining the Royal Air Force. He served with 3 Squadron at Castletown during the latter part of the Battle of Britain, in 1940 flying his first operational sortie. Gardner was later commissioned as a Warrant Officer.

P/O J. R. Gardener, a pilot from No. 141 Squadron was on patrol on July 19th, 1940 in a Defiant (L7016) when he was shot down by a Bf 109 of JG 51 and injured near Dover at 12: 45 hours.

Sgt. B. G. D. Gardner joined No. 610 Squadron on July 27th, 1940 and Gardner shot down three Bf 109's on August 12th, 1940 and another on August 14th, 1940 when he was wounded in the arm. On June 28th, 1941, he was shot down by friendly fire. Gardner died while serving with 75 Signals Wing.

F/O Peter Melvill Gardner claimed three victories in France while attached to No. 3 Squadron. On returning to No. 32 Squadron after France fell, he added another before the start of the Battle of Britain. Gardner destroyed two Bf 109's on August 12th, 1940, a Ju 88 on the 15th and another Bf 109 on the 16th of that month. Gardner was awarded the Distinguished Flying Cross on August 30th, 1940 and on July 11th, 1941 he was shot down over France and spent the rest of the war as a prisoner of war, returning to the Royal Air Force. He was known as a powerboat and sports car racer. Later he removed to the Bahamas where he owned a popular restaurant called "*Sun and...*"

Sub/Lt. (FAA) Richard Exton Gardner joined the Royal Navy and began flying, later being commissioned as a Sub – Lieutenant. He was awarded his wings at RAF Netheravon in April of 1940 and joined 760 Squadron (FAA). Later, he joined 242 Squadron and claimed a He111 that he destroyed on July 10th, 1940, shared a Do17 on August 21st, and destroyed a Do17 on September 7th of that year. Later, Gardner took part in Operation Tiger in Egypt and on May 8th, 1941, he destroyed two Ju87's and shared a SM79, later being awarded the DSC, shooting down a Ju52, a Cant Z506B, and a Fiat BR20, later being an instructor at 760 Squadron.

References:
http://bbm.org.uk/the-airmen/british-airmen-list-g/

CAPT. PERCY GARDNER

Capt. Percy Gardner, the Canadian Warrior, fought for his country during the Great War. He was awarded the Military Cross for his gallantry. Gardner was a World War I hero.

Percy Harold Gardner was born on June 28th, 1895 in Arnprior, Ontario, Canada. His father was Herbert Winter Wills Gardner. Percy Gardner was member of the 42nd Regiment and on March 26th, 1915, he joined the 38th Battalion, CEF, in Ottawa, Ontario, serving garrison duty in Bermuda and on August 13th, 1916 the battalion landed in France during World War I.

"As No.1 party approached the parapet of the German trench, Lance-Sergeant Howe waved the soldiers down. Some of them took refuge in a deep shell hole partly filled with water. Lieutenant Gardner and Howe reportedly entered the German trench at 5.36 p.m., followed by the rest of the party, and were met with "considerable resistance at this point from an enemy party numbering about ten who engaged the Raiders with bombs and rifle fire." Canadian grenades and small arms fire from the group moving southward—Howe later reported that Gardner shot two Germans with his revolver—killed eight of the enemy and that two other Germans fled to a dugout. That dugout was immediately bombed."

Awarded the Military Cross - official citation: "For conspicuous gallantry and devotion to duty. In the course of five days the enemy made three attempts to raid his company's front, but on no occasion did any of the enemy succeed in entering the front line. This was largely due to his skillful dispositions and organization and to the splendid example of courage and devotion to duty which was an inspiration to his men." - unit recommendation dated 31 March 1918: "Recommended for consistent good work. He was in command of "D" Company when three attacks were launched against them in five days. None of the enemy reached our trenches. This was largely due to the efficient and effective organization of the front line garrison as made by Capt. Gardner".

Awarded a Mention-in-Dispatches - London Gazette Number 30107, 1 June 1917 - no citation - unit recommendation dated 3 March 1917: **"For distinguished and gallant services and devotion to duty."** Recommended for a Military Cross - unit recommendation dated 3 March 1917: **"This Officer displayed splendid courage and leadership while in command of No.2 Party during raid on enemy trenches Feb 22/17." - no award made".**

References:
Four Names on the Vimy Memorial: The 38TH Battalion's Trench Raid of 22 February 1917 by Dr. Ken Reynolds, Canadian Army Journal, Vol. 9.2
www.army.forces.gc.ca.caj./documents/vol_09/iss.2/CAJ_vol.9.2_14_e.pdf

2ND LT. CYRIL GARDNER

2nd Lt. Cyril Gardner, the World War I Hero, was a Newfoundland warrior. He was the only Allied Forces soldier to earn the German Cross. Gardner captured 72 of the enemy single – handedly.

Distinguished Conduct Medal
London Gazette, 11th December 1916
Action Date, 12th October 1916 - Gueudecourt
"For conspicuous gallantry in action. With two men he attacked a hostile bombing party, defeated them, and took one officer and fifteen men prisoners."
Bar to Distinguished Conduct Medal
London Gazette, 12th March 1917.
Action Date, 27th January 1917 - Lesboeufs
"For conspicuous gallantry and devotion to duty. He led a party of stretcher-bearers into No Man's Land. Later, he succeeded in securing the surrender of seventy-two of the enemy, whom he handed over to a party of another regiment."

Cyril Gardner was born on August 15th, 1885 and was from British Harbor, Trinity, Newfoundland, and Canada, then British territory. His parents were Arthur Gardner and Mary Colbourne Gardner, both of Newfoundland, and his brothers were John, Edward (Ned), Arthur, Eric, and a sister Grace.

There is not much known of him. His civilian occupation was accountant before he found his calling at age 29 as a soldier. On December 22nd, 1914, he enlisted in the 1st Battalion, Newfoundland Infantry Regiment in the British Army.

On February 5th, 1915, he embarked with the second draft on the troopship *Dominion* and served at Gallipoli, being promoted to Lance Corporal on November 14th of that year. Afterwards, on February 27th, 1916 he was promoted to Corporal and on July 1st, 1916, he was wounded at Beaumont Hamel. Gardner rejoined a month later and on August 24th, 1916 he was promoted to Sergeant.

On October 12th, 1916, Sergeant Gardner was awarded the Distinguished Conduct Medal for conspicuous gallantry in action at Gueudecourt.
"Through a gap in the trench which "C" Company was holding Sergeant-Major Gardner... sighted a German bombing party withdrawing from a fruitless assault on another part of the Newfoundland line. Acting quickly, Gardner with two of his men launched an attack on the enemy detachment, catching them by surprise. They cut down a number of them, took some prisoners, including an officer, and put the rest to flight."
(p.317) – The Fighting Newfoundlander by Col. G. W. L. Nicholson

On November 11th, 1916, Gardner was promoted to Company Sergeant – Major.

On January 27th, 1917, Sergeant – Major Cyril Gardner earned his status as a legendary soldier of Newfoundland when he single – handedly captured 72 of the enemy at Lesboeufs.

The book *The Fighting Newfoundlander*, by Colonel G.W.L. Nicholson stated: **"Although no one was sure why he was wandering around No Man's Land unarmed on January 27th, of 1917. He came upon a trench that held a whole company of the enemy. Gardner took a revolver from one of the Germans and called upon them to surrender. He told them "Tres bon. You're late. Everyone else has camaraded." The Germans understood his gestures, if not his words. As he was marching 72 prisoners back to his own lines, he was challenged by a British officer who was ready to fire on the Germans. After Gardner stopped him, one of the German officers removed the Iron Cross from his own breast and pinned it on Sergeant Major Gardner."**

On March 12th, 1917, Sgt. Maj. Gardner was awarded the Distinguished Conduct Medal and Bar.

On April 14th, 1917, legendary 2nd Lt. Cyril Gardner died at age 31 (some reports state age 32) while fighting at the Battle of the Somme. He has no known resting place. His brother Ned also died in the Great War.
There is a memorial at Beaumont – Hamel (Newfoundland) Memorial in Monchy – le – Preux, France.

Gardner's medals earned were the Distinguished Conduct Medal and Bar; 1914 – 1915 Star; British War Medal; Victory Medal (Royal Newfoundland Regiment)

References:
The Fighting Newfoundlander by Col. G. W. L. Nicholson
http://www.rnfldr.ca/history.aspx?item=262
(1917) *Newfoundland Quarterly* (photograph of Cyril Gardner)

SGT. JOHN H. GARDNER

Sgt. John H. Gardner, the American Warrior, was a deadly marksman who was cool under fire. He earned the Distinguished Service Cross during the First World War. Gardner was one of America's greatest warriors.

"From my association with the boys from the good state of South Carolina, I feel that I will not be taken as a rank outsider, when I ask your support in behalf of John Gardner, a man whom I learned to admire and trust from his conduct, bravery and devotion to duty under every condition existing in the field of war. Though a Sergeant, his interest was the welfare of his men. Never seeking a commission, asking only to be left with the men from Hartsville, always on the job in the interest of his Company. After I was disabled and sent to the hospital and I am informed all of his officers gone, John Gardner rose to the occasion and with his coolness and bravery under fire, led his men through some of the hardest fighting, reflecting honor upon himself and upon his State. For this he was decorated by the British and American Governments. Surely the good people of Darlington County will not forget him now in his ambition to be Sheriff of his county." – Major Howell, U. S. Army

John Henry Gardner was born on May 25th, 1884 in Hartsville, Darlington County, South Carolina, descended from Daniel Gardner of Kershaw County, South Carolina. He was a farmer, then enlisted in the South Carolina National Guard in June of 1916 at age 32, serving as an infantryman. It was during World War I as a U. S. Army soldier at age 34, Gardner earned the Distinguished Service Cross for his extraordinary heroism. His citation states:

"Sergeant John H. Gardner, United States Army, for extraordinary heroism in action while serving with Company L, 118th Infantry Regiment, 30th Division, A.E.F., near Brancourt, France, 8 October 1918. After his company commander had been wounded immediately before an attack, Sergeant Gardner took command of the company and led it throughout the action. When his company was held up by machine-gun fire, he went forward and killed four German machine-gunners, thereby enabling his company to continue the advance. On another occasion he picked up the rifle of a wounded soldier and killed three of the enemy. Later, when his company was almost surrounded by hostile machine gunners, under his cool direction his men fought their way out, reached their objective, and consolidated the position."

Gardner killed seven enemy machine gunners under heavy fire earning the Distinguished Service Cross, the Silver Star, the Purple Heart, and the British Distinguished Conduct Medal, being promoted to first sergeant.

Gardner, John Henry, 1312150, sergeant, Company L, 118th Infantry, 30th Division.

British Distinguished Conduct Medal, list No. 35, dated January 31, 1919, British War Office.

Details of the acts of gallantry performed:

"Sergeant Gardner, after his company commander had been wounded just prior to an attack near Brancourt on October 8th, 1918, took command of the company and led it throughout the day in the attack. He displayed the utmost courage and heroism during the day. Early in the attack he worked his way ahead of his company which was being held up by machine gun fire and killed four Boche machine gunners, allowing his company to advance.

On another occasion he picked up the rifle of a wounded comrade and killed three more Boche machine gunners.

Later the company became almost completely surrounded by enemy machine guns and under his cool direction and foresight fought its way out of the difficult position it was in and successfully gained and consolidated its objective. His utter disregard for personal safety and heroic example he set for the rest of the men was responsible largely for the successful advance of his company."

On March 9th, 1920, Gardner married Lida Camp and they had one daughter named Margaret. John Gardner served as a rural policeman, then ran for Sheriff of Darlington County in 1924, and worked at Sonoco Products Co. until his retirement. It was reported in January of 1929, he attempted suicide, shooting himself in the chest twice, but he survived.

He later died from an illness on January 23rd, 1958 at age 73, being buried at Magnolia Cemetery in Hartsville, Darlington County, South Carolina.

His tombstone reads he earned the Distinguished Service Cross, the Purple Heart, and the Silver Star.

Distinguished Service Cross

AWARDED FOR ACTIONS
during World War I
Service: Army
Rank: Sergeant
Division: 30th Division, American Expeditionary Forces

GENERAL ORDERS:
War Department, General Orders No. 21 (1919)

CITATION:
The President of the United States of America, authorized by Act of Congress, July 9, 1918, takes pleasure in presenting the Distinguished Service Cross to Sergeant John H. Gardner (ASN: 1312150), United States Army, for extraordinary heroism in action while serving with Company L, 118th Infantry Regiment, 30th Division, A.E.F., near Brancourt, France, 8 October 1918. After his company commander had been wounded immediately before an attack, Sergeant Gardner took command of the company and led it throughout the action. When his company was held up by machine-gun fire, he went forward and killed four German machine-gunners, thereby enabling his company to continue the advance. On another occasion he picked up the rifle of a wounded soldier and killed three of the enemy. Later, when his company was almost surrounded by hostile machine gunners, under his cool direction his men fought their way out, reached their objective, and consolidated the position.

References:
History of South Carolina, Vol. 2 edited by Yates Snowden, Harry Gardner Cutler
https://valor.militarytimes.com/hero/12041

John Gardner is a distant cousin, being a descendant of Daniel Gardner.

COL. LARRY GARDNER

Col. Larry Gardner, the Aviator, was a legendary pilot. He had more than 300 combat missions in three major wars. Gardner was one of the U. S. Air Force's most distinguished pilots.

Laurence F. Gardner was born on September 3rd, 1926 and served in the U. S. Air Force. He began his career as a pilot in 1943 when he enlisted in the U. S. Army Air Force during World War II. His first combat mission was as a gunner on a B – 24 over the oil refineries over Ploesti, considered the most dangerous mission of the war, one – third of the crews were lost.

He had his finger shot off when an enemy shell ripped through his turret and he had also been shot down behind enemy lines, later being reunited with the Allied Forces. After World War II, it was in 1951 he was assigned to 52 – Charlie and became one of its most distinguished pilots. He was posted to the 8th Fighter/Bomber squadron at K – 2 in Taegu.

Gardner married his wife Clare and was then sent to fight in the Korean War where he had over 100 combat missions.

After his service in Korea, Gardner served with the CIA in Bangkok where he was a fighter pilot advisor to the Royal Thailand Air Force and he flew a number of covert operations throughout Asia. Afterwards, Gardner flew another 100 combat missions during the Vietnam War, earning the Silver Star.

"Altogether, Larry Gardner flew more than three hundred combat missions in three major wars before he was forty years old. He was shot. He was shot down. He was shot up and lived through the most frightening moments a pilot could imagine." – *52 – Charlie: Members of a Legendary Pilot Training Class Share Their Stories...* by Edward T. Gushee

After his return from Vietnam, he was slated for the Apollo program but was disqualified for being too tall.

On July 8th, 1999, American hero Laurence "Larry" Gardner died at age 72 in Hartwood, Stafford County, Virginia and was buried at Arlington National Cemetery with full military honors.

References:
52 – Charlie: Members of a Legendary Pilot Training Class Share Their Stories... by Edward T. Gushee

MAJ. MADISON D. GARDNER

Maj. Madison D. Gardner, U. S. Army Soldier, was a World War II hero. He was a career soldier. Gardner killed, wounded, or captured 17 of the enemy, earning the Distinguished Service Cross.

Madison Dillard Gardner was born on April 8th, 1921 in Arkansas, his parents being Albert Sidney Gardner and Effie Rogers Gardner. He was an officer in the U. S. Army. Gardner was 6' 2, 165 pounds, served in World War II and the Korean War where he distinguished himself, earning the rank of Major.

On November 4th, 1944 at Les Baroques, 2nd Lt. Madison Gardner killed, wounded, or captured 17 Germans single handedly, smashing four German strongpoints.

History of 30th Infantry Regiment, World War II by Rupert Prohme on Page 270 states:

"2nd Lt. Madison D. Gardner, Company A platoon leader, fired approximately 125 rounds with his carbine killing one machine gunner, wounding another and taking four prisoners. Then his accurate fire on a second enemy position wounded one German and drove the rest to cover inside a house.

Delivering heavy carbine fire on the enemy elements in foxholes around the house, Lieutenant Gardner forced four to surrender. Then, seizing an enemy grenade launcher, he advanced alone, alternately running and crawling forty yards to within twenty yards of the house.

As three Germans rushed out of the house, Lieutenant Gardner shot and killed two, capturing the third. He continued to clear houses and organized a defense of Les Baroques while under fire from machine guns three hundred yards distant. Only after this was completed did he allow himself to be evacuated.

For this outstanding action in which he smashed four German strongpoints and killed, wounded, or captured 17 Germans, Lieutenant Gardner was awarded the Distinguished Service Cross."

He married Edna Forsythe and they had two children during his 23 year career as a soldier. On March 11th, 1989, Madison D. Gardner died at age 67 from natural causes. He was buried at Garden of Memories in Salinas, Monterey County, California.

References:
History of 30th Infantry Regiment, World War II by Rupert Prohme

CAPT. PHILIP GARDNER

Capt. Philip Gardner, the Victoria Cross Recipient, was a World War II hero. He served in the British Army as a captain. Gardner was legendary even before he earned the highest award for gallantry in the British and Commonwealth forces.

Philip John Gardner was born on November 18th, 1914 in Sydenham, London, England. He was educated at Dulwich College and served in the British Army from 1938 to 1945 as a captain. "Pip" Gardner, as he was known, served with the Westminster Dragoons, 4th Royal Tank Regiment.

He was attached to the 70th Infantry Division during World War II at the Siege of Tobruk and it was at Operation Crusader in Tobruk, Libya in northern Africa, he became a legend.

On November 23rd, 1941, Capt. Gardner was ordered to take two tanks to the rescue of two armored cars of the King's Dragoon Guards which were under heavy enemy attack and out of action. It was while one of his tanks fired on the enemy, Gardner dismounted from the other while under enemy fire. He then hitched a tow rope to one of the cars and lifted it to an officer whose legs had been blown off.

Afterwards, the top rope broke and Gardner returned to the armored car being wounded in the neck, arm, and leg. He transferred the wounded man to the second tank and returned to British lines through intense shell fire. Following his heroic action, after the Battle of Gazala, he was captured and was a Prisoner of War until the end of the war.

Captain Philip "Pip" Gardner was awarded the Victoria Cross and he always shunned the spotlight.

On February 16th, 2003, he died at age 88 in Hove, East Sussex, England.

References:
Monuments of Courage by David Harvey
British VCs of World War 2 by John Laffin

CAPT. WILLIAM A. GARDNER

Capt. William A. Gardner, the American Ace, was a World War II fighter pilot. He was the first American pilot to land on the airstrip at Tacloban. Capt. Gardner had eight kills on his record.

William Alfred Gardner was born on March 3rd, 1923 in Gorham, New Hampshire. He earned a Bachelor of Science degree in mechanical engineering in 1941 from the University of New Hampshire. Afterwards, he joined the Army Reserves as a second lieutenant in the Coastal Reserves.

Then in 1942, he transferred to the Army Air Corps, becoming a pilot in the 35th Fighter Squadron, 8th Fighter Group in New Guinea and the Philippines, later being Operations Officer with the 8th Air Force in the European Theater. On September 22nd, 1943, Gardner scored his first victory while flying a P – 40N, shooting down a G4M 'Betty' bomber.

On January 16th, 1944, north of Saidor, he and 14 other P – 40 pilots fought against a force of 40 Japanese fighters. Gardner shot down three of the enemy, downing a trio of 'Hamp' victories. Then on June 16th, 1944, he achieved ace status when he shot down a A6M 'Zeke' over the East Dutch Indies, his fifth notch. Gardner shot down a Ki – 61 'Tony' in July and then in August he claimed a K – 21 'Sally' bomber. On November 1st, 1944, he claimed his eighth notch, shooting down a 'Zeke' during the Leyte Campaign over Negros Island.

Gardner had 172 combat missions and flew 887 combat flight hours, earning the Silver Star and two Distinguished Flying Crosses. He was discharged in April of 1945 and later served as chief test pilot for the Curtiss Propeller Division of Wright Aueronautical Corporation. Afterwards, he was involved in defence contracting for the U. S. Air Force and served as director of Sands National Laboratories in New Mexico.

References:
'Twelve to One' V Fighter Command Aces of the Pacific by Tony Holmes

SGT. FRANK GARDNER

Sgt. Frank Gardner, U. S. Marine, was part of Landing Force, Air Support Control Unit One, participating at the Battles of Saipan, Iwo Jima, and Okinawa. He was a poet in later years, telling his tales of some of the bloodiest battles of World War II. Gardner was later a Special Agent in the Federal Bureau of Investigation.

"We would not have to fight in combat any more, to be wounded any more, or die any more. We, as warriors, had not been programmed for any alternative other than war. We were not exuberant individuals, prone to independent self – expression. We were United States Marines who had learned how to fight a war, and now we would have to learn how to be at peace. Now, I can admit that I was quietly thanking God that I was going home alive. I suspect my other Marines were doing the same."

Francis Victor Gardner was born on December 2nd, 1922 in Washington, District of Columbia, his father, Ivory V. Gardner, a World War I Veteran and U. S. Army sharpshooter, dying in a work related accident a couple of years later. Frank attended Mount Saint Mary's College in Maryland and worked odd jobs. Gardner enlisted on September 30th, 1942 in the United States Marine Corps.

Afterwards, as a radio operator, he attended Marine Air Detachment, Naval Training School, Texas A & M College, College Station, Texas.

Staff Sergeant Frank Gardner was an expert rifleman, firing 310 scores, and participated as a radio operator at the Battle of Saipan, the Battle of Iwo Jima, and the Battle of Okinawa.

He was awarded the Navy Unit Commendation for action in Iwo Jima, which reads:

HEADQUARTERS

MARINE AIR SUPPORT CONTROL UNITS,
AMPHIBIOUS FORCES, PACIFIC FLEET,
C/O FLEET POST OFFICE
SAN FRANCISCO, CALIFORNIA

The Commanding Officer takes pleasure in COMMENDING

Staff Sergeant Francis V. Gardner, USMCR, for services
as set forth in the following

CITATION

"For excellent service in the line of his profession in connection with the operation of Marine Landing Force, Air Support Control Unit One during the assault and occupation of both Iwo Jima and Okinawa. In both operations against the enemy, Staff Sergeant Francis V. Gardner, (481357), USMCR, under difficult conditions, performed his duties in a highly satisfactory manner. His devotion to duty, technical skill, and resourcefulness during the critical phases of the Iwo Jima and Okinawa campaigns contributed materially to the successful operation of Marine Landing Force, Air Support Control Unit One. His conduct under combat conditions was in keeping with the highest traditions of the Naval Service."

Vernon E. Megee, Colonel, USMC, Commanding

Gardner was honorably discharged on October 18th, 1945 from the U. S. Marine Corps at Cherry Point, North Carolina. He graduated with a Bachelor's Degree in Social Science from Mount Saint Mary's College in Maryland. Afterwards, in May of 1948, Gardner served as a Special Agent in the Federal Bureau of Investigation.

He married Geraldine Donahue in 1951, having nine children. Gardner served as a FBI agent for 13 years and moved to the U. S. Department of State where he served for 16 years, traveling from Central and South America to Europe. Gardner retired from the Foreign Service in 1986 and began writing poetry about his life as a United States Marine.

References:
Landing Force 48 by Frank V. Gardner

CPL. CLIFF GARDNER

Cpl. Cliff Gardner, the World War II Hero, was an American operative who was among the first to liberate the Jews from the Holocaust internment camps. He stood 6' 3, weighing 230 pounds, he was at the Invasion of Normandy and the Battle of the Bulge. Gardner was a top marksman serving in the Office of Strategic Services, precursor to the Central Intelligence Agency.

"He was an absolutely likeable guy." – Gov. Carruthers

Clifford Gardner was born in 1924 in Valleyhead, Alabama. The Gardner family moved three years later to Santa Rosa, New Mexico. Cliff became co – valedictorian of Santa Rosa High School.

As a top marksman, Gardner served in World War II with a branch of the Office of Strategic Services, which became the CIA, specializing in counter espionage and covert operations. He was in the Invasion of Normandy and the Battle of the Bulge. Gardner was assigned as the bodyguard to protect and drive legendary journalist and writer Ernest Hemingway from Paris to Luxembourg and back.

Gardner met several high profile correspondents such as Charles Collingwood, John Larner, and Ernie Pyle.

After the war, he excelled working with the Timpte Brothers trailer manufacturers in Albuquerque, New Mexico, designing a hydraulics system. Then he moved to Torc where he was elected to the Sierra County Commission. He helped found KSNM – FM and KHQT – FM radio stations.

Gardner was known for his engineering talents, along with his humility, and also helped with Gov. Carruthers gubernatorial campaign in Sierra County, New Mexico.

On April 9th, 2003, the "humble giant", Cliff Gardner died at age 78 from cancer at a Truth or Consequences veterans' home.

References:
Albuquerque Journal (April 13th, 2003)
www.ancestry.com

ALVY GARDNER

Alvy Gardner, the UDT Operator, was a "Frogman" during World War II. The "frogmen" were the ancestors of the U. S. Navy SEALs. Gardner was an underwater demolition team operator.

Alvy Gordon Gardner was born on November 22nd, 1925 in Silverton, Briscoe County, Texas. He enlisted in the U. S. Navy during World War II. Gardner served in Underwater Demolition Team Four, serving with merit at Okinawa Shima in 1945, earning the Asiatic – Pacific Area Ribbon.

It was during World War II while he was in the Pacific Theatre working on detonating explosives to destroy a bridge, he was confronted by two Japanese "frogmen" under water and Gardner killed both of the enemy with a knife.

Gardner earned the Bronze Star while his brother William Douglas Gardner earned the Purple Heart during World War II. He suffered from PTSD most of his life. Alvy Gardner later died at age 73 on January 23rd, 1999 in Coleman, Coleman County, Texas.

Photograph of William Douglas Gardner, fought at the Battle of Leyte Gulf during World War II, brother of Alvy Gardner, both served in the U. S. Navy during World War II.

Courtesy to Britt Gardner, U. S. Secret Service agent for photographs and information on his grandfather William Douglas Gardner and his great uncle Alvy Gardner.

LT. RUSS GARDNER

Lt. Russ Gardner, the Canadian Officer, was a tall, handsome warrior who earned the Military Cross. He was from Ontario and served in the Korean War. Gardner killed five of the enemy with his tommy – gun.

On November 6th, 1952, *The Calgary Herald* reported:

'TOMMY GUN' GARDNER TELLS HOW HE DID IT

Canadian Officer Killed Five Chinese

WITH THE CANADIANS IN KOREA (CP) –

Lt. Russ Gardner, tall, handsome Military Cross winner from Arnprior, Ont., who has been wounded four times in Korea, isn't sure he killed six Chinese in the battle of Gilraltar Spur as his comrades reported.

But he's positive he mowed down five of them with the tommy – gun he is reputed to take to bed with him.

WOUNDED in the right arm and both legs by shell fragments in the Oct. 23 engagement, the 25 – year – old former Algonquin Park summer – time guide was well enough to sit up in a field dressing station and tell his story of the battle. He suffered his first wound in an earlier action.

"I'm QUITE sure I killed five, in fact I'm positive I killed five Chinese."

References:
Calgary Herald

MEREDITH KNOX GARDNER

Meredith Knox Gardner, the Cold War Hero, was a linguist and codebreaker. He was a genius who worked in counter – intelligence decoding Soviet intelligence traffic involved in espionage in the United States, later known as the Venona project. Gardner was a legend in the intelligence community, pulling off one of the greatest coups of the 20th Century.

"He was a quiet, scholarly man, entirely unaware of the awe in which he was held by other cryptanalysts." – Peter Wright

Meredith Knox Gardner was born on October 20th, 1912 in Okolona, Mississippi, being raised in Austin, Texas. He taught himself how to read by age three, teaching himself Yiddish, Hebrew, German, and Spanish by age eight, graduating from the University of Texas at Austin and later earned a master's degree in German from the University of Wisconsin – Madison, where he was a teaching assistant. Afterwards, he was a linguist and professor of German at the University of Akron.

Gardner was recruited by the U. S. Army's Signals Intelligence Service, precursor of the National Security Agency, as a codebreaker and soon after he mastered the Japanese language in only a few months during World War II.

He was the first person to say the words, "Atomic bomb" in Japanese, and he was fluent in French, German, Greek, Italian, Japanese, Latin, Lithuanian, Spanish and Russian.

After the war in 1946, he began working on a highly secret project later codenamed VENONA, breaking the Soviet cryptosystems. It was thought to be unbreakeable reusing certain pages of their pads. Later that year, Gardner identified the ciphers used for spelling English words and he had read a decrypt that implied Soviets ran an agent who had information from the War Department Staff, U. S. Army Air Corps Major William Ludwig Ullmann.

On December 20th, 1946, Gardner discovered KGB messages exposing Soviet espionage in the United States. The message was from 1944 and contained a list of the leading scientists on the Manhattan Project, developing the atomic bomb. He and his colleagues discovered a reference to an agent code named Liberal who had a wife named Ethel.

The atom spies were the infamous Julius Rosenberg and Ethel Rosenberg, both being executed in 1953, and despite smashing an espionage ring, he was disappointed that his art form, VENONA, had resulted in McCarthyism.

Then in 1949, he deciphered part of a Soviet message which identified the text of a 1945 telegram from British Prime Minister Winston Churchill to U. S. President Harry S. Truman. It was proof that the Soviets had a spy who had access to secret communication between the British and the Americans. It was Gardner's biggest breakthrough.

Gardner smashed an espinoge ring and retired in 1972, his work remaining secret unil 1996 when the NSA, the CIA, and the Center for Democracy honored him and his colleagues in a formal ceremony.

He married Blanche Hatfield, they had two children, and on August 9th, 2002, Meredith Gardner died at age 89 in Chevy Chase, Maryland.

Courtesy to his son Arthur Gardner and his daughter Ann Gardner Martin

References:
Meredith Gardner 89, Dies; Broke Code in Rosenberg Case by David Stout, Aug. 18, 2002, *New York Times*
Obituaries – Blanche Hatfield Gardner Teacher Sept. 3, 2005, *Washington Post*
Spymaster by Peter Wright
The Code – Breaker and the G – Man by Candice Gaukel Andrews
In the Enemy's House: The Secret Saga of the FBI Agent and the Code Breaker Who Caught the Russian Spies by Howard Blum
Hall of Honor 2004 Inductee - Meredith Gardner – NSA/CSS

MAJ. ALAN GARDNER

Maj. Alan Gardner, the Green Beret, was an American hero. He died for our freedom in the Vietnam War. Gardner was a Special Forces soldier.

"His personality was a daredevil one, always willing to push everything to the edge and yet a tender side." – Carl Keil

Alan David Gardner was born on March 3rd, 1939, a native of Lewisburg, Pennsylvania. He attended Bucknell University where he studied civil engineering, earning his Bachelor of Science. Gardner was a member of the American Society of Civil Engineering, was involved in varsity wrestling, and was President of the Parachute Club.

He married and fathered a son, and when his best friend, Carl Keil was going through a traumatic time with his son being born premature, Gardner stayed with him in the hospital.

Gardner served in the U. S. Army in the Corp of Engineers through the ROTC Program and became an officer of the Golden Knights, the parachute team. As an officer, he earned the rank of Captain, and joined U. S. Army Special Forces. Gardner deployed to Vietnam and Cambodia.

Gardner parachuted down during Bob Hope's show and was mentioned in his book titled, *Bob Hope's Vietnam Story: Five Women I Love*.

Hope stated:

"One thing happened at Cam Ranh Bay which was quite a switch – the GIs entertained us. Captain Allen Gardner of Lewisburg, Pennsylvania, treated us to a "free fall" exhibition which really had us gasping.

It really takes guts to fall thousands of feet and not pull the ripcord on your parachute until the very last second. I know I could never do it. I get nosebleeds just watching Wilt the Stilt.

As we watched Captain Gardner hurtling toward the earth, we were all subconsciously pulling the ripcord of his chute for him. The suspense was almost unbearable. It was like waiting for Pamela Mason to finish a sentence. Finally, after what seemed an eternity, the parachute mushroomed out over him. We all breathed a great sigh of relief and broke into spontaneous applause.

When he landed, Kaye Stevens, overwhelmed by the excitement of it all, rushed over to Captain Gardner, threw her arms around him, and gave him a big kiss. It turned out to be a mistake. She didn't realize that he still hadn't defrosted from his high altitude leap, and it was like kissing the penguin in the Kool commercial. It took her about an hour to unpucker.

Later I interviewed Captain Gardner on stage and he turned out to be very quick with the ad libs. I asked him, "Do you have any control over where you land?" And he replied, "I landed right on the girls' dressing room, didn't I?" I said, "What were you thinking of all the time you were falling?" And he came back with, "I landed right on the girls' dressing room, didn't I?"

If there's anything I hate, it's a show – off who gets laughs."

Maj. Alan Gardner was in the 31st Eng. Det., HQ Co, 5th Special Forces Group. As he was on board a helicopter flying a high ranking officer's body back out to one of the bases, the helicopter he was in was shot down. He died on June 27th, 1970, at age 31, in the Kontom Province over South Vietnam and his body was recovered.

Gardner was buried at Arlington National Cemetery. He is listed on Panel/Row 9W, 98 on the Vietnam War Memorial Wall. The famous World War II hero and actor, Audie Murphy was buried in the plot next to him.

His father Capt. Robert Gardner was World War II Veteran, and both of Maj. Alan Gardner's sons served, one as an officer in the U. S. Army and one in the U. S. Marine Corps.

Courtesy to his daughter Wendy Gardner Beistline and his best friend Carl Keil

CAPT. GREGORY E. GARDNER

(Public Domain 75th Infantry Regiment (Ranger) Distinctive Unit Insignia)

Capt. Gregory E. Gardner, U. S. Army Ranger, earned the Soldier's Medal after dying for his fellow comrades during a training exercise. He was a Vietnam War veteran and Special Operations soldier. Gardner was inducted in 1994 into the U. S. Army Ranger Hall of Fame.

A native of Huntsville, Alabama, Capt. Gardner, 34 years old, 75th Ranger Regiment, earned the Soldier's Medal, dying for his fellow Rangers. The 2nd Ranger Battalion, 75th Infantry, while at a training exercise, a helicopter crashed in Indian Springs, Oklahoma. Capt. Gardner was last seen pulling his comrades out of the helicopter before dying.

The crash killed seven soldiers, wounding sixty – one soldiers.

Gregory Eldon Gardner died at age 34 on September 21st, 1981 in Indian Springs, Oklahoma.

References:
https://www.ranger.org/Ranger-Hall-of-Fame

1ST LT. JIM GARDNER

1st Lt. Jim Gardner, U. S. Army Ranger, was one of America's greatest warriors. He was a true American soldier, heart and soul. Gardner was a fearless warrior and earned the Medal of Honor for giving his life to his country, dying for our freedom.

James Alton Gardner was born on February 7th, 1943 in Dyersburg, Tennessee. He attended Dyersburg High School and was a star athlete, playing football as an interior lineman and fullback. Gardner was remembered for his sense of humor, red hair, foot speed, and most of all, his fearless nature.

He was recruited as a football player for West Point Military Academy by Coach Tony Bullotta after taking his entrance exam in the spring of 1960 in Fort Campbell, Kentucky. Gardner began his career as a cadet at the United States Military Academy in 1961 in the Second New Cadet Company. However, he was homesick and dropped out of West Point, but did not give up on his dream of being an officer.

Gardner attended the University of Tennessee a year before he received U. S. Army basic training at Fort Polk, Louisiana, then joined OCS Class 4 – 64, 52nd Company (OC), 5th Student Battalion, in Fort Benning, Georgia in 1964 and he excelled in sports as well as military aptitude. He "maxed" the PT test twice and was a star on the 4 – 64 football team. Gardner was an excellent marksman with the M – 14 and afterwards he was commissioned as an officer in the U. S. Army.

2nd Lt. James A. Gardner was a U. S. Army Ranger and joined the 101st Airborne Division. He was assigned to the 1st Battalion (Airborne), 327th Infantry, 1st Brigade in Vietnam and was in Operation Gibraltar. Although he had dropped out of West Point, he graduated from OCS a year before the Class of 65'.

He married Joella McManus in June of 1965, a month before being sent to Vietnam. A girl drew a portrait of him before he was deployed from Fort Campbell, Kentucky. The painting now is displayed in the lobby of the Dyer County courthouse.

Gardner was the first commander of the Special Operations elite platoon known as Tiger Force, which he organized to "out guerrilla the guerrillas" in the jungles of the Vietnam War.

On February 7th, 1966, Lt. Gardner led his platoon into battle to relieve a company of the 1st Battalion that had been pinned down by a superior enemy force in the village of My Cahn, Vietnam. As the platoon moved to begin the attack, the enemy fire intensified. The company of the 1st Battalion and Tiger Force were under heavy enemy fire.

Gardner charged through a hail of fire across an open field. He threw a grenade into a bunker and destroyed it. Then he dashed to a second bunker and destroyed the Viet Cong with another grenade.

Gardner shot and killed an enemy gunner who was firing at him, and destroyed the Viet Cong in the third bunker with a grenade. Afterwards, he reorganized his platoon and advanced to a new assault position, collecting several grenades. Gardner charged the enemy position, firing his rifle as he advanced towards the fourth bunker, blowing up the Viet Cong with a grenade.

As the bunker blew up, he came under fire again. He rolled into a ditch to gain cover and moved towards the new source of fire. Gardner leaped from the ditch and charged with a grenade in one hand and firing his rifle with the other.

As he checked to see if he had taken out the enemy, he was shot across his chest four times from another enemy position. Gardner reportedly turned around and said, **"That's the best I can do."** He was mortally wounded before he reached the fifth bunker, but staggered forward and destroyed the Viet Cong with a grenade.

1st Lt. James A. Gardner died on his 23rd birthday and was awarded the Congressional Medal of Honor.

Gardner killed several Viet Cong before he died valiantly on the battlefield. He was a true action hero. The fallen warrior was buried at Fairview Cemetery in Dyersburg, Tennessee.

On October 19th, 1967, his widow, Joella McManus Gardner received his Medal of Honor at the Pentagon in Arlington, Virginia, presented by Secretary of the Army Stanley A. Resor during the administration of President Lyndon B. Johnson.

Col. David Hackworth described Gardner as someone of **"gentle demeanor"** whose hard work habits helped build a **"mean, two-platoon Tiger Force."** **"When someone dies for you, as Jim Gardner died for me...it's the worst of all crosses a combat leader has to bear,"** Hackworth wrote.

Capt. Dennis Foley wrote: **"It was one of the most incredible acts of courage that I have ever seen."**

1st Lt. James A. Gardner was inducted into the U. S. Army Ranger Hall of Fame on June 29th, 2006 at a ceremony in Fort Benning, Georgia. The Medal of Honor awarded to him was donated by his family to the 101st Airborne Division (Air Assault) on August 14th, 2009 and it is displayed at the Headquarters' Atrium in its Hall of Heroes. A bowling center in Fort Campbell, an athletic field in Fort Benning, the National Guard Armory in Dyersburg, and a primary conference room at the Pentagon are fittingly named after Gardner.

http://en.wikipedia.org/wiki/James_A._Gardner

During his military career, from 1964 to 1966, Gardner received the Congressional Medal of Honor, the Bronze Star, the Purple Heart, and the Vietnam Gallantry Cross with Palm; his citation signed by President Johnson.

1st Lt. James A. GARDNER
The Congressional Medal of Honor

Rank and organization: First Lieutenant, U. S. Army, Headquarters and Headquarters Company, 1st Battalion (Airborne), 327th Infantry, 1st Brigade, 101st Airborne Division. Place and date: My Canh, Vietnam, 7 February 1966. Entered service at: Memphis, Tenn. Born: 7 February 1943, Dyersburg, Tenn.

Citation: For conspicuous gallantry and intrepidity in action at the risk of his life above and beyond the call of duty. 1st Lt. Gardner's platoon was advancing to relieve a company of the 1st Battalion that had been pinned down for several hours by a numerically superior enemy force in the village of My Canh, Vietnam. The enemy occupied a series of strongly fortified bunker positions which were mutually supporting and expertly concealed. Approaches to the position were well covered by an integrated pattern of fire including automatic weapons, machine guns and mortars. Air strikes and artillery placed on the fortifications had little effect. 1st Lt. Gardner's platoon was to relieve the friendly company by encircling and destroying the enemy force. Even as it moved to begin the attack, the platoon was under heavy enemy fire. During the attack, the enemy fire intensified. Leading the assault and disregarding his own safety, 1st Lt. Gardner charged through a withering hail of fire across an open rice paddy. On reaching the first bunker he destroyed it with a grenade and without hesitation dashed to the second bunker and eliminated it by tossing a grenade inside. Then, crawling swiftly along the dike of a rice paddy, he reached the third bunker. Before he could arm a grenade, the enemy gunner leaped forth, firing at him. 1st Lt. Gardner instantly returned the fire and killed the enemy gunner at a distance of 6 feet. Following the seizure of the main enemy position, he reorganized the platoon to continue the attack. Advancing to the new assault position, the platoon was pinned down by an enemy machine gun emplaced in a fortified bunker. 1st Lt. Gardner immediately collected several grenades and charged the enemy position, firing his rifle as he advanced to neutralize the defenders. He dropped a grenade into the bunker and vaulted beyond. As the bunker blew up, he came under fire again. Rolling into a ditch to gain cover, he moved toward the new source of fire. Nearing the position, he leaped from the ditch and advanced with a grenade in one hand and firing his rifle with the other. He was gravely wounded just before he reached the bunker, but with a last valiant effort he staggered forward and destroyed the bunker, and its defenders with a grenade. Although he fell dead on the rim of the bunker, his extraordinary actions so inspired the men of his platoon that they resumed the attack and completely routed the enemy. 1st Lt. Gardner's conspicuous gallantry were in the highest traditions of the U. S. Army.

Gardner's Congressional Medal of Honor was donated to the U. S. Army's 101st Airborne Division, along with his Republic of Vietnam (RVN) Gallantry Cross Medal with Palm, Bronze Star, and Purple Heart.

Courtesy to the Vietnam Memorial Fund for photograph

References:
Vietnam Medal of Honor Heroes by Edward F. Murphy
Dyersburg Gazette
http://www.west-point.org/users/usma1965/624620/
http://www.stategazette.com/story/1566626.html
http://fortcampbellcourier.com/news/article_ada4e7dd-960a-517b-96f7-133777711fcb.html

LT. BILL GARDNER

Lt. Bill Gardner, U. S. Navy SEAL, is one of America's bravest heroes who fought against communism in the jungles of Vietnam. He is the author of the book titled, _Hell Week_, an account of his training as an elite commando. Gardner is one of America's elite warriors.

"My father and his fellow warriors come from a different time in the history of the SEALs. They truly were the silent warriors. There were no movies or books, no publicity about their victories, and certainly no praise for their service during those days. I am extremely proud of my father and his service to our country." – Jon Gardner

"He loved his men almost to a fault." – Chief Tom Blais

William E. Gardner was born on April 22nd, 1941, a native of North Carolina. He was a country boy and was no stranger to living off the land. Gardner was practicing war games as a young child and he was destined to become a man o' war.

After he graduated from high school in 1959, he attended North Carolina State College, even being a cadet in the R. O. T. C. for the Air Force. He graduated in 1963 with a degree in mechanical engineering and then volunteered for Officer Candidate School in Newport, Rhode Island. Gardner earned the rank of Ensign in the U. S. Navy in 1964 and as an officer he served as a SEABEE in the Civil Engineering Corp, earning the rank of Lieutenant.

Bill Gardner began his career as a U. S. Navy SEAL in August of 1966 when he attended BUD/S class #38, then known as UDTRA, and on December 19th, 1966, he received his BUD/S diploma, but went through underwater swimmer's school in Key West, Florida as well as jump school in Fort Benning, Georgia before he was assigned to the Teams. As an officer in the U. S. Navy, carrying a Car - 15 rifle and a .38 Smith & Wesson revolver, standing 6' 1, weighing 205 pounds, Lt. Gardner was the platoon commander of SEAL Team Two, Fourth Platoon, during the Vietnam War. He participated in a number of special operations, served as Operations Officer of Underwater Demolition Team 22 and Executive Officer of Underwater Demolition Team 21 afterwards.

Gardner served as Second - in - Command with LCDR Jack Schropp on a two month deployment to Greenham AFB in England to run joint ops with Special Forces in Germany. He later retired in February of 1972 from the U. S. Navy. Gardner married in 1969 and helped his wife with their travel agency, and now maintains rental property in Virginia Beach after having written a book titled, _Hell Week_, published in 2004, which describes in detail the rigorous training of a U. S. Navy SEAL.

I personally spoke with Bill Gardner over the phone and it was a very memorable moment. He sounded like a Navy SEAL. Gardner has a very masculine, deep, baritone voice and speaks with a slow Southern drawl. He is kind enough to let me use his own words and pictures from his book.

It is a true honor to have spoken to and share the same name as Lt. Bill Gardner.

On March 18th, 2004, in Virginia Beach Beacon section of *The Virginian – Pilot*:

"On a slow day at the travel agency where Bill Gardner works with his wife Ann, he began jotting down a few thoughts about the week of intense training to become a Navy SEAL.

The words "Wednesday night of Hell Week" popped in his head, and from there, the pages unfolded.

"I'd hit a certain remembrance, and I couldn't write fast enough," said Gardner, 62, a first – time author and retired Navy SEAL."

<u>Hell Week</u> by William E. Gardner
Pg. 65

     "Hand to Hand Combat, in one simple, single word, was "Aggressive!" Hand to Hand was drawn from any and all forms of the martial arts, street fighting, you name it.

There was no bowing in the middle of the mat, and no points awarded for take downs. You did not have an opponent, you had the enemy. Your objective was not to take the enemy down, but rather to take him out.

Some moves were defensive as in countering someone wielding a club or knife, but for the most part the moves were aggressively designed to break bones, render the nerve endings useless or deal death blows."

Pg. 102

"Weapons instruction was excellent. From how to fire a Chinese B – 40 rocket to learning how to break – down a 50 caliber machine gun, a 30 cal. air – cooled machine gun, an AK – 47, a 9mm Swedish K, M- 16, a Colt 45 hand gun, and many others. Still engraved in my mind is the small spring with the metal cap in the main block of the 30 cal. air cooled machine gun that if not properly removed could put a hole through you before hitting the opposite bulkhead.

John Wayne never had any problem with firing his weapons at night; he just flipped up his hand gun, or rifle, sighted in and blew the bad guy away. What happens when it is so dark you can not see the back sight, much less the front sight, on the barrel?

Enter "Quick Kill", or as some people refer to as instinct shooting (practicing over and over again bringing your weapon to your shoulder in the same position, and in the same alignment every time). By practicing over and over again bringing your hand gun up to the firing position in both hands, arms extended, elbows flexed, and with the same alignment every time. With both eyes open you squeeze off a round. With enough practice the round will travel the same line as the line of your eye – sight. "Enough Practice" cannot be over stressed.

With Daisy pump air rifles and plenty of BB's we would pair off with one tosser and one shooter. Initially the tosser would throw a tin can into the air and the shooter would fire. When the shooter could consistently hit 9 out of 10 tosses, the size of the target would be reduced to a metal disk about the size of a silver dollar. When the shooter could consistently hit the silver dollar size target 9 out of 10 times, a smaller size metal disk would be used. All shooters progressed until we were hitting tossed dimes."

Pg. 105

"Individual weapon selection depended mainly on what normal position an individual occupied in a squad or platoon; rear security – machine gun, radio man – M – 16 with grenade launcher, etc. Working point, I preferred the Car – 15 with extra short barrel and telescoping stock. My second consideration would have been the 12 gage pump Ithaca feather weight shot gun with double "00" buck shot. In addition to being longer than the Car – 15, after five rounds the shot gun had to be reloaded. The shot gun shells were heavier and more difficult to carry than the .223 caliber for the Car – 15.

If you are the only man carrying the shot gun on a given operation and you expend all of your ammunition you essentially end up with a club without a bayonet.

Personally my two main reasons for preferring the Car – 15 on point were ease of movement through thick shit and the one hand operation of the weapon.

We were honed and fine tuned. On December 12 1969, myself, LTJG Ace Sarich, DMCS Tom Blaise, EMI Ken McDonald, BM1 Pat Martin, DM1 Davey Sutherland, PR2 Steve Dunthorn, MR2 Ron Rogers, GMG2 Dan Olson, HM2 Steve Elson, PR3 Greg Frisch, EN3 Bob Shamberger, BM3 Bill Bibby, RM3 Jim Burison, SN Dick Peters, and AE1 Curtis Ashton boarded our U. S. Navy transport at NAS Norfolk for our 5 ½ day flight to Viet Nam."

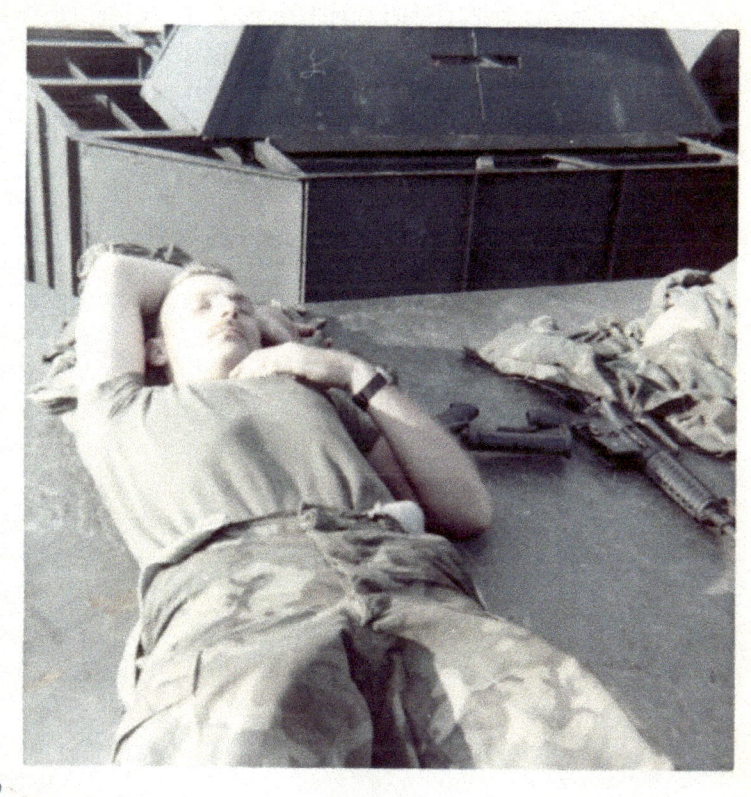

Pg. 107

"One individual in our platoon really had a problem with falling asleep. On one particular night ambush, early in our tour, he fell asleep. Before any of the guys could arouse him, he let out a snoring "snort". After the post – op. de – briefing, I had a very serious nose to nose discussion with this individual on falling asleep not being a future option. The discussion worked well for the next month or so, but damned if he didn't fall asleep again on another all night ambush.

The snorer's position was about four men down from me in the ambush line. After hearing the first snort I passed the word I was coming down the line. We had a good moon that night, and I was able to work down the line without too much difficulty.

When I crawled up next to the snorer I could see he was laying flat on his back, his weapon next to him pointing down towards his feet, mouth wide open, and getting ready to let out another snort any second. Very slowly I eased into a crouched position and stepped over the snorer's body with one foot. Now I am straddling the snorer with my ass almost touching his stomach. Simultaneously I dropped a knee on each of his shoulders, one hand over his mouth, and the other hand around his neck completely pinning him to the ground. The snorer's eye balls popped wide open with nothing but white showing. They looked like two hard boiled eggs.

By now the snorer is trying to suck air, and my mouth is by his left ear. I whispered three short words "you are dead" in his ear. I rolled off him and crawled back to my position. Not one word was mentioned at the de – briefing about the incident. To the best of my knowledge, not one of us ever went to sleep on another ambush. At least I never heard any more snoring."

Pg. 112

"Being the designated initiator, I proceeded to mark the target with tracer rounds. All hell broke loose! M – 60's hammering, Stoners ripping, M – 79 grenade launchers whomping, and claymores Ka – booming. Seemingly over before it began, we were not taking incoming fire, so we put up a pop flare to help retrieve documents etc."

Pg. 114

"Except for all but two operations I ran in Viet Nam, I served as the point man. Standard platoon, and squad, operations do not have the platoon commander as the point man. However, after trying several different platoon members at point, during pre – deployment operations, I found what worked best for me was to be on point. Not to infer my walking point was any feather in my cap. There were plenty of experienced people behind me who could take control if I screwed up and got my ass shot off."

Pg. 115

"They are here, but where? All senses are all ahead full. Your ears actually hurt from straining to pick up any and all sounds. Even though you smoke, your sense of smell is acute. Your vision is dazzling, and you are afraid to blink for fear of missing some slight movement. The old pump in your chest is going like a trip hammer, and you think the veins in your neck are going to explode! Fear or adrenaline, whatever you want to call it, but you are jacked - up to an all time unforgettable high. Sweat is pouring from every pore, to the extent you would swear you were bleeding. Even though you are drenched in sweat on the outside, the inside of your mouth has that dry brassy taste. On the exact opposite end of the fulcrum, from brain dead stupor during Hell Week, you are like a fine tuned banjo string with every brain wave twanging at a high pitched vibration."

Pg. 116

"Leaving my ammo vest and Car – 15 with McDonald, I slid into the canal with my trusty Smith & Wesson 38 Combat Master Piece in my shoulder holster, and very slowly kicked, stroked and glided to the other side of the canal.

Trying to stay as low as a mud fish, I inched up the far bank hoping to see some opening or objective we could maneuver towards. No such luck, same old thick shit. Sliding back into the canal I was about half way back to the other side when suddenly I heard loud Vietnamese chatter to my left. Glancing to my left I saw two guys walking and talking loudly, with their rifles slung over their shoulders. They had not spotted me, and I was not about to stick around to see how many more were behind these two. Executing a turtle dive as slowly as I could, then all ahead full underwater towards the bank. Underwater oxygen depletion never crossed my mind.

After bumping head first into the bank and slowly easing my head above water the whole world exploded. The two lead guys had literally bumped into McDonald on our flank without ever knowing he was there. McDonald had his Stoner singing, and shit was starting to fly. I came out of that canal like I had a rocket up my ass; got back into my ammo vest, and was wired to the hilt and ready to go.

By now Shamberger is chomping with his M – 60, and Dunthorn is spitting M – 79 grenades. What had I walked us into? One thing was for sure, we could not sit tight. Surely there would be more coming our way!"

Courtesy to Bill Gardner, his lovely wife Ann, and their two sons, Jon Gardner and Owen Gardner, along with Trafford Publishing, for information and photographs on this biography for my relative, friend, and mentor, dedicated to a great warrior, a great SEAL, and a great man, Lt. Bill Gardner.

MASTER CHIEF BUD GARDNER

Master Chief Bud Gardner, U. S. Navy SEAL, is one of America's elite warriors. He fought against communism in the jungles of Vietnam. Gardner was a special operator, a complete weapons expert, and a legend of the SEAL Teams.

"An original from the old school way of looking at things, a real character, a weapons expert, and a weapons handling expert. He personified what it was & meant to be a "STONER AW Man" in the 60s and early 70s. If you had to go to combat and hand-pick some guys, Bud would have to be one of the 'A Team' members right off the git-go." – Steven Frisk

"He was the rear security in our squad, and yes, he would be on my "A" list of men you wanted with you in an ass kicking contest. Fearless to a fault and one of the hardest hitters I've seen. One punch, goodnight. Also, he could take a box of parts and build a Ferrari. An incredible mechanic and welder (nuke sub qualified)." – Don Crawford

"I always thought of Bud as super calm, cool and collected - He had a great reputation as an "Operator" - always one of the highest complements you can be paid. Bud always laughed easily and sometimes when he was drinking adult beverages it was difficult to understand him, what with his heavy accent. A good man to have watching your six." – Chip Maury

David "Bud" Gardner was born in 1944 and was from Wagener, Aiken County, South Carolina. He stood 6 feet tall and had a Southern drawl. Gardner enlisted in the U. S. Navy on September 21st, 1964, his father Henry Gardner's birthday, and was a hull technician.

He graduated from BUD/S Class #42, then known as UDTRA in 1967, along with Don Crawford and Steven Frisk, being in SEAL Team One during the Vietnam War and later served in SEAL Team Three which he helped create.

Gardner was a weapons expert and used a Stoner machine gun. A renowned photograph was taken of him by combat photographer Chip Maury. Gardner earned the rank of (E – 9) Master Chief retiring as a U. S. Navy SEAL.

TEAMMATES: SEALs AT WAR by Barry Enoch on pages 174 – 178 stated:
"It was December 19, 1968, when Lieutenant Bliss issued the patrol order. Our objective was to destroy the VC village and to bring back it civilians for questioning and then relocation to a safe area under government control. The platoon was inserted by two Army slicks with an additional two Cobra gunships flying support. This would be a daylight operation with time on target set for 1200 hours, or noon straight up. Mr. Bliss had conducted a helicopter reconnaissance flight of the target area and told us to expect it to be completely defoliated.
Twelve SEALs would participate in the operation. This would include Mr. Moses, David Wilson, and Chip Maury. The first Huey was to take Mr. Bliss, Frisk, Beanan, Crawford, Chip, and myself. Our squad would be the strike force tasked with taking out any armed or evading VC. The second helicopter's personnel was tasked to round up the civilians after

searching/destroying the village. Mr. Lyon was in charge of Second Squad which included John Ware, Bud Gardner, Hubbard, Wilson, and Mr. Moses."

After he retired, Gardner taught shooting part – time for Mid – South Shooting Institute and it is said he worked for the Naval Support Activity in Panama City, spending his last years in Florida.

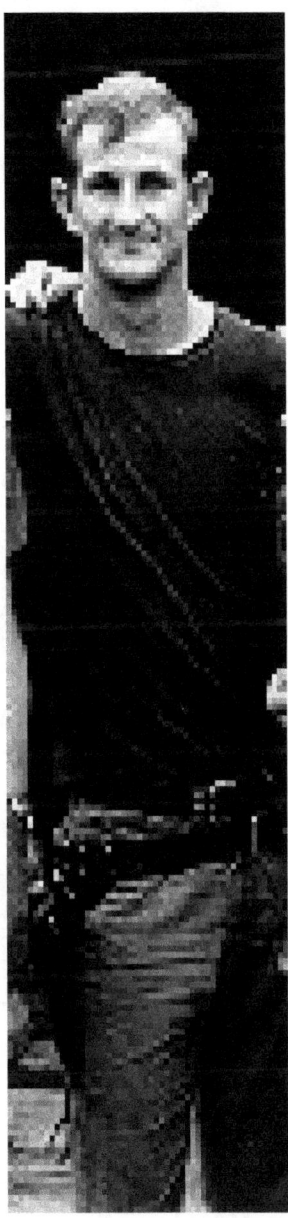

Courtesy to Bud Gardner and Chip Maury

**The Art of Combat: Artists and the Vietnam War, Then and Now
at THE INDIANAPOLIS ART CENTER
October 27, 2000 - January 7, 2001
Chip Maury**

"Bud has the reputation of being one of the Finest Kind of operators. Bud Gardner is a real life legend in our lifetime." – Chip Maury

Courtesy to Bernie Campoli, Chip Maury, Steven Frisk, Don Crawford, and Bud Gardner

MASTER CHIEF JASON GARDNER

Master Chief Jason Gardner, U. S. Navy SEAL, is one of America's bravest heroes. He fights against terrorists who try and harm the United States of America. Gardner is one of America's elite warriors.

Jason N. Gardner was born in the summer of 1969 in Camp Lejuene, North Carolina. His father was a Lieutenant Colonel in the U. S. Marine Corps and as a child Jason knew he wanted to join the military. After he graduated from Dana Hills High School in California, Gardner enlisted in the U. S. Navy.

Afterwards, he graduated from BUD/S Class #155 in 1989 and Gardner became a U. S. Navy SEAL. He served with SEAL Team Five as a frontline SEAL sniper and was SEAL Team Five Command Master Chief. Later, he separated from active duty in 1998, beginning his career as a private investigator, but he soon returned to his career as a commando in SEAL Team Seven.

Chief Gardner served in the first Gulf War, Somalia, Iraq, and Afghanistan. He was deployed all over Asia during his career. Gardner had seen more people killed in Somalia than anywhere else.

However, it was in Afghanistan that he saw the most combat of his career with 23 operations and over 340 hours of being under fire, or "Troops in contact". As a Senior Chief, Gardner was awarded the Silver Star for his heroic actions from July 16th to 17th, 2009 in the enemy terrain of northern Kandahar. Gardner had "**fearlessly exposed himself to return fire and coordinate counterattacks, preventing his task unit from being overrun.**"

The book titled, *The Red Circle: My Life in the Navy SEAL Sniper Corps and How I Trained America's Deadliest Marksmen* by Brandon Webb, John David Mann, and Marcus Luttrell mentioned Jason Gardner as the commander of Sniper Cell, stating:

"Another reason I felt so fortunate was Chief Gardner himself. Chief Gardner has an amazing resume of service as a SEAL. He fought in the first Gulf War; he shot a half a dozen guys in Somalia. In Afghanistan he put in more than 340 hours of "troops in contact", meaning under fire, and led troops in 196 KIA and the capture of six HVT. In 2009 he was awarded the Silver Star. He is the nicest guy you'll ever meet, but you do not want to go up against him in combat. The man is a killing machine. He was also a fantastic boss to work for."

Gardner served as lead instructor for Naval Special Warfare Group One Training Detachment and in 2019 he retired after 30 years as a U. S. Navy SEAL, being a recipient of the Silver Star, two Bronze Stars, the Purple Heart and several other awards.

He is married with children, owned a small farm on the West Coast, and now is a leadership instructor, speaker, and strategic advisor at Echelon Front, a team of combat leaders who offer practical solutions to get your team across every industry to develop leadership skills, from web based training to field training exercises.
https://echelonfront.com/jason-gardner/

I spoke with Jason Gardner over the phone and he is very straight forward and personable. He was generous enough to tell his story of being a U. S. Navy SEAL. It is an honor to share the same name as Master Chief Jason Gardner.

https://valor.militarytimes.com/hero/315813

CHIEF OF NAVAL OPERATIONS
The President of the United States takes pleasure in presenting the SILVER STAR MEDAL to
SENIOR CHIEF SPECIAL WARFARE OPERATOR (SEA, AIR AND LAND)
JASON N. GARDNER
UNITED STATES NAVY
for service as set forth in the following
CITATION:

For conspicuous gallantry and intrepidity in action against the enemy while serving as SEAL Team SEVEN Task Unit TRIDENT Senior Enlisted Advisor, in direct support of Operation ENDURING FREEDOM from 9 April to 1 October 2009. Senior Chief Gardner commanded his task unit during a two – day direct action mission in enemy terrain in Northern Kandahar from 16 to 17 July 2009. He led seven positions which were encircled by enemy forces and sustained a barrage of enemy fire from all sides. Senior Chief Gardner fearlessly exposed himself to return fire and coordinate counterattacks, preventing his task unit from being overrun. Although he was shut off from seven observation positions by an enemy machine gunner, he continued to expose himself to spot and direct fire, silencing the automatic weapon which had pinned down his task unit. Senior Chief Gardner's heroic actions inspired his platoons and contributed to 56 enemy killed in action. He fearlessly led his task unit during 357 hours of troops in contact, resulting in 196 enemy killed in action and six high – value individuals captured. By his bold leadership, courageous actions, and total dedication to duty, Senior Chief Gardner reflected great credit upon himself and upheld the highest traditions of the United States Naval Service.

WORLD WAR I HEROES

Alexander M. Gardner, Private, U. S. Army; Kings County, New York.

Alfred W. Gardner, 1st Lieutenant, U. S. Army; New York County, New York; earned the Distinguished Service Cross.

Beniard J. Gardner, Private, U. S. Army; Allegheny County, Pennsylvania.

Benjamin H. Gardner, Lieutenant, U. S. Army; Anderson County, Texas.

Calvin C. Gardner, Corporal, U. S. Army; Hill County, Texas.

Charles T. Gardner, 2nd Lieutenant, U. S. Army; Kentucky.

Clarence L. Gardner, Private, U. S. Army; Ohio.

Clarence R. Gardner, Private, U. S. Army; Jefferson County, Ohio.

Coley W. Gardner, Private, U. S. Army; Accomack County, Virginia.

Dayton M. Gardner, Private, U. S. Army; Napa County, California.

Earl Gardner, Private, U. S. Army; St. Charles County, Missouri.

Earl R. Gardner, Corporal, U. S. Army; Otsego County, New York.

Edward Gardner, Private, U. S. Army; Fairfield County, Connecticut.

Elbert R. Gardner, Sergeant, U. S. Army; Passaic County, New Jersey.

Elmer F. Gardner, Corporal, U. S. Army; Lycoming County, Pennsylvania.

Emmett Gardner, Wagoner, U. S. Army; Jefferson County, Oklahoma.

Eugene Gardner, Private, U. S. Army; Missouri.

Eugene Gardner, Private, U. S. Army; Weakley County, Tennessee.

Francis W. Gardner, Lieutenant, U. S. Army; Mississippi.

Frank R. Gardner, Private, U. S. Army; Ashley County, Arkansas.

Frank E. Gardner, Private, U. S. Army; Adams County, Pennsylvania.

George William Gardner, Private, U. S. Army; Maricopa County, Arizona.

George W. Gardner, Corporal, U. S. Army; Cherokee County, Kansas.

Grover A. Gardner, Officer NCO, U. S. Army; Mercer County, New Jersey.

Harry E. Gardner, Private, U. S. Army; Audrain County, Missouri.

Herman Gardner, Private, U. S. Army; Deschutes County, Oregon.

Hincley Gardner, Private, U. S. Army; Texas.

Howard J. Gardner, Private, U. S. Army; Blair County, Pennsylvania.

Jas. H. Gardner, Private, U. S. Army; Pitt County, North Carolina.

Jas. C. Gardner, Private First Class, U. S. Army; Multnomah County, Oregon.

Jas. E. Gardner, Corporal, U. S. Army; Marion County, Oregon.

Jas. Gardner, Private, U. S. Army; Hamilton County, Tennessee.

Jessie Gardner, Private, U. S. Army; Troup County, Georgia.

John Martin Gardner, Corporal, U. S. Marine Corps; Harnett County, North Carolina.

John F. Gardner, Private, U. S. Army; York County, South Carolina.

John L. Gardner, Private, U. S. Army; Richmond County, New York.

John Anthony Gardner, Sergeant, U. S. Army; Fremont County, Idaho.

Joseph M. Gardner, Private, U. S. Army; Chester County, Pennsylvania.

Leroy W. Gardner, Corporal, U. S. Army; Worcester County, Massachusetts.

Leroy E. Gardner, Private, U. S. Army; Pennsylvania.

Luther M. Gardner, Private, U. S. Army; Tuscaloosa County, Alabama.

Martin E. Gardner, Sergeant, U. S. Army; Washington County, Maryland; earned the Distinguished Service Cross.

Oscar Gardner, Private, U. S. Army; Kershaw County, South Carolina.

Paul A. Gardner, Private First Class, U. S. Army; New York County, New York.

Ralph Gardner, Private, U. S. Army; Hardin County, Ohio.

Raymond A. Gardner, Private, U. S. Army; Harnett County, North Carolina.

Richard A. Gardner, Corporal, U. S. Army; Connecticut.

Richard A. Gardner, Private, U. S. Army; Orange County, New York.

Robert Gardner, Private First Class, U. S. Army; Illinois.

Robert Gardner, Private, U. S. Army; Rensselaer County, New York.

Robert Gardner, Lieutenant, U. S. Army; Worcester County, Massachusetts.

Robert Gardner, Private, U. S. Army; Kankakee County, Illinois.

Russell L. Gardner, Private, U. S. Army; Alameda County, California.

Rubin P. Gardner, Private, U. S. Army; Isle of Wight County, Virginia.

Tom F. Gardner, Corporal, U. S. Army; Georgia.

Verne W. Gardner, Private, U. S. Marine Corps; Illinois.

Verne W. Gardner, Private, U. S. Army; District of Columbia.

Wayland S. Gardner, Private, U. S. Army; North Carolina.

William H. Gardner, Private, U. S. Army; New York.

William S. Gardner, Corporal, U. S. Army; Duplin County, North Carolina.

William J. Gardner, Corporal, U. S. Army; Wayne County, North Carolina.

Willie L. Gardner, Private, U. S. Army; Obion County, Tennessee.

Charles T. Gardiner, U. S. Army; Kentucky

Edward H. Gardiner, U. S. Army; Massachusetts

Elmer L. Gardiner, U. S. Army; Washington

Frank Gardiner, U. S. Army; New York

Herat Gardiner, U. S. Army; Ohio

Sydney H. Gardiner, U. S. Army; New York

Tommie B. Gardiner, U. S. Army; Texas

Courtesy to www.honorstates.org

WORLD WAR II HEROES

Howard Gardner, U. S. Army Ranger, was one of the first American commandos. He was one of the heroes who died in the D – Day Invasion. Gardner was one of America's bravest heroes who fought and died for freedom. Howard J. Gardner was born in 1922 and was from New York. His father was likely Ray B. Gardner, listed as his next of kin, residing in Liverpool, New York. Howard Gardner resided in Onondaga County, New York and was employed in warehousing, being a single man without any children and on November 18th, 1942, he enlisted in Syracuse, New York. Gardner served in the U. S. Army during World War II, serving as a Private First Class in the 5th Ranger Battalion. On June 6th, 1944, he died in the D – Day Invasion of Normandy, France. He was buried at Normandy American Cemetery and Memorial in Colleville – sur – Mer, Departement du Calvados, Basse – Normandie, France. Gardner is listed in Plot G, Row 11, Grave 23, and earned the Purple Heart.

William Gardner, U. S. Army soldier, was born on May 4th, 1916 and was from Allegheny County, Pennsylvania. He served in the U. S. Army as a 1st Lieutenant in Company D, 116th Infantry Regiment, 29th Division, killed in action on D – Day, June 6th, 1944 at Omaha Beach, Normandy, France. Gardner was buried at Arlington National Cemetery, earning the Purple Heart.

George H. Gardner, U. S. Army soldier, was born in 1921 in Mississippi. He enlisted as a private and died on June 10th, 1944 at age 22 or 23 in Caen, Departement du Calvados, Basse – Normandie, France. Gardner was buried at the Normandy American Cemetery and Memorial, Plot E, Row 16, Grave 37, earning the Purple Heart.

Emory G. Gardner, U. S. Army soldier, was born on January 11th, 1925 in Bedford, Pennsylvania. He was with the 508th Parachute Infantry Regiment and died on July 4th, 1944 at age 19 in Normandy, France. Gardner was buried at the Normandy American Cemetery and Memorial in Colleville – sur – Mer, Departement du Calvados, Basse – Normandie, France, Plot G, Row 8, Grave 15, earning the Purple Heart.

Roy D. Gardner, U. S. Army soldier, enlisted as a private in Michigan. He died on July 11th, 1944 in Normandy, France. Gardner was buried at the Normandy American Cemetery and Memorial, earning the Purple Heart.

Arthur Joseph Gardner, U. S. Navy sailor, was born on April 10th, 1920, the son of an Austrian immigrant named Sylvester I. Gardner. He was from Pennsylvania and enlisted in the U. S. Navy, serving as a WT2G on the *U. S. S. Helena* dying on December 7th, 1941 at age 21 at Pearl Harbor in Honolulu County, Hawaii. The U. S. Navy sailor was buried at Tyrolean Catholic Cemetery in Sheppton, Schuylkill County, Pennsylvania.

A.G. Gardner, Corporal, U. S. Army; Chicot County, Arkansas.

Aaron S. Gardner, Master Sergeant, U. S. Army Air Corps; Salt Lake City, Utah; earned the Air Medal.

Abraham Gardner, Private First Class, U. S. Army; Kings County, New York.

Alfred W. Gardner, Seaman First Class, U. S. Navy; Indiana.

Andrew J. Gardner, Lieutenant, U. S. Navy; Kentucky.

Arthur B. Gardner, Jr., 2nd Lieutenant, U. S. Marine Corps; Queens County, New York; earned the Silver Star.

Arthur Joseph Gardner, Petty Officer Second Class, U. S. Navy; Carbon County, Pennsylvania; (KIA at Pearl Harbor).

Arthur W. Gardner, Major, U. S. Army; Ingham County, Michigan.

Benjamin Gardner, Private First Class, U. S. Army; Philadelphia County, Pennsylvania.

Bill A. Gardner, Private, U. S. Army; Dimmit County, Texas.

Bradley C. Gardner, Technical Sergeant, U. S. Army; Essex County, New Jersey.

Cadmus B. Gardner, Jr., Private First Class, U. S. Army; Carroll County, Kentucky.

Calvin R. Gardner, Private First Class, U. S. Army; Pennsylvania.

Carl A. Gardner, Staff Sergeant, U. S. Army; Essex County, New Jersey.

Cecil Eldon Gardner, Fireman Second Class, U. S. Navy; Missouri.

Cecil Gardner, Corporal, U. S. Army; Preble County, Ohio.

Charles A. Gardner, Sergeant, U. S. Army Air Corps; San Francisco County, California; earned the Air Medal.

Charles W. Gardner, Jr., Private, U. S. Army; Greene County, New York.

Charlie R. Gardner, Private First Class, U. S. Army; Cabarrus County, North Carolina; earned the Silver Star.

Charlie T. Gardner, Private, U. S. Army; Vance County, North Carolina.

Clarence E. Gardner, Staff Sergeant, U. S. Army; Fremont County, Iowa.

Cleo H. Gardner, Staff Sergeant, U. S. Army Air Corps; Marion County, Indiana; earned the Air Medal.

David B. Gardner, 2nd Lieutenant, U. S. Army; Millard County, Utah.

David F. Gardner, Private, U. S. Army; Halifax County, North Carolina.

Delmar Gardner, Seaman, U. S. Navy; Illinois.

Donald W. Gardner, Petty Officer Second Class, U. S. Navy; South Dakota; earned the Distinguished Flying Cross.

Donald A. Gardner, 1st Lieutenant, U. S. Army Air Corps; Lake County, Utah; earned the Air Medal.

Doyle N. Gardner, Private First Class, U. S. Army; Centre County, Pennsylvania.

Doyle D. Gardner, Private First Class, U. S. Army; Jasper County, Texas.

Earle Watson Gardner, Petty Officer Third Class, U. S. Navy; Butler County, Alabama.

Edward T. Gardner, 1st Lieutenant, U. S. Army Air Corps; Cass County, Michigan; earned the Air Medal.

Edward A. Gardner, Sergeant, U. S. Army; Chase County, Kansas.

Edwin P. Gardner, Staff Sergeant, U. S. Army; Jefferson County, Kentucky; earned the Bronze Star.

Elmer W. Gardner, Sergeant, U. S. Army; Salt Lake County, Utah.

Elmer L. Gardner, Staff Sergeant, U. S. Army; Tioga County, Pennsylvania.

Elon F. Gardner, Private First Class, U. S. Army; Logan County, Illinois.

Elwyn G. Gardner, Staff Sergeant, U. S. Army; Bristol County, Massachusetts.

Emory G. Gardner, Private First Class, U. S. Army; Bedford County, Pennsylvania; (KIA Normandy).

Enos B. Gardner, Private, U. S. Army; Monroe County, Tennessee.

Ernest J. Gardner, Staff Sergeant, U. S. Army; Madison County, Indiana.

Eugene E. Gardner, Private, U. S. Army; Arizona.

Eugene John Gardner, Merchant Seaman, U. S. Merchant Marine; Oswego County, New York.

Everett K. Gardner, Petty Officer Second Class, U. S. Navy; Maryland.

Everett O. Gardner, Technical Sergeant, U. S. Army; Cheshire County, New Hampshire.

Francis N. Gardner, Private First Class, U. S. Army; Kanawha County, West Virginia.

Frank W. Gardner, Captain, U. S. Army; Middlesex County, Massachusetts; earned the Silver Star twice.

Frank A. Gardner, Private, U. S. Army; Maryland; earned the Bronze Star.

Frank W. Gardner, 1st Lieutenant, U. S. Army; Tarrant County, Texas.

Fred Gardner, Corporal, U. S. Army; Bryan County, Oklahoma.

Frederick J. Gardner, Private, U. S. Army; Bronx County, New York.

Frederick F. Gardner, Private First Class, U. S. Marine Corps; New York.

Garland G. Gardner, Seaman Second Class, U. S. Navy; Maryland.

Garrett E. Gardner, Captain, U. S. Army Air Corps; New Jersey.

Gene Gardner, Staff Sergeant, U. S. Army; Bonneville County, Idaho.

George Hayward Gardner, Private, U. S. Army; Poinsett County, Arkansas; (KIA Normandy).

George H. Gardner, Chief Petty Officer, U. S. Navy; California.

George A. Gardner, Staff Sergeant, U. S. Army Air Corps; New Haven County, Connecticut; earned the Air Medal.

George H. Gardner, Private, U. S. Army; Fleming County, Kentucky.

George T. Gardner, 2nd Lieutenant, U. S. Army; Middlesex County, New Jersey.

George Anthony Gardner, Merchant Seaman, U. S. Merchant Marine; Jefferson County, Texas.

George Elwood Gardner, Merchant Seaman, U. S. Merchant Marine; Morris County, New Jersey.

George H. Gardner, Private, U. S. Army; Franklin County, Massachusetts.

George E. Gardner, Corporal, U. S. Army; Grafton County, New Hampshire.

George C. Gardner, Private, U. S. Army; Cabarrus County, North Carolina.

Glen W. Gardner, Staff Sergeant, U. S. Army; Canadian County, Oklahoma.

Gordon Bryant Gardner, Staff Sergeant, U. S. Army Air Corps; Juab County, Utah.

Harold G. Gardner, Staff Sergeant, U. S. Army Air Corps; Los Angeles County, California; earned the Air Medal.

Harold Edwin Gardner, Captain, U. S. Marine Corps; Los Angeles County, California; earned the Distinguished Flying Cross and the Air Medal.

Harry C. Gardner, Jr., Private, U. S. Army; Los Angeles County, California.

Harry C. Gardner, Private, U. S. Army; Rockingham County, Virginia.

Harvey Gardner, Jr., Merchant Seaman, U. S. Merchant Marine; Camden County, New Jersey.

Harvey E. Gardner, Staff Sergeant, U. S. Army; Snohomish County, Washington.

Henry L. Gardner, Staff Sergeant, U. S. Army; Okaloosa County, Florida.

Herbert H. Gardner, 2nd Lieutenant, U. S. Army Air Corps; DeKalb County, Georgia; earned the Air Medal.

Herbert Gardner, 2nd Lieutenant, U. S. Army; Suffolk County, Massachusetts.

Howard J. Gardner, Private First Class, U. S. Army; Onondaga County, New York; (KIA Normandy).

Howard N. Gardner, Petty Officer First Class, U. S. Navy; New York.

Howard F. Gardner, Jr., 2nd Lieutenant, U. S. Army; Wilbarger County, Texas.

Howard W. Gardner, Major, U. S. Army; Windsor County, Vermont.

Ivy N. Gardner, 2nd Lieutenant, U. S. Army; Pulaski County, Arkansas.

Jack C. Gardner, Sergeant, U. S. Army Air Corps; Massachusetts.

Jack Raymond Gardner, Private First Class, U. S. Marine Corps; Michigan.

Jack Henry Gardner, Private First Class, U. S. Marine Corps; New York.

Jack W. Gardner, Private First Class, U. S. Army; Tulsa County, Oklahoma.

Jack C. Gardner, Technician Fifth Grade, U. S. Army; Kenton County, Kentucky.

Jack S. Gardner, Staff Sergeant, U. S. Army; Hamilton County, Ohio.

James E. Gardner, Private First Class, U. S. Army Air Corps; Noble County, Indiana.

James R. Gardner, Petty Officer First Class, U. S. Navy; Kentucky.

James F. Gardner, Corporal, U. S. Army; Mississippi.

James Gardner, 2nd Lieutenant, U. S. Army Air Corps; Washington County, Pennsylvania.

James H. Gardner, 1st Lieutenant, U. S. Army; Riverside County, California.

James H. Gardner, Corporal, U. S. Army; Franklin County, Pennsylvania.

James G. Gardner, Technician Fifth Grade, U. S. Army; Kent County, Michigan.

James W. Gardner, Staff Sergeant, U. S. Army; Hamilton County, Texas.

Jeffrie T. Gardner, Master Sergeant, U. S. Army; South Carolina.

John H. Gardner, 1st Lieutenant, U. S. Army; Baltimore County, Maryland.

John K. Gardner, 1st Lieutenant, U. S. Army Air Corps; New Jersey; earned the Air Medal.

John W. Gardner, Flight Officer, U. S. Army Air Corps; Los Angeles County, California.

John D. Gardner, Private First Class, U. S. Army; Carbon County, Utah.

John T. Gardner, Captain, U. S. Army; Walla Walla County, Washington.

John H. Gardner, Brigadier General, U. S. Army; Middlesex County, New Jersey.

Joseph H. Gardner, 2nd Lieutenant, U. S. Army; Hudspeth County, Texas.

Julies D. Gardner, Private, U. S. Army; Marengo County, Alabama.

Kenneth L. Gardner, Sergeant, U. S. Army Air Corps; Arizona; earned the Air Medal.

Kenneth E. Gardner, Private, U. S. Army; New Haven County, Connecticut.

Lawrence D. Gardner, Private, U. S. Army; Arlington County, Virginia.

Lee Gardner, Private First Class, U. S. Army; Cook County, Illinois.

Leland V. Gardner, Sergeant, U. S. Army; California; earned the Silver Star.

Lester J. Gardner, Private, U. S. Army; Knox County, Tennessee.

Lester Gardner, Private, U. S. Army; Bonneville County, Idaho.

Lewis S. Gardner, 2nd Lieutenant, U. S. Army Air Corps; Mecklenburg County, North Carolina; earned the Air Medal.

Lewis Gardner, Private, U. S. Army; Bucks County, Pennsylvania.

Lloyd L. Gardner, Private First Class, U. S. Army; Wexford County, Michigan.

Lloyd E. Gardner, Sergeant, U. S. Army; Pitt County, North Carolina.

Lorne J. Gardner, Private First Class, U. S. Army; Kent County, Michigan.

Louis K. Gardner, Jr., Staff Sergeant, U. S. Army; Dallas County, Texas.

Mannon J. Gardner, Staff Sergeant, U. S. Army; Calhoun County, Alabama.

Matthew S. Gardner, Sergeant, U. S. Army; Missouri.

Melvin J. Gardner, Staff Sergeant, U. S. Army; Maricopa County, Arizona; earned the Distinguished Flying Cross.

Merle A. Gardner, Private First Class, U. S. Army; Lincoln County, Oklahoma.

Nial Ira Gardner, Private First Class, U. S. Marine Corps; New York.

Onward L. Gardner, Private First Class, U. S. Army; Martin County, North Carolina.

Oral W. Gardner, 2nd Lieutenant, U. S. Army; Gray County, Kansas.

Oral C. Gardner, Private, U. S. Army; Kalkaska County, Michigan.

Orrin W. Gardner, Private First Class, U. S. Army; LaPorte County, Indiana.

Otis L. Gardner, Private, U. S. Army; Dallas County, Alabama.

Parson E. Gardner, Private, U. S. Army; Rapides Parish, Louisiana.

Paul W. Gardner, Private, U. S. Army; Lycoming County, Pennsylvania.

Ralph Gardner, Seaman Second Class, U. S. Navy; Iowa.

Ralph B. Gardner, Private First Class, U. S. Army; Adams County, Pennsylvania.

Raymond K. Gardner, Private, U. S. Army; Stanislaus County, California.

Raymond R. Gardner, Petty Officer Second Class, U. S. Navy; California.

Raymond C. Gardner, Corporal, U. S. Army; Monroe County, New York.

Rex C. Gardner, Private First Class, U. S. Army; Taylor County, Texas.

Richard L. Gardner, Private, U. S. Army; Cook County, Illinois.

Richard A. Gardner, Private, U. S. Army; Erie County, New York.

Richard Robert Gardner, Private First Class, U. S. Marine Corps; Sioux Falls, South Dakota; earned the Silver Star.

Richard W. Gardner, Private First Class, U. S. Army; Philadelphia County, Pennsylvania.

Richard J. Gardner, Private First Class, U. S. Army; LaPorte County, Indiana.
Robert R. Gardner, Petty Officer Second Class, U. S. Navy; Illinois.
Robert E. Gardner, Sergeant, U. S. Army Air Corps; Lawrence County, Indiana.
Robert E. Gardner, Lieutenant, U. S. Navy; Mississippi; earned the Air Medal.
Robert E. Gardner, 1st Lieutenant, U. S. Army; Stanislaus County, California.
Robert W. Gardner, Private First Class, U. S. Army; Fayette County, Pennsylvania.
Robert E. Gardner, Private, U. S. Army; Greene County, Indiana.
Robert E. Gardner, 2nd Lieutenant, U. S. Army; Polk County, Iowa.
Robert W. Gardner, Private First Class, U. S. Army; Van Buren County, Iowa.
Robert C. Gardner, Private First Class, U. S. Army; Barry County, Michigan.
Robert L. Gardner, Private First Class, U. S. Army; Ingham County, Michigan.
Robert L. Gardner, Jr., Sergeant, U. S. Army; Wilson County, North Carolina.
Robert W. Gardner, Staff Sergeant, U. S. Army; Belmont County, Ohio.
Robert Gardner, Private First Class, U. S. Army; Sweetwater County, Wyoming.
Roger Lee Gardner, Chief Petty Officer, U. S. Navy; King County, Washington.
Ronald Gardner, Private First Class, U. S. Army; Tioga County, Pennsylvania.
Roy D. Gardner, Private, U. S. Army; Genesee County, Michigan; (KIA Normandy).
Ruben J. Gardner, Private, U. S. Army; Scott County, Virginia.
Rudolph S. Gardner, Petty Officer Third Class, U. S. Navy; California.
Ruel L. Gardner, Private First Class, U. S. Army; Roger Mills County, Oklahoma.
Russel Gardner, Seaman Second Class, U. S. Navy; Iowa.
Russell Thomas Gardner, Fireman Second Class, U. S. Navy; Polk County, Missouri.
Samuel Ervin Gardner, Jr., Merchant Seaman, U. S. Merchant Marine; Baltimore County, Maryland.
Shirley E. Gardner, 1st Lieutenant, U. S. Army Air Corps; Berkshire County, Massachusetts; earned the Air Medal.
Sidney D. Gardner, Private First Class, U. S. Army; St. Lawrence County, New York.
Stephen Partridge Gardner, Lieutenant, U. S. Navy; Hidalgo County, Texas; earned the Bronze Star.
Theodore O. Gardner, Private, U. S. Army; Pennsylvania.
Thomas J. Gardner, Petty Officer First Class, U. S. Navy; Ohio.
Thomas C. Gardner, Private, U. S. Army; Los Angeles County, California.
Vernon Eugene Gardner, Fireman First Class, U. S. Navy; Lancaster County, Nebraska.
Virgil W. Gardner, Private, U. S. Army; Osage County, Oklahoma.
Walter Gardner, Technician Fifth Grade, U. S. Army; Missouri.
Walter S. Gardner, Staff Sergeant, U. S. Army; Greene County, Arkansas.
Walter F. Gardner, 1st Lieutenant, U. S. Army; Albany County, New York.
Walter G. Gardner, Staff Sergeant, U. S. Army; New York County, New York.

Wendell S. Gardner, Private First Class, U. S. Army; Cleburne County, Arkansas.

Willard Gardner, Merchant Seaman, U. S. Merchant Marine; New York.

Willard E. Gardner, Private First Class, U. S. Army; Shelby County, Tennessee.

William E. Gardner, Seaman Second Class, U. S. Navy; Illinois.

William T. Gardner, Ensign, U. S. Navy; Illinois.

William H. Gardner, 2nd Lieutenant, U. S. Army; Queens County, New York.

William E. Gardner, Sergeant, U. S. Army; Williamson County, Texas.

William H. Gardner, Private, U. S. Army; Butler County, Pennsylvania.

William T. Gardner, Private First Class, U. S. Army; Allegheny County, Pennsylvania.

William M. Gardner, Sergeant, U. S. Army; Salt Lake County, Utah.

William Gardner, 1st Lieutenant, U. S. Army; Allegheny County, Pennsylvania; (KIA Normandy).

William N. Gardner, Private, U. S. Army; Cook County, Illinois.

William A. Gardner, Technician Fifth Grade, U. S. Army; Dearborn County, Indiana.

William W. Gardner, Private First Class, U. S. Army; Sedgwick County, Kansas.

William R. Gardner, 2nd Lieutenant, U. S. Army; Warren County, Kentucky.

William Gardner, Private First Class, U. S. Army; Middlesex County, Massachusetts.

Wilfred Gardner, Staff Sergeant, U. S. Army; Union County, Arkansas.

Winslow G. Gardner, 1st Lieutenant, U. S. Army Air Corps; Weber County, Utah; earned the Air Medal.

Romeo Gardner, Private First Class, U. S. Army; Franklin County, New York.

Richard W. Gardener, U. S. Army; Arkansas

Arnold J. Gardiner, U. S. Army; New York

Blake F. Gardiner, U. S. Army; South Dakota

Carl T. Gardiner, U. S. Navy; Maine

Charles E. Gardner, U. S. Army; Iowa

Clarence A. Gardiner, U. S. Army; Rhode Island

Clovis C. Gardiner, U. S. Army; Maine

George E. Gardiner, U. S. Navy; California

Harold Walter Gardiner, U. S. Merchant Marine; Oregon

Hugh R. Gardiner, U. S. Army, New York

John C. Gardiner, U. S. Army Air Corps; California

John D. Gardiner, U. S. Army; Pennsylvania

Keith K. Gardiner, U. S. Army; Utah

Kenneth S. Gardiner, U. S. Army; Maine

Leland V. Gardiner, U. S. Army; Utah

Leon J. Gardiner, U. S. Army; Pennsylvania

Lorenzo Alfonso Gardiner, U. S. Merchant Marine; Louisiana

Maynard F. Gardiner, U. S. Army; New York

Ralph F. Gardiner, U. S. Army; Rhode Island

Ruth M. Gardiner, U. S. Army; Indiana
Thomas A. Gardiner, U. S. Army; Pennsylvania
Walker W. Gardiner, U. S. Army; South Carolina
Warren H. Gardiner, U. S. Army; Rhode Island
Wilbert M. Gardiner, U. S. Navy; Washington
William V. Gardiner, U. S. Army; Michigan

KOREAN WAR HEROES

Beverly A. Gardner was from Kern County, California and was a Private First Class as a Light Weapons Infantryman in the U. S. Army, 8th Cavalry Regiment, 1st Cavalry Division, killed in action on June 23rd, 1951 during the Korean War.

Channing Gardner was from St. Louis County, Minnesota and was a Lieutenant Junior Grade in the U. S. Navy as a Pilot in Fighter Squadron 653, declared dead while missing on May 29th, 1952, missing in action, earning the Distinguished Flying Cross and Air Medal during the Korean War.

Charles T. Gardner was from Fulton County, Georgia and was a Private First Class as a Light Weapons Infantryman in the U. S. Army, 23rd Infantry Regiment, 2nd Infantry Division, killed in action on September 21st, 1951 during the Korean War.

Charles E. Gardner was from Amite County, Mississippi and was a Corporal as a Rigger in the U. S. Army, 76th Engineer Construction Battalion, killed in action on January 16th, 1951 during the Korean War.

Elmer D. Gardner was from Oklahoma County, Oklahoma and was a Private E – 2 as a Light Weapons Infantryman in the U. S. Army, 48th Field Artillery Battalion, 7th Infantry Division, reported dead on December 5th, 1950, while captured, prisoner of war during the Korean War.

Frederick G. Gardner was from Bennington County, Vermont and was a Private First Class as a Light Weapons Infantryman in the U. S. Army, Company L, 3rd Battalion, 5th Infantry Regiment, killed in action on April 25th, 1951 during the Korean War.

Glenn Gardner was from Henderson County, Tennessee and was a Sergeant in the U. S. Army, Company G, 2nd Battalion, 5th Infantry Regimental Combat Team, killed in action on August 8th, 1950 during the Korean War.

Henry Lee Gardner was from Franklin County, Ohio and was a Corporal in the U. S. Army, 595th Engineer Dump Truck Company, died non – hostile death on July 3rd, 1951 working on an embankment when it collapsed suffocating him during the Korean War.

James Douglas Gardner was born on July 23rd, 1932 and was from Baltimore County, Maryland, serving as a Private E – 2 as a Light Weapons Infantryman in the U. S. Army, 29th Infantry Regimental Combat Team, killed in action on July 27th, 1950 during the Korean War.

James O. Gardner was from Norfolk County, Virginia and was a Major in the U. S. Army, 24th Infantry Regiment, 25th Infantry Division, killed in action on November 28th, 1950 during the Korean War.

James D. Gardner was from Fleming County, Kentucky and was a Private First Class as a Heavy Weapons Infantryman, 19th Infantry Regiment, 24th Division, killed in action on October 14th, 1951 during the Korean War.

Koeling B. Gardner was from Jefferson County, Kentucky and was a 1st Lieutenant in the U. S. Army, 5th Cavalry Regiment, 1st Cavalry Division, killed in action on October 25th, 1951, earning the Silver Star during the Korean War.

Ladon A. Gardner was from Alexander County, Illinois and was a Private E – 2 as a Light Weapons Infantryman in the U. S. Army, 9th Infantry Regiment, 2nd Infantry Division, killed in action on February 12th, 1951 during the Korean War.

Lawrence N. Gardner was from Franklin County, Vermont and was a Corporal in the U. S. Army, 187th Airborne Infantry Regimental Combat Team, killed in action on March 28th, 1951, earning the Distinguished Service Cross during the Korean War.

Lawrence Benjamin Gardner was born on February 12th, 1931 and was from Fayette County, Pennsylvania, serving as a Private First Class as a Light Weapons Assault Crewman in the U. S. Army, 65th Infantry Regiment, 3rd Infantry Division, killed in action on May 23rd, 1953 during the Korean War.

Maurice P. Gardner was from Franklin County, Vermont and was a Private First Class as a Fire Direction and Liaison Operator in the U. S. Army, Battery B, 38th Field Artillery Battalion, 2nd Infantry Division, reported dead on November 30th, 1950 while captured during the Korean War.

Merritt H. Gardner was from Windham County, Connecticut and was a Corporal as a Light Weapons Infantryman in the U. S. Army, 279th Infantry Regiment, 45th Infantry Division, killed in action on July 4th, 1952 during the Korean War.

Ralph Henry Gardner was from Matagorda County, Texas and was a Private First Class in the U. S. Marine Corps, 1st Battalion, 7th Marines, 1st Marine Division, killed in action on April 16th, 1951 during the Korean War.

Tennie Gardner was from Fairfield County, Connecticut and was a Sergeant in the U. S. Army, Headquarters Company, 24th Infantry Regiment, 25th Infantry Division, died non – hostile on October 30th, 1950 during the Korean War.

Weldon Danforth Gardner was from McLennan County, Texas and was a 1st Lieutenant as a Pilot in the U. S. Air Force, 7th Fighter – Bomber Squadron, 49th Fighter – Bomber Group, died in a non – hostile crash on May 30th, 1953 during the Korean War.

William Gardner was from Baltimore County, Maryland and was a Corporal as a Field Artillery Cannoneer in the U. S. Army, Battery C, 503rd Field Artillery Battalion, 2nd Infantry Division, reported dead on December 1st, 1950 while captured during the Korean War.

William B. Gardner was from Luzerne County, Pennsylvania and was a Sergeant First Class as a Light Weapons Assault Crewman in the U. S. Army, 23rd Infantry Regiment, 2nd Infantry Division, killed in action on April 5th, 1951 during the Korean War.

Curtis C. Gardiner, U. S. Army; South Dakota
Donald F. Gardiner, U. S. Army; New York
Joseph William Gardiner, U. S. Navy; Missouri
Murvee Daniel Gardiner, U. S. Army; New Jersey

Courtesy to www.honorstates.org

VIETNAM WAR HEROES

SGT. ROBERT LOUIS GARDNER

Sgt. Robert Louis Gardner was born on July 1st, 1922 and was from Nashua, Hillsborough County, New Hampshire. He was a Sergeant in the U. S. Army and died on June 13th, 1962 in Vietnam. Gardner is on panel/row 1E, 9 on the Vietnam Veterans Memorial Wall.

CPL. JAMES L. GARDNER

Cpl. James Lee Gardner was born on November 9th, 1945 and was from Portland, Oregon. He was a Corporal in the U. S. Marine Corps and died on February 2nd, 1966 in the province of Quang Ngai, Vietnam. Gardner is on panel/row 4E, 133 on the Vietnam Veterans Memorial Wall.

1st LT. JAMES A. GARDNER

1st Lt. James A. Gardner was born on February 7th, 1943 and was from Dyersburg, Dyer County, Tennessee. He was a 1st Lieutenant in the U. S. Army, 101st Airborne, 327th Infantry, Tiger Force Recon and died on February 7th, 1966 in My Canh, Vietnam. Gardner is on panel/row 5E, 11 on the Vietnam Veterans Memorial Wall.

Note: Gardner is mentioned in previous biography.

PFC. JACK E. GARDNER

Pfc. Jack Elroy Gardner was born on November 10th, 1944 and was from Vacaville, Solano County, California. He was a Private First Class in the U. S. Army and died on May 20th, 1966 in Vietnam. Gardner is on panel/row 7E, 89 on the Vietnam Veterans Memorial Wall.

SP4 WILLIAM H. GARDNER

SP4 William Hugh Gardner, Jr., was born on May 24th, 1940 and was from Montgomery, Montgomery County, Alabama. He was a SP4 in the U. S. Army and died on August 2nd, 1966 in Vietnam. Gardner is on panel/row 9E, 97 on the Vietnam Veterans Memorial Wall.

1ST LT. JAMES E. GARDNER

1st Lt. James E. Gardner was born on March 19th, 1941 and was from Kalamazoo, Michigan. He was a 1st Lieutenant in the U. S. Army and died on October 13th, 1966 in Vietnam. Gardner is on panel/row 11E, 71 on the Vietnam Veterans Memorial Wall.

LT. FRANK MAYNARD GARDNER

Lt. Frank Maynard Gardner was born on September 12th, 1923 and was from Cranston, Providence County, Rhode Island. He served as a Lieutenant in the U. S. Navy and died on October 26th, 1966 in Vietnam. Gardner is on panel/row 11E, 109 on the Vietnam Veterans Memorial Wall.

PVT. GLENN V. GARDNER

Pvt. Glenn Virgil Gardner was born on August 14th, 1947 and was from San Bernardino, California. He was a Private in the U. S. Army and died on November 25th, 1966, missing in action, offshore aboard a military troop transport en route to Vietnam. Gardner is on panel/row 12E, 116 on the Vietnam Veterans Memorial Wall.

SGT. LARRY W. GARDNER

Sgt. Larry Wayne Gardner was born on October 10th, 1946 and was from Ridgway, Elk County, Pennsylvania. He served as a Sergeant in the U. S. Marine Corps and died on January 21st, 1967 in Vietnam. Gardner is on panel/row 14E, 62 at the Vietnam Veterans Memorial Wall.

SSGT. ROY E. GARDNER

SSgt. Roy Edward Gardner was born on July 7th, 1941 and was from Brookside, Jefferson County, Alabama. He was a Staff Sergeant in the U. S. Army and died on March 11th, 1967 in the province of Binh Dinh, Vietnam. Gardner is on panel/row 16E, 58 on the Vietnam Veterans Memorial Wall.

Note: Gardner was awarded the Silver Star and Bronze Star.

PFC. ALEN L. GARDNER

Pfc. Alen Louis Gardner was born on August 11th, 1947 and was from Elmira, Chemung County, New York. He was a Private First Class in the U. S. Army and died on April 22nd, 1967 in the province of Binh Dinh, Vietnam. Gardner is on panel/row 18E, 69 on the Vietnam Veterans Memorial Wall.

CAPT. JOHN G. GARDNER

Capt. John Garrett Gardner was born on July 28th, 1940 and was from Hot Springs, Madison County, North Carolina. He was a Captain in the U. S. Marine Corps and as a helicopter pilot he was missing in action on June 3rd, 1967 in Vietnam, later being found and buried at Arlington National Cemetery. Gardner is on panel/row 21E, 45 on the Vietnam Veterans Memorial Wall.

CPL. FRED MICHAEL GARDNER

Cpl. Fred Michael Gardner was born on December 4th, 1947 and was from Mobile, Alabama. He was a Corporal in the U. S. Army and died on August 3rd, 1967 in the province of Dinh Tuong, Vietnam. Gardner is on panel/row 24E, 72 on the Vietnam Veterans Memorial Wall.

Note: Cpl. Mike Gardner is a distant cousin and he is buried at the Cederlawn Cemetery in Philadelphia, Mississippi.

SGT. BOBBY R. GARDNER

Sgt. Bobby Ray Gardner was born on April 25th, 1946 and was from Ahoskie, Hertford County, North Carolina. He was a Sergeant in the U. S. Army and died on August 8th, 1967 in the province of Binh Duong, Vietnam. Gardner is on panel/row 24E, 90 on the Vietnam Veterans Memorial Wall.

Note: Gardner was awarded the Bronze Star.

AN LAWRENCE L. GARDNER

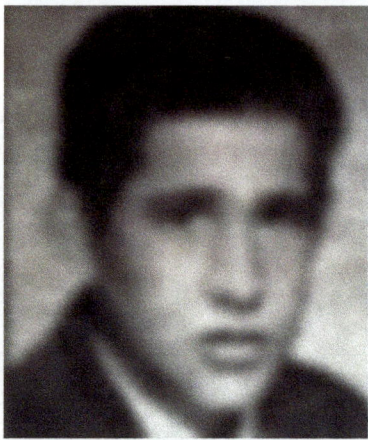

AN. Lawrence Lee Gardner was born on December 6th, 1947 and was from Las Vegas, Nevada. He was a AN in the U. S. Navy and died on October 25th, 1967 offshore. Gardner is on panel/row 28E, 66 on the Vietnam Veterans Memorial Wall.

CPL. DANIEL E. GARDNER

Cpl. Daniel Eli Gardner was born on February 19th, 1947 and was from Oklahoma City, Oklahoma. He was a Corporal in the U. S. Army and died on December 10th, 1967 in the province of Long An, Vietnam and was buried at Evergreen Cemetery in Tucson, Arizona. Gardner is on panel/row 31E, 74 on the Vietnam Veterans Memorial Wall.

SP4 ROBERT E. GARDNER

SP4. Robert Eugene Gardner was born on September 22nd, 1942 and was from Sylacauga, Talladega County, Alabama. He was a SP4 in the U. S. Army and died on April 19th, 1968 in the province of Quang Tri, Vietnam. Gardner is on panel/row 50E, 46 on the Vietnam Veterans Memorial Wall.

CPL. EDDIE A. GARDNER

Cpl. Eddie Augustus Gardner was born on February 2nd, 1947 and was from Jackson, Hinds County, Mississippi. He was a Corporal in the U. S. Army and died on April 30th, 1968 in the province of Quang Tri, Vietnam. Gardner is on panel/row 53E, 13 on the Vietnam Veterans Memorial Wall.

1ST LT. SAMUEL R. GARDNER

1st Lt. Samuel Ray Gardner was born on May 7th, 1943 and was from Wichita, Sedgwick County, Kansas. He served as a 1st Lieutenant in the U. S. Army and died on May 5th, 1968 in the province of Quang Tin, Vietnam. Gardner is on panel/row 55E, 12 on the Vietnam Veterans Memorial Wall.
Note: Gardner was awarded the Distinguished Flying Cross and Bronze Star.

PFC. MICHAEL J. GARDNER

Pfc. Michael John Gardner was born on May 13th, 1948 and was from Minneapolis, Minnesota. He was a Private First Class in the U. S. Marine Corps and died on May 26th, 1968 in the province of Quang Tri, Vietnam. Gardner is on panel/row 66W, 6 on the Vietnam Veterans Memorial Wall.

LCPL. STEPHEN M. GARDNER

LCpl. Stephen Mark Gardner was born on September 2nd, 1948 and was from Wenatchee, Chelan County, Washington. He was a Lance Corporal in the U. S. Marine Corps and died on June 28th, 1968 in the province of Quang Tri, Vietnam. Gardner is on panel/row 54W, 10 on the Vietnam Veterans Memorial Wall.

TSGT. ROBERT L. GARDNER

TSgt. Robert Linley Gardner was born on January 22nd, 1927 and was from Findlay, Hancock County, Ohio. He was a TSgt. in the U. S. Air Force and died on July 30th, 1968 in Vietnam. Gardner is on panel/row 50W, 35 on the Vietnam Veterans Memorial Wall.

CPL. ROBERT C. GARDNER

Cpl. Robert Charles Gardner was born on January 5th, 1948 and was from Chicago, Illinois. He was a Corporal in the U. S. Marine Corps and died on August 16th, 1968 in the province of Quang Nam, Vietnam. Gardner is on panel/row 48W, 25 on the Vietnam Veterans Memorial Wall.

PFC. DAVID E. GARDNER

Pfc. David Ernest Gardner was born on May 29th, 1948 and was from Walpole, Cheshire County, New Hampshire. He was a Private First Class in the U. S. Army and died on December 11th, 1968 in the province of Dinh Tuong, Vietnam. Gardner is on panel/row 36W, 2 on the Vietnam Veterans Memorial Wall.
Note: Gardner was awarded the Bronze Star.

SGT. GORDON D. GARDNER

Sgt. Gordon Dwight Gardner was born on March 18th, 1949 and was from Sunnyvale, Santa Clara County, California. He was a Sergeant in the U. S. Army and died on February 3rd, 1969 in the province of Quang Tri, Vietnam. Gardner is on panel/row 33W, 48 on the Vietnam Veterans Memorial Wall.

PFC. MARION L. GARDNER

Pfc. Marion Lora Gardner was born on December 26th, 1948 and was from Tulsa, Osage County, Oklahoma. Gardner was a Private First Class in the U. S. Army and died on May 13th, 1969 in the province of Tay Ninh, Vietnam. Gardner is on panel/row 25W, 99 on the Vietnam Veterans Memorial Wall.

CPL. PHILLIP D. GARDNER

Cpl. Phillip D. Gardner was born on May 1st, 1948 and was from Odessa, Texas. He was a Corporal in the U. S. Army and died on June 6th, 1969 in the province of Quang Tin, Vietnam. Gardner is on panel/row 23W, 86 on the Vietnam Veterans Memorial Wall.

PFC. WILHIMON GARDNER

Pfc. Wilhimon Gardner was born on December 18th, 1948 and was from New York City, New York. He was a Private First Class in the U. S. Army and died on August 26th, 1969 in the province of Quang Ngai in Vietnam. Gardner is on panel/row 19W, 118 on the Vietnam Veterans Memorial Wall.

PFC. GERALD L. GARDNER

Pfc. Gerald Lee Gardner was born on August 3rd, 1949 and was from Cedar Rapids, Iowa. He was a Private First Class in the U. S. Marine Corps and died on February 2nd, 1970 in the province of Quang Nam, Vietnam. Gardner is on panel/row 14W, 93 on the Vietnam Veterans Memorial Wall.

1ST LT. RICHARD GEORGE GARDNER

1st Lt. Richard George Gardner was born on November 3rd, 1946 and was from Washington, D. C. He served as a 1st Lieutenant in the U. S. Army and died on April 24th, 1970 in Quang Ngai province in Vietnam. Gardner is on panel/row 11W, 45 on the Vietnam Veterans Memorial Wall.

CWO ROBERT W. GARDNER

CWO Robert Wayne Gardner was born on June 2nd, 1947 and was from Wheaton, Montgomery County, Maryland. He served in the U. S. Army as a Chief Warrant Officer in the 281st Assault Helicopter Company as an aviator and died after his helicopter was shot down on April 27th, 1970 in the province of Pleiku in South Vietnam and was buried at Arlington National Cemetery. Gardner is on panel/row 11W, 58 on the Vietnam Veterans Memorial Wall.

SSGT. JAMES D. GARDNER

SSGT. James Dale Gardner was born on September 16th, 1948 and was from Daytona Beach, Florida. He was a Staff Sergeant in the U. S. Army and died on June 21st, 1970 in the province of Tay Ninh, Vietnam. Gardner is on panel/row 9W, 76 on the Vietnam Veterans Memorial Wall.

MAJ. ALAN DAVID GARDNER

Maj. Alan D. Gardner was born on March 3rd, 1939 and was from Lewisburg, Pennsylvania. He served as a Major in the U. S. Army, 31st Engineer Detachment, Headquarters and Headquarters Company, 5th Special Forces Group and died on June 27th, 1970 in the Kontum Province, Vietnam. Gardner is on panel/row 9W, 98 on the Vietnam Veterans Memorial Wall.
Note: Gardner is mentioned in a previous biography.

SP4 WILLIE GARDNER

SP4 Willie Gardner, Jr. was born on July 12th, 1950 and was from Brent, Bibb County, Alabama. He was a SP4 in the U. S. Army and died on February 12th, 1971 in the province of Quang Tin, Vietnam. Gardner is on panel/row 5W, 99 on the Vietnam Veterans Memorial Wall.

WO ROBERT PAUL GARDINER

WO Robert Paul Gardiner was born on May 1st, 1948 and was from Orange County, California. He was a Warrant Officer in the U. S. Army as a helicopter pilot in the 1st Cavalry Division, 1st Squadron, 9th Cavalry, B Troop and died on July 4th, 1969 when his helicopter was shot down in South Vietnam. Gardiner is on panel/row 21W, 60 on the Vietnam Veterans Memorial Wall.

SP4 ROY WILLIAM GARDINER

SP4 Roy William Gardiner was born on May 17th, 1949 and was from Vernal, Uintah County, Utah. He was a SP4 in the U. S. Army and died on April 18th, 1970 in Bien Hoa Province in Vietnam. Gardiner is on panel/row 11W/21 on the Vietnam Veterans Memorial Wall.

Courtesy to the Vietnam Memorial Fund for photographs and information
References:
http://www.vvmf.org/search
www.honorstates.org

9/11 HEROES

Christopher S. Gardner, 36, died on September 11th, 2001, at the World Trade Center, was an executive at Aon who had a large staff reporting to him on the company's global risk services. He was a natural leader, always the "captain of the ship" who had a lifelong passion for the sea. Gardner was never worried and always in control, described as a great family man to his wife and two children. Profile submitted Dec. 23rd, 2001, *The New York Times*

Douglas Benjamin Gardner, 39, died on September 11th, 2001, at the World Trade Center, was a businessman who worked for Lehman Brothers, his father's real estate business, and was also an executive managing director. He loved basketball, sports, and was a good athlete. Gardner was a great family man to his wife and two children.
Profile submitted Nov. 18th, 2001, *The New York Times*

Harvey Joseph Gardner III, 35, died on September 11th, 2001, at the World Trade Center, was described as a **"true American hero, forever strong and loved"**, who reportedly comforted others during the tragedy, telling them it was okay and he was being his **"normal, level – headed self"**. He was a certified computer technician and consultant for General Telecom on the 83rd floor, working at the World Trade Center for two years. Gardner was an American patriot, a student of history, martial arts, built computers from scratch, and he lived in Lakewood, New Jersey, his family described as being **"FOREVER PROUD"**.
Profile submitted Dec. 12th, 2001, *The New York Times*

Jeffrey Brian Gardner, 36, died on September 11th, 2001, at the World Trade Center, was an insurance salesman, but his appearance was that of an adventurer. He worked for Marsh & McLennan as an environmental insurance broker. Gardner loved wine, opera, smoking hand – carved pipes, and was an adventurer on a motorcycle touring around rough country. He had a great sense of humor and built homes in Newark, Honduras and Brazil while on vacation. Gardner worked for Habitat for Humanity, which involved his favorite activities, carpentry and making friends with volunteers.
Profile submitted Feb. 17th, 2002, *The New York Times*

Thomas A. Gardner, 39, died on September 11th, 2001, at the World Trade Center, was a firefighter on the New York City Fire Department. He was an aspiring science teacher with a great sense of humor, who played hockey for a Long Island team with his older brother, he loved animals, and he was described as humble. Gardner was a firefighter for 13 years battling fires in Harlem, then moved on to the city's elite hazardous – materials unit known as HazMat 1 in Queens, serving a total of 17 years as a New York City firefighter.

He had a B. A. in Biology and Education, as well as a teacher of hazardous materials and weapons of mass destruction, being a Master Instructor for the IAFF and Louisiana State University. Gardner also taught a course in HazMat at the Fire Science Program of New Jersey City University, developing a web course at NJCU, which was one of the first of its kind in the country. Queens College now has the Thomas A. Gardner Award for students planning to teach science. Gardner was one of New York City's bravest heroes.
Profile submitted Aug. 11th, 2002, *The New York Times*

William Arthur Gardner, 45, died on September 11th, 2001, at the World Trade Center, was a systems analyst at eSpeed. He was a great husband according to his wife. Gardner was the father of two children.
Profile submitted Feb. 17th, 2002, *The New York Times*

References:
http://www.legacy.com/Sept11/Home.aspx

IRAQ WAR HEROES

LCPL. DEREK GARDNER

Lance Cpl. Derek L. Gardner, U. S. Marine, died for our freedom during Operation Iraqi Freedom. He was from San Juan Capistrano, California and was engaged to marry his girlfriend, telling her, **"This isn't goodbye sweetheart, this is hello to our new beginning."** Gardner was assigned to Headquarters Battalion, 1st Marine Division, I Marine Expeditionary Force, Camp Pendleton, California.

He was a motor vehicle operator and was killed on September 6th, 2004 by a car bomb in Iraq's Anbar province.

Gardner was from a military family. His father, Ken Gardner was a U. S. Marine during the Vietnam War. His grandfathers served in the Korean War and World War II. His great grandfather served in World War I.

"He was a proud Marine. He walked like a Marine, he talked like a Marine. He was just doing his job." – Vickey De Lacour, his mother.

SPC. JAMES "WILL" GARDNER

Spc. James "Will" Gardner, U. S. Army soldier, died for our freedom in Operation Iraqi Freedom. He was from Glasgow, Kentucky. Gardner was assigned to 1st Battalion, 101st Aviation Regiment, 101st Combat Aviation Brigade, 101st Airborne Division (Air Assault), Fort Campbell, Kentucky. He was known for his fearless nature and died at age 22 on April 10th, 2006 in Tal Afar, Iraq from a non – combat related cause.

Gardner was survived by his parents, siblings, and his wife.

SGT. FREEMAN L. GARDNER

Sgt. Freeman L. Gardner, Jr., U. S. Army soldier, died for our freedom in Operation Iraqi Freedom. He was from Little Rock, Arkansas. Gardner was assigned to the 18th Engineer Company, 3rd Stryker Brigade Combat Team, 2nd Infantry Division, Fort Lewis, Washington.

He died at age 26 after he was killed on March 22nd, 2007 in Baghdad, Iraq when an improvised explosive device detonated near his unit while on combat patrol.

Courtesy to www.valor.militarytimes.com

Note: Respect and honor to all of those who were wounded or died fighting for their country and freedom.

MEDAL OF HONOR

WILLIAM GARDNER

Born: 1832 Ireland
Home: New York, New York
Service: Union Navy
Rank: Seaman
Division: U. S. S. Galena
Action Date: August 5, 1864 (awarded December 31, 1864)
He entered the Union Navy at New York, New York. He served as a Ship's Cook. His CMOH was issued by General Order Number 45, dated December 31, 1864. His citation reads: **"As seaman on board the USS Galena in the engagement at Mobile Bay, 5 August 1864. Serving gallantly during this fierce battle which resulted in the capture of the rebel ram Tennessee and the damaging of Fort Morgan, Gardner behaved with conspicuous coolness under the fire of the enemy."**

Medal of Honor awarded to William Gardner

JAMES DANIEL GARDINER

Born: September 16, 1839 Gloucester, Virginia
Home: Yorktown, Virginia
Died: September 29, 1905 Clarks Summit, Pennsylvania
Service: Union Army, 36th Regiment United States Colored Troops
Rank: Private
Action Date: September 29, 1864 at Chapins Farm, Virginia. His citation reads: **"Rushed in advance of his brigade, shot a rebel officer who was on the parapet rallying his men, and then ran him through with his bayonet."**

CHARLES N. GARDNER

Born: March 29, 1845 South Scituate, Massachusetts
Died: September 22, 1919 Massachusetts
Service: Union Army, Company E, 32nd Massachusetts Infantry
Rank: Second Lieutenant
Action Date: April 1, 1865 Five Forks, Virginia, his citation reads: **"The President of the United States of America, in the name of Congress, takes pleasure in presenting the Medal of Honor to Private Charles N. Gardner, United States Army, for extraordinary heroism on 1 April 1865, while serving with Company E, 32d Massachusetts Infantry, in action at Five Forks, Virginia, for capture of flag."**

ROBERT J. GARDNER

Born: September 28, 1837 Livingston, New York
Home: Egremont, Massachusetts
Died: September 23, 1902 Parkers Corners, Michigan
Service: Union Army, Company K, 34th Massachusetts Infantry
Rank: Sergeant

Action Date: April 2, 1865 Petersburg, Virginia, his citation reads: **"The President of the United States of America, in the name of Congress, takes pleasure in presenting the Medal of Honor to Sergeant Robert J. Gardner, United States Army, for extraordinary heroism on 2 April 1865, while serving with Company K, 34th Massachusetts Infantry, in action at Petersburg, Virginia. Sergeant Gardner was among the first to enter Fort Gregg, clearing his way by using his musket on the heads of the enemy."**

CHARLES GARDNER

Alias: Simon Suhler
Born: 1844 Bavaria, Germany
Home: San Francisco, California
Died: May 16, 1895 San Antonio, Texas
Service: U. S. Army, Company B, 8th U. S. Cavalry
Rank: Private
Action Date: August to October 1868, issued on July 24, 1869, his citation reads: **"The President of the United States of America, in the name of Congress, takes pleasure in presenting the Medal of Honor to Private Charles Gardner, United States Army, for bravery in scouts and actions against Indians from August to October 1868, while serving with Company B, 8th U.S. Cavalry, in action in Arizona Territory."**

PETER W. GARDNER

Alias: Peter W. Gardiner
Home: Fort Lowell, Arizona Territory (acknowledged January 1877 Camp Bowie, Arizona Territory)
Service: U. S. Army, Company H, 6th U. S. Cavalry
Rank: Private
Action Date: April 23, 1875, Sappa Creek, Kansas, his citation reads: **"With 5 other men he waded in mud and water up the creek to a position directly behind an entrenched Cheyenne position, who were using natural bank pits to good advantage against the main column. This surprise attack from the enemy rear broke their resistance."**

JAMES ALTON GARDNER

Born: February 7, 1943 Dyersburg, Tennessee
Died: February 7, 1966 Vietnam
Note: 1st Lt. James A. Gardner received the Congressional Medal of Honor, the Bronze Star, the Purple Heart, and the Vietnam Gallantry Cross with Palm; his citation is mentioned previously in his biography.

Courtesy to https://valor.militarytimes.com/

DISTINGUISHED SERVICE CROSS

ELMER W. GARDNER

World War I Veteran
Home: Marydale, New York
Service: U. S. Army
Rank: Private, Company G, 9th Infantry Regiment, 2d Division, A. E. F.
Action Date: July 18, 1918

The President of the United States of America, authorized by Act of Congress, July 9, 1918, takes pleasure in presenting the Distinguished Service Cross to Private Elmer W. Gardner (ASN: 39586), United States Army, for extraordinary heroism in action while serving with Company G, 9th Infantry Regiment, 2d Division, A.E.F., south of Soissons, France, 18 July 1918. While acting as a runner, Private Gardner was seriously wounded, but in spite of his injury, he struggled forward and delivered his message.

ALFRED W. GARDNER

World War I Veteran (KIA)
Home: Sharon Springs, New York
Rank: First Lieutenant, 305th Infantry Regiment, 77th Division, A. E. F.
Action Date: October 3, 1918

The President of the United States of America, authorized by Act of Congress, July 9, 1918, takes pride in presenting the Distinguished Service Cross (Posthumously) to First Lieutenant (Infantry) Alfred W. Gardner, United States Army, for extraordinary heroism in action while serving with 305th Infantry Regiment, 77th Division, A.E.F., in the Argonne Forest, France, 3 October 1918. Attacking enemy machine-gun nests, Lieutenant Gardner displayed the highest courage when he led his company up a steep slope in the face of murderous fire. Before he could accomplish his objective he was killed.

JOHN H. GARDNER

World War I Veteran
Home: Hartsville, South Carolina
Service: U. S. Army
Rank: Sergeant, 118th Infantry Regiment, 30th Division, A. E. F.
Action Date: October 8, 1918

The President of the United States of America, authorized by Act of Congress, July 9, 1918, takes pleasure in presenting the Distinguished Service Cross to Sergeant John H. Gardner (ASN: 1312150), United States Army, for extraordinary heroism in action while serving with Company L, 118th Infantry Regiment, 30th Division, A.E.F., near Brancourt, France, 8 October 1918. After his company commander had been wounded immediately before an attack, Sergeant Gardner took command of the company and led it throughout the action. When his company was held up by machine-gun fire, he went forward and killed four German machine-gunners, thereby enabling his company to continue the advance. On another occasion he picked up the rifle of a wounded soldier and killed three of the enemy. Later, when his company was almost surrounded by hostile machine gunners, under his cool direction his men fought their way out, reached their objective, and consolidated the position.

MARTIN E. GARDNER

World War I Veteran (KIA)
Home: Sharpsburg, Maryland
Rank: Sergeant, Company A, 326th Infantry Regiment, 82d Division, A. E. F.
Action Date: October 15, 1918

The President of the United States of America, authorized by Act of Congress, July 9, 1918, takes pride in presenting the Distinguished Service Cross (Posthumously) to Sergeant Martin E. Gardner (ASN: 1900435), United States Army, for extraordinary heroism in action while serving with Company A, 326th Infantry Regiment, 82d Division, A.E.F., near St. Juvin, France, 15 October 1918. After his commanding officer had been severely wounded, Sergeant Gardner took command of the detachment, and although severely wounded himself, he gallantly led his group in the attack against enemy machine-gun fire. At the conclusion of this successful attack, he was shot and killed by an enemy sniper.

GEORGE W. GARDNER

World War I Veteran
Home: Traer, Kansas
Rank: Sergeant, Company F, 353d Infantry Regiment, 89th Division, A. E. F.
Action Date: November 2, 1918

The President of the United States of America, authorized by Act of Congress, July 9, 1918, takes pleasure in presenting the Distinguished Service Cross to Sergeant George W. Gardner (ASN: 2176371), United States Army, for extraordinary heroism in action while serving with Company F, 353d Infantry

Regiment, 89th Division, A.E.F., in Bois-de-Barricourt, France, 2 November 1918. Sergeant Gardner led his platoon through shell and machine-gun fire in an attack on strong enemy positions, capturing two machine-guns and assisting in the destruction of several others that were holding up our advance.

MADISON D. GARDNER

World War II Veteran
Service: U. S. Army
Rank: Second Lieutenant, Company A, 30th Infantry Regiment, 3d Division
Action Date: November 4, 1944

Second Lieutenant Madison D. Gardner, United States Army, was awarded the Distinguished Service Cross for extraordinary heroism in connection with military operations against an armed enemy while serving with Company A, 30th Infantry Regiment, 3d Infantry Division, in action against enemy forces on 4 November 1944. Second Lieutenant Gardner's intrepid actions, personal bravery and zealous devotion to duty exemplify the highest traditions of the military forces of the United States and reflect great credit upon himself, the 3d Infantry Division, and the United States Army.

HESTER N. GARDNER

World War II Veteran
Home: Denver, Colorado
Service: U. S. Army
Rank: Staff Sergeant
Action Date: November 12, 1944

The President of the United States of America, authorized by Act of Congress July 9, 1918, takes pleasure in presenting the Distinguished Service Cross to Staff Sergeant Hester N. Gardner, United States Army, for extraordinary heroism in connection with military operations against an armed enemy while serving with Company L, 143d Infantry Regiment, 36th Infantry Division, in action on 12 November 1944, near La Chappelle, France. While leading his squad in an attack against a heavily defended enemy stronghold, Sergeant Gardner was subjected to intense machine gun fire which pinned down the squad and severely wounded him in the head. Although he was the target for concentrated enemy machine gun fire, Sergeant Gardner fearlessly raised himself from the ground and continued to fire his Thompson sub-machine gun. Killing the gunner and destroying the gun, he enabled his squad to safely withdraw. Having exhausted his supply of ammunition, he dropped unconscious to the ground. By his magnificent courage and fortitude, Sergeant Gardner enabled his squad to withdraw from a precarious position and friendly mortar fire was then directed against the enemy stronghold, forcing the hostile force to withdraw in disorder. Staff Sergeant Gardner's intrepid actions, personal bravery and zealous devotion to duty exemplify the highest traditions of the military forces of the United States and reflect great credit upon himself, his unit, and the United States Army.

LAWRENCE N. GARDNER

Korean War Veteran (KIA)
Home: Franklin, Vermont
Service: U. S. Army
Rank: Corporal, Company G, 3d Battalion, 187th Airborne Regimental Combat Team
Action Date: March 28, 1951

The President of the United States of America, under the provisions of the Act of Congress approved July 9, 1918, takes pride in presenting the Distinguished Service Cross (Posthumously) to Corporal Lawrence N. Gardner (ASN: RA-11143331), United States Army, for extraordinary heroism in connection with military operations against an armed enemy of the United Nations while serving with Company G, 3d Battalion, 187th Airborne Regimental Combat Team, 11th Airborne Division. Corporal Gardner distinguished himself by extraordinary heroism in action against enemy aggressor forces in the vicinity of Parun-ni, Korea, on 28 March 1951. On that date, Company G was assigned the mission of capturing Hill 507, a hostile strong point. As the company approached the summit of the hill, the stubbornly resisting enemy began tossing hand grenades among the friendly troops. Seeing the grenades fall among his comrades, Corporal Gardner, with complete disregard for his personal safety, and with heroic determination to save the lives of his gravely endangered comrades, began hurling them back into the enemy positions. He succeeded in recovering two of the grenades and throwing them at the enemy and was attempting to throw a third grenade toward an enemy entrenchment when it exploded in his hand, killing him instantly.

Corporal Kenneth Gardiner, U. S. Army, Battery A, 10th Field Artillery, 3d Division, A. E. F., from Council Bluffs, Iowa, awarded the Distinguished Service Cross for extraordinary heroism in action on July 17th, 1918 near St. Eugene, France, for carrying messages while under enemy fire during World War I.

Lieutenant Colonel Henry E. Gardiner, U. S. Army, awarded the Distinguished Service Cross for extraordinary heroism for military operations against an armed enemy, in February of 1943 during World War II.

Courtesy to https://valor.militarytimes.com/

NAVY CROSS

ALFRED GARDNER

World War I Veteran
Service: U. S. Navy
Rank: Lieutenant, Junior Grade, Commander of a Dirigible, Naval Aviation Forces

The President of the United States of America takes pleasure in presenting the Navy Cross to Lieutenant, Junior Grade Alfred Gardner, United States Navy (Reserve Force), for distinguished service in the line of his profession as Commanding Officer of a dirigible engaged in patrol and convoy flights, in the War Zone, in which operations he did exceptional work, pushing his flights to the limits of physical and material endurance and upon one occasion broke all records for length of flight for her type of ship.

CLYDE "G" GARDNER

World War II Veteran
Service: U. S. Navy
Rank: Lieutenant, Junior Grade, Commander 2d Carrier Task Force Pacific
Action Date: October 24, 1944, Bombing Squadron

The President of the United States of America takes pleasure in presenting the Navy Cross to Lieutenant, Junior Grade Clyde "G" Gardner, Jr., United States Naval Reserve, for extraordinary heroism in operations against the enemy while serving as Pilot of a carrier-based Navy Dive Bomber in Bombing Squadron FIFTEEN (VB-15, attached to the U.S.S. ESSEX (CV-9), in action against major units of the Japanese Fleet in the Sibuyan Sea during the Battle for Leyte gulf, on 24 October 1944. Fearlessly pressing his attack to low altitude in the face of accurate and intense anti-aircraft fire from the entire enemy disposition, Lieutenant, Junior Grade, Gardner skillfully obtained a direct hit upon a Japanese battleship of the YAMATO class. By his superb airmanship, exceptional courage and steadfast devotion to duty throughout a perilous assignment, Lieutenant, Junior Grade, Gardner contributed directly to the success of this historic Battle and upheld the highest traditions of the United States Naval Service.
Courtesy to https://valor.militarytimes.com/

SILVER STAR

JOHN F. GARDNER

World War I Veteran
Service: U. S. Army, 125th Infantry Regiment, 32d Division, American Expeditionary Forces
By direction of the President, under the provisions of the act of Congress approved July 9, 1918 (Bul. No. 43, W.D., 1918), Major (Infantry) John F. Gardner, United States Army, is cited by the Commanding General, American Expeditionary Forces, for gallantry in action and a silver star may be placed upon the ribbon of the Victory Medals awarded him. Major Gardner distinguished himself by gallantry in action while serving with the 125th Infantry Regiment, 32d Division, American Expeditionary Forces, in action on 31 August 1918, near Juvigny, France, in helping the wounded under terrific enemy fire.

GEORGE W. GARDNER

World War I Veteran
Service: U. S. Marine Corps
Rank: Sergeant
Division: 2d Division, American Expeditionary Forces
By direction of the President, under the provisions of the act of Congress approved July 9, 1918 (Bul. No. 43, W.D. 1918), Sergeant George W. Gardner (MCSN: 67202), United States Marine Corps, is cited by the Commanding General, SECOND DIVISION, American Expeditionary Forces, for gallantry in action and a silver star may be placed upon the ribbon of the Victory Medals awarded him. Sergeant Gardner distinguished himself while serving with the 43d Company, Fifth Regiment (Marines), 2d Division, American Expeditionary Forces at Blanc Mont, France, 1 to 10 October 1918. (Silver Star Citation).

ALONZO J. GARDNER

World War II Veteran
Service: U. S. Army, 91st Infantry Division
Alonzo J. Gardner, United States Army, is reported to have been awarded the Silver Star under the below listed General Orders for conspicuous gallantry

and intrepidity in action against the enemy while serving with the 91st Infantry Division during World War II.

ARTHUR B. GARDNER
World War II Veteran (KIA)
Born: Long Island, New York
Died: January 2, 1944; buried Manila, Philippine Islands
Service: U. S. Marine Corps, 1st Marine Division
Rank: Second Lieutenant

The President of the United States of America takes pride in presenting the Silver Star (Posthumously) to Second Lieutenant Arthur B. Gardner, Jr. (MCSN: 0-15850), United States Marine Corps Reserve, for conspicuous gallantry and intrepidity while attached to the FIRST Marine Division during combat against enemy Japanese forces on Cape Gloucester, New Britain, January 2, 1944. When his platoon became pinned down at a river crossing by heavy enemy machine-gun fire from well-concealed encampments which inflicted serious casualties, Second Lieutenant Gardner unhesitatingly made his way forward over difficult terrain to assist in extricating his men. Courageously remaining exposed to hostile fire, with utter disregard for his own personal safety, he succeeded in withdrawing his command to a position of safety before he himself was mortally injured. Second Lieutenant Gardner's determined leadership and selfless devotion to duty in the face of grave peril were in keeping with the highest traditions of the United States Naval Service. He gallantly gave his life for his country.

BRUCE A. GARDNER
World War II Veteran
General Orders: Headquarters, 8th Air Force, General Orders No. 102 (1943)
Service: U. S. Army Air Forces

Bruce A. Gardner, United States Army Air Forces, was awarded the Silver Star for conspicuous gallantry and intrepidity in action during World War II.

BURTON H. GARDNER
World War II Veteran
Service: U. S. Army Air Forces, 8th Air Force

Burton H. Gardner, United States Army Air Forces, was awarded the Silver Star for conspicuous gallantry in action against the enemy while serving with the EIGHTH Air Force in the European Theater of Operations during World War II.

CARL M. GARDNER
World War II Veteran
Service: U. S. Army, 6th Infantry Divison

Carl M. Gardner, United States Army, is reported to have been awarded the Silver Star under the below-listed General Orders for conspicuous gallantry and intrepidity in action against the enemy while serving with the 6th Infantry Division during World War II.

CHARLES L. GARDNER

World War II Veteran
Service: U. S. Navy, 2d Marine Division
Rank: Hospitalman Apprentice First Class
Action Date: June 27, 1944
Hospitalman Apprentice First Class Charles L. Gardner, United States Navy, was awarded the Silver Star for conspicuous gallantry and intrepidity in action on June 27, 1944, while serving as a Corpsman attached to the SECOND Marine Division at Saipan.

CHARLES R. GARDNER

World War II Veteran
Service: U. S. Army, 24th Infantry Division
Charles R. Gardner, United States Army, is reported to have been awarded the Silver Star under the below-listed General Orders for conspicuous gallantry and intrepidity in action against the enemy while serving with the 24th Infantry Division during World War II.

ELDON C. GARDNER

World War II Veteran
Home: Iowa
Service: U. S. Army, 80th Infantry Division
Rank: Second Lieutenant
Action Date: December 4, 1944
The President of the United States of America, authorized by Act of Congress July 9, 1918, takes pleasure in presenting the Silver Star to Second Lieutenant (Infantry) Eldon C. Gardner (ASN: 0-1319273), United States Army, for gallantry in action while serving with the 80th Infantry Division in connection with military operations against an enemy of the United States on 4 December 1944 in France. While leading his rifle platoon in an attack on the enemy, Lieutenant Gardner assaulted an enemy truck and antitank gun escaping down a road covered by enemy machine guns and bordered by trenches occupied by the enemy. With utter disregard for his own safety, Lieutenant Gardner ran directly into the face of the raking enemy fire, firing his carbine to kill the driver, and hurling hand grenades to destroy the truck and the remainder of the crew. His courage, aggressiveness, and loyal devotion to duty were in keeping with the highest traditions of the military service and reflect great credit upon himself, his unit and the United States Army.

ELMER GARDNER

World War II Veteran
Service: U. S. Army, 26th Infantry Division

Elmer Gardner, United States Army, is reported to have been awarded the Silver Star under the below listed General Orders, for conspicuous gallantry and intrepidity in action against the enemy, while serving with the 26th Infantry Division during World War II.

FRANCIS A. GARDNER

World War II Veteran
Service: U. S. Army, 8th Infantry Division

Francis A. Gardner, United States Army, is reported to have been awarded the Silver Star under the below-listed General Orders for conspicuous gallantry and intrepidity in action against the enemy while serving with the 8th Infantry Division during World War II.

FRANK W. GARDNER

World War II Veteran (KIA) (2 Silver Star Medals)
Home: Belmont, Massachusetts
Service: U. S. Army, Company B, 320th Infantry Regiment, 35th Division
Rank: First Lieutenant; Captain
1st Action Date: August 10 – 11, 1944

The President of the United States of America, authorized by Act of Congress July 9, 1918, takes pleasure in presenting the Silver Star to First Lieutenant (Infantry) Frank W. Gardner (ASN: 0-1298382), United States Army, for gallantry in action while serving with the 35th Infantry Division, in action in the vicinity of ****, France, on 10 - 11 August 1944. Lieutenant Gardner, commanding Company B, 320th Infantry Regiment, led his troops in an attack, on tanks, against Hill Number 317 in the face of direct fire from enemy anti-tank guns the afternoon of 10 August. He succeeded in reaching the hillside that evening, then attached his unit to another company of riflemen and established joint defensive positions. This position was isolated from the remainder of the battalion for approximately thirty hours, during which time five sharp enemy counterattacks, supported by tanks, were successfully repulsed. Although twice wounded, Lieutenant Gardner remained in active command until the morning of 12 August, when the severity of his wounds necessitated his evacuation. His dynamic leadership, resourcefulness, and disregard for personal safety in establishing and holding the forward position against strong enemy opposition, was largely responsible for the successful assault on Hill Number 317 by his battalion on 12 August.

2nd Action Date: November 8 – 10, 1944

The President of the United States of America, authorized by Act of Congress July 9, 1918, takes pride in presenting a Bronze Oak Leaf Cluster in lieu of a Second Award of the Silver Star (Posthumously) to Captain (Infantry) Frank W. Gardner (ASN: 0-1298382), United States Army, for gallantry in action while serving with the 35th Infantry Division, in action in the vicinity of ****, France, from 8 to 10 November 1944. On the night of 8 November, Captain Gardner, Commanding Officer of Company B, 320th Infantry Regiment, 35th Infantry

Division, personally led his company in a drive to clear the enemy from positions along a railroad southeast of ****. So skillfully did he direct the fire and movement of his troops that the enemy was routed from strongly dug-in positions and an 88-mm. gun was captured before its crew could fire a shot. About dusk on 10 November, the enemy counterattacked sharply and one group with two machine guns broke through the right flank and attacked the 1st Battalion command post. Captain Gardner was the first in the area to become cognizant of the threat and, with complete disregard for personal safety, exposed himself to the attacking enemy and attempted to warn the occupants of the command post. His actions brought heavy machine gun and rifle fire upon him, resulting in his death. By drawing enemy fire, Captain Gardner provided the necessary warning which otherwise would not have come until the enemy opened fire upon the battalion commander and his staff. Captain Gardner's gallant leadership was a source of inspiration to the troops under his command. His heroic self-sacrifice reflects the highest credit upon his character as an officer and upon the military service.

GEORGE H. GARDNER

World War II Veteran
Service: U. S. Army, 8th Infantry Division
George H. Gardner, United States Army, is reported to have been awarded the Silver Star under the below-listed General Orders for conspicuous gallantry and intrepidity in action against the enemy while serving with the 8th Infantry Division during World War II.

GEORGE W. GARDNER

World War II Veteran
Born: St. Louis, Missouri
Service: U. S. Marine Corps, 1st Battalion, 2d Marine Division
Rank: Sergeant
Action Date: July 9, 1944

The President of the United States of America takes pleasure in presenting the Silver Star to Sergeant George W. Gardner (MCSN: 319259), United States Marine Corps, for conspicuous gallantry and intrepidity while serving with the First Battalion, Second Marines, SECOND Marine Division, in action against enemy Japanese forces on Saipan, Marianas Islands, 9 July 1944. Volunteering to assist the Platoon leader on a hazardous mission, Sergeant Gardner courageously worked his way to an enemy-occupied strong point to rescue two Marine casualties. Although wounded himself during this encounter, he brought the men back to safety, thereby undoubtedly saving their lives. His courage, devotion to duty and grave concern for the welfare of others were in keeping with the highest traditions of the United States Naval Service.

GLEN R. GARDNER

World War II Veteran
Home: Vigo Park, Texas
Service: U. S. Army, Company I, 232d Infantry Reg., 42d Infantry Division
Rank: Technician Fifth Grade
Action Date:

The President of the United States of America, authorized by Act of Congress July 9, 1918, takes pleasure in presenting the Silver Star to Technician Fifth Grade Glen R. Gardner (ASN: 38066237), United States Army, for gallantry in action while serving with Company I, 232d Infantry Regiment, 42d Infantry Division, in action on 12 April 1945, near Kronungen, Germany. When his platoon was pinned down by enemy machine gun fire while attacking Kronungen, Corporal Gardner advanced with another bazookaman toward the enemy position. When the gunner was suddenly killed by a burst of machine gun fire, Corporal Gardner immediately loaded the bazooka, and fired directly into the machine gun nest, knocking it out. His prompt action and courage under fire thus relieved the pressure on his platoon and enabled them to advance on their objective.

HARRY E. GARDNER

World War II Veteran
Home: Waco, Texas
Service: U. S. Navy
Rank: Ensign
Action Date:

Ensign Harry E. Gardner, United States Navy, was awarded the Silver Star for gallantry in action as a member of an Underwater Demolition Team (UDT), in action against the Japanese during the Iwo Jima assault, on 17 February 1945. His gallant actions and dedicated devotion to duty, without regard for his own life, were in keeping with the highest traditions of military service and reflect great credit upon himself and the United States Naval Service.

JAMES M. GARDNER

World War II Veteran
Home: Mississippi
Service: U. S. Army, 90th Infantry Division, Medical Detachment
Rank: Technician Fifth Grade
Action Date: July 22, 1944

The President of the United States of America, authorized by Act of Congress July 9, 1918, takes pleasure in presenting the Silver Star to Technician Fifth Grade James M. Gardner (ASN: 34473750), United States Army, for gallantry in action against an armed enemy while serving with the Medical Detachment, 90th Infantry Division, in France, on 22 July 1944 during World War II.

JESSIE A. GARDNER

World War II Veteran
Born: Burkburnett, Texas
Home: Wichita Falls, Texas
Service: U. S. Marine Corps, 4th Marine Division, 4th Tank Battalion,
Company B
Rank: Private First Class
Action Date: June 15, 1944

The President of the United States of America takes pleasure in presenting the Silver Star to Private First Class Jessie A. Gardner (MCSN: 488608), United States Marine Corps Reserve, for conspicuous gallantry and intrepidity while serving with Company B, Fourth Tank Battalion, FOURTH Marine Division, in action against enemy Japanese forces on Saipan, Marianas Islands, 15 June 1944. Courageously volunteering his weight to help correct a dangerous list on a landing craft loaded with a tank, Private First Class Gardner exposed himself to heavy hostile artillery fire falling the craft and the beach. Fearless and determined, he sat at his position post instead of seeking the shelter of the hull, and was seriously wounded when an enemy shell hit the craft. His self-sacrificing efforts and gallant devotion to duty were in keeping with the highest traditions of The United States Naval Service.

LAWRENCE B. GARDNER

World War II Veteran
Service: U. S. Army Air Forces

Lawrence B. Gardner, United States Army Air Forces, was awarded the Silver Star for conspicuous gallantry and intrepidity in action during World War II.

LEON P. GARDNER

World War II Veteran
Service: U. S. Army, 4th Armored Division

Leon P. Gardner, United States Army, is reported to have been awarded the Silver Star under the below-listed General Orders, for conspicuous gallantry and intrepidity in action against the enemy while serving with the 4th Armored Division during World War II.

LEONARD A. GARDNER

World War II Veteran
Service: U. S. Army, 90th Infantry Division

Leonard A. Gardner, United States Army, is reported to have been awarded the Silver Star under the below-listed General Orders, for conspicuous gallantry and intrepidity in action against the enemy while serving with the 90th Infantry Division during World War II.

LELAND V. GARDNER

World War II Veteran

Service: U. S. Army, 2d Armored Division

Leland V. Gardner, United States Army, is reported to have been awarded the Silver Star under the below-listed General Orders for conspicuous gallantry and intrepidity in action while serving with the 2d Armored Division during World War II.

LLOYD H. GARDNER

World War II Veteran

Service: U. S. Army, 7th Infantry Divison

Lloyd H. Gardner, United States Army, is reported to have been awarded the Silver Star under the below-listed General Orders for conspicuous gallantry and intrepidity in action against the enemy while serving with the 7th Infantry Division during World War II.

RICHARD C. GARDNER

World War II Veteran

Home: Minnesota

Service: U. S. Army, 9th Infantry Division

Rank: First Lieutenant

Action Date: March 11 – 14, 1945

The President of the United States of America, authorized by Act of Congress July 9, 1918, takes pleasure in presenting the Silver Star to First Lieutenant (Field Artillery) Richard C. Gardner (ASN: 0-1173253), United States Army, for conspicuous gallantry and intrepidity in connection with military operations against the enemy while serving with the 9th Infantry Division from 11 March 1945 to 14 March 1945, during operations in Germany. His gallantry and disregard for personal safety reflects highest credit upon himself and the Armed Forces of the United States.

RICHARD ROBERT GARDNER

World War II Veteran (KIA)

Born: Sioux Falls, South Dakota

Died: March 13, 1945

Service: U. S. Marine Corps, 1st Battalion, 9th Marines, 3d Marine Division

Rank: Private First Class

Action Date: March 13, 1945

The President of the United States of America takes pride in presenting the Silver Star (Posthumously) to Private First Class Richard Robert Gardner (MCSN: 419667), United States Marine Corps Reserve, for conspicuous gallantry and intrepidity as a Squad Leader, serving with Company C, First Battalion, Ninth Marines, THIRD Marine Division, in action against enemy Japanese forces on Iwo Jima, Volcano Islands, 13 March 1945. Assigned the mission of storming the nose of a savagely-defended ridge, Private First Class Gardner courageously led his squad one hundred yards out on the ridge where he and men were assaulted by a tremendous volume of Japanese machine-gun and rifle fire as they maneuvered into position. When one of his squad fell seriously wounded under the sudden barrage, Private First Class Gardner disregarded personal danger to pull his comrade to a place of comparative safety, but was himself fatally wounded by the intense enemy fire. His fearless initiative, aggressive fighting spirit and selfless devotion to duty reflect the highest credit upon Private First Class Gardner and the United States Naval Service. He gallantly gave his life for his country.

STEVEN J. GARDNER

World War II Veteran
Service: U. S. Army, 41st Infantry Division
Steven J. Gardner, United States Army, is reported to have been awarded the Silver Star under the below-listed General Orders for conspicuous gallantry and intrepidity in action against the enemy while serving with the 41st Infantry Division during World War II.

VERNON W. GARDNER

World War II Veteran
Service: U. S. Army, 30th Infantry Division
Vernon W. Gardner, United States Army, is reported to have been awarded the Silver Star under the below-listed General Orders for conspicuous gallantry and intrepidity in action against the enemy while serving with the 30th Infantry Division during World War II.

WARREN F. GARDNER

World War II Veteran
Service: U. S. Army, 26th Division
Warren F. Gardner, United States Army, is reported to have been awarded the Silver Star under the below listed General Orders, for conspicuous gallantry and intrepidity in action against the enemy, while serving with the 26th Infantry Division during World War II.

WILLIAM A. GARDNER

World War II Veteran
Service: U. S. Army Air Force (Air Corps)
Captain William Alfred Gardner, United States Army Air Forces, was awarded the Silver Star for gallantry in action against the enemy as a P-40 Fighter Pilot of the 35th Fighter Squadron, 8th Fighter Group, FIFTH Air Force, in action against the enemy in aerial combat in the Pacific Theater of Action during World War II.

WILLIAM C. GARDNER

World War II Veteran
Service: U. S. Army, 37th Infantry Division

William C. Gardner, United States Army, is reported to have been awarded the Silver Star under the below-listed General Orders for conspicuous gallantry and intrepidity in action against the enemy while serving with the 37th Infantry Division during World War II.

CHARLES G. GARDNER

Korean War Veteran
Service: U. S. Army
Charles G. Gardner, United States Army, is reported to have been awarded the Silver Star under the below-listed General Orders for conspicuous gallantry and intrepidity in action against the enemy in Korea.

CLAUDE D. GARDNER

Korean War Veteran
Service: U. S. Army, 24th Infantry Division
Claude D. Gardner, United States Army, is reported to have been awarded the Silver Star under the below-listed General Orders for conspicuous gallantry and intrepidity in action against the enemy while serving with the 24th Infantry Division in Korea.

FRANK H. GARDNER

Korean War Veteran
Home: Northampton County, Pennsylvania
Service: U. S. Army, 23d Infantry Regiment, 2d Infantry Division, Company D
Rank: Second Lieutenant
The President of the United States of America, authorized by Act of Congress July 9, 1918, takes pleasure in presenting the Silver Star to Second Lieutenant (Infantry) Frank H. Gardner, Jr. (ASN: 0-954783), United States Army, for gallantry in action as a member of Company D, 23d Infantry Regiment, 2d Infantry Division, in action against an armed enemy on 2 September 1950, in the vicinity of Changnyong, Korea. The enemy had seized a commanding hill which was a key position in the defense line of the 1st Battalion, 23d Infantry Regiment, and had set up a 120-mm. Mortar and a machine gun which dominated the battalion perimeter. To prevent a very serious attack to American forces it was absolutely necessary to eliminate this enemy strong point. Lieutenant Gardner led his platoon up the hill, setting an example of inspiring leadership by his grim determination to wipe out this threat to our lines. Disregarding the intense mortar, machine gun and small arms fire delivered by the enemy in his emplaced position, he continued to lead his platoon forward up the slope of the hill in a determined charge. The enemy was completely routed, leaving behind an estimated 12 dead and many wounded. As a result of this timely, well-executed, and brilliantly led attack, the battalion was able to hold its position and keep its casualties to a minimum. The gallantry displayed on this occasion by Lieutenant Gardner was an inspiration

to all who witnessed it and reflects great credit upon himself and the military service.

FRED GARDNER

Korean War Veteran
Home: North Carolina
Service: U. S. Army, 1st Battalion, 25th Infantry Division
Rank: Master Sergeant
Action Date: September 19, 1950

The President of the United States of America, authorized by Act of Congress July 9, 1918, takes pleasure in presenting the Silver Star to Master Sergeant Fred Gardner (ASN: RA-6359521), United States Army, for gallantry in action as a member of Company C, 1st Battalion, 35th Infantry Regiment, 25th Infantry Division, in action against an armed enemy in Korea. At about 0300 hours on 19 September 1950, Master Sergeant Gardner's platoon in defensive position near Uiryong, Korea, was subjected to a severe hostile attack. Despite the intense machine gun and small arms fire, he moved about among the men to lend encouragement and better direct fire of all weapons. He himself, killed six of the enemy. Inspiring his men by his personal courage, determination and skill, he made possible complete route of the numerically superior hostile force. Master Sergeant Gardner's gallant and exemplary leadership were in keeping with the highest traditions of the military service and reflect great credit upon himself, his unit, and the United States Army.

GEORGE W. GARDNER

Korean War Veteran
Home: Neosho County, Kansas
Service: U. S. Army, 38th Infantry Regiment, 2d Infantry Division
Rank: First Lieutenant
Action Date: August 27, 1950

First Lieutenant (Infantry) George W. Gardner (ASN: 0-1313392), United States Army, was awarded the Silver Star for conspicuous gallantry and intrepidity in connection with military operations against the enemy in Korea, while serving with Company A, 38th Infantry Regiment, 2d Infantry Division, on 27 August 1950 during the Korean War.

KOELING B. GARDNER

Korean War Veteran (KIA)
Service: U. S. Army, 1st Cavalry Division

Koeling B. Gardner, United States Army, is reported to have been awarded the Silver Star under the below-listed General Orders for conspicuous gallantry and intrepidity in action against the enemy while serving with the 1st Cavalry Division in Korea.

ROBERT C. GARDNER

Korean War Veteran
Home: Peekskill, New York
Service: U. S. Army, 5th Cavalry Regiment, 1st Cavalry Division
Rank: First Lieutenant
Action Date: February 11, 1951

The President of the United States of America, authorized by Act of Congress July 9, 1918, takes pleasure in presenting the Silver Star to First Lieutenant (Infantry) Robert C. Gardner (ASN: 0-1330175), United States Army, for gallantry in action against the enemy while serving with Company F, 5th Cavalry Regiment, 1st Cavalry Division, in action on 11 February 1951, near Hoedong-ni, Korea. After Company F had captured the right knob of a hill, it was necessary to secure the center knob of the objective to hold the already taken ground. After two assaults had failed and darkness began to set in, Lieutenant Gardner moved to the front of the platoon and started another attack. As he led the unit forward, he shouted words of encouragement, urging the men on, annihilating one enemy position after another until the objective was secured. Lieutenant Gardner's gallantry reflects great credit upon himself and the military service.

WALTER A. GARDNER

Korean War Veteran
Service: U. S. Army, 1st Cavalry Division

Walter A. Gardner, United States Army, is reported to have been awarded the Silver Star under the below-listed General Orders for conspicuous gallantry and intrepidity in action against the enemy while serving with the 1st Cavalry Division in Korea.

DONALD RAY GARDNER

Vietnam War Veteran
Service: U. S. Marine Corps, 3d Reconnaissance Battalion, 3d Marine Division
Rank: Captain
Action Date: August 18, 1966

Captain Donald R. Gardner (MCSN: 0-79807), United States Marine Corps, was awarded the Silver Star for conspicuous gallantry and intrepidity in action while serving with Company C, Third Reconnaissance Battalion, THIRD Marine Division (Rein.), FMF, in connection with combat operations against the enemy in the Republic of Vietnam on August 18, 1966. By his courage, aggressive fighting spirit and steadfast devotion to duty in the face of extreme personal danger, Captain Gardner upheld the highest traditions of the Marine Corps and the United States Naval Service.

Note: Donald Ray Gardner is a retired U. S. Marine Corps General who had been awarded the Silver Star, the Navy Distinguished Service Medal, and two Legions of Merit.

JAMES L. GARDNER

Vietnam War Veteran
Born: 1929 Memphis, Tennessee
Home: Wynne, Arkansas
Service: U. S. Air Force, 504th Tactical Air Support Group
Rank: Major
Action Date: March 31, 1967

The President of the United States of America, authorized by Act of Congress, July 8, 1918 (amended by act of July 25, 1963), takes pleasure in presenting the Silver Star to Major James L. Gardner, Jr. (AFSN: FR-43743), United States Air Force, for gallantry in connection with military operations against an opposing armed force as a Forward Air Controller and Pilot of an O-1 Bird Dog of the 504th Tactical Air Support Group, Bien Hoa Air Base, Vietnam, in action near Kontum, Republic of Vietnam, on 31 March 1967. On that date, Major Gardner was flying his O-1 Bird Dog aircraft in support of friendly forces engaged in defense of their besieged outpost. Small arms, automatic weapons and three machine guns had already inflicted numerous casualties, when the opposition turned their fire power on Major Gardner. With complete disregard for his own personal safety, Major Gardner made repeated low passes over the opposing forces to draw their fire and expose themselves to attacks from the fighter aircraft. By his gallantry and devotion to duty, Major Gardner has reflected great credit upon himself and the United States Air Force.

Note: James L. Gardner is a retired U. S. Air Force General who has been awarded the Silver Star, the Distinguished Flying Cross, and three Legions of Merit.

JASON GARDNER

Iraq/Afghanistan War Veteran (Global War on Terror)
Service: U. S. Navy

The President of the United States of America takes pleasure in presenting the Silver Star to Senior Chief Special Warfare Operator (SEAL) Jason Gardner, United States Navy, for conspicuous gallantry and intrepidity in action against the enemy while serving as SEAL Team SEVEN Task Unit TRIDENT Senior Enlisted Advisor, in direct support of Operation ENDURING FREEDOM from 9 April to 1 October 2009. Senior Chief Gardner commanded his task unit during a two-day direct action mission in enemy terrain in Northern Kandahar from 16 to 17 July 2009. He led seven positions which were encircled by enemy forces and sustained a barrage of enemy fire from all sides. Senior Chief Gardner fearlessly exposed himself to return fire and coordinated counterattacks, preventing his task unit from being overrun. Although he was shut off from seven observation positions by an enemy machine gunner, he continued to expose himself to spot and direct fire, silencing the automatic weapon which had pinned down his task unit. Senior Chief Gardner's heroic actions inspired his platoons and contributed to 56 enemy killed in action. He fearlessly led his task unit during 357 hours of troops in contact, resulting in

196 enemy killed in action and six high-value individuals captured. By his bold leadership, courageous actions, and total dedication to duty, Senior Chief Gardner reflected great credit upon himself and upheld the highest traditions of the United States Naval Service.

Charles L. Gardiner, U. S. Army, 6th Armored Division, awarded the Silver Star for extraordinary heroism during World War II.

David B. Gardiner, Jr., U. S. Army, 104th Infantry Division, awarded the Silver Star for extraordinary heroism during World War II.

Douglas Gardiner, U. S. Army, 6th Armored Division, awarded the Silver Star for extraordinary heroism during World War II.

James W. Gardiner, U. S. Army, 4th Infantry Division, awarded the Silver Star for extraordinary heroism during World War II.

Peter L. Gardiner, U. S. Army, 104th Infantry Division, awarded the Silver Star for extraordinary heroism during World War II.

Robert M. Gardiner, U. S. Army, 78th Infantry Division, awarded the Silver Star for extraordinary heroism during World War II.

Courtesy to https://valor.militarytimes.com/

DISTINGUISHED FLYING CROSS

MELVIN J. GARDNER

World War II Veteran (MIA June 2nd, 1942 following a bombing mission in Burma)
Home: Mesa, Arizona
Service: U. S. Army Air Forces
Rank: Sergeant, 1st Special Aviation Project, Doolittle Tokyo Raider Force
Action Date: April 18, 1942
The President of the United States of America, authorized by Act of Congress, July 2, 1926, takes pleasure in presenting the Distinguished Flying Cross to Sergeant Melvin J. Gardner (ASN: 6296448), United States Army Air Forces, for extraordinary achievement as Engineer/Gunner of a B-25 Bomber of the 1st Special Aviation Project (Doolittle Raider Force), while participating in a highly destructive raid on the Japanese mainland on 18 April 1942. Sergeant Gardner with 79 other officers and enlisted men volunteered for this mission knowing full well that the chances of survival were extremely remote, and executed his part in it with great skill and daring. This achievement reflects high credit on himself and the military service.

DONALD W. GARDNER

World War II Veteran (MIA August 11th, 1943)
Home: Huron, South Dakota
Service: U. S. Navy
Rank: Aviation Radioman Second Class, Bombing Squadron 107 (VB – 107)
The President of the United States of America takes pride in presenting the Distinguished Flying Cross (Posthumously) to Aviation Radioman Second Class Donald W. Gardner (NSN: 6480239), United States Naval Reserve, for extraordinary achievement in the line of his profession while participating in aerial flight in a U.S. heavy bombing plane, which led to the ultimate destruction of an enemy submarine. Aviation Radioman Second Class Gardner, on a special anti-submarine mission which commenced on 3 August 1943, and finally culminated on 11 August 1943, performed all duties at his battle station with such courage and valor that the final destruction of the enemy was assured. His last action, in which he gave his life, is a great credit to his country and was in keeping with the highest traditions of the United States Naval Service.

HAROLD EDWIN GARDNER

World War II Veteran
Service: U. S. Marine Corps
Rank: Captain
Died: July 1, 1945

Captain Harold Edwin Gardner (MCSN: 0-10564), United States Marine Corps, was awarded the Distinguished Flying Cross for extraordinary achievement while participating in aerial flight, in actions against enemy Japanese forces in the Pacific Theater of Operations during World War II.

FELLOWS D. GARDNER

World War II Veteran
Service: U. S. Marine Corps

Fellows D. Gardner (MCSN: 0-10714), United States Marine Corps, was awarded the Distinguished Flying Cross for extraordinary achievement while participating in aerial flight, in actions against enemy Japanese forces in the Pacific Theater of Operations during World War II.

BURTIS G. GARDNER

World War II Veteran
Service: U. S. Marine Corps

Burtis G. Gardner (MCSN: 255326), United States Marine Corps, was awarded the Distinguished Flying Cross for extraordinary achievement while participating in aerial flight, in actions against enemy Japanese forces in the Pacific Theater of Operations during World War II.

ARTHUR F. GARDNER

World War II Veteran
Service: U. S. Marine Corps

Arthur F. Gardner (MCSN: 0-12740), United States Marine Corps, was awarded the Distinguished Flying Cross for extraordinary achievement while participating in aerial flight, in actions against enemy Japanese forces in the Pacific Theater of Operations during World War II.

WILLIAM A. GARDNER

World War II Veteran
Service: U. S. Marine Corps

William A. Gardner (MCSN: 0-27437), United States Marine Corps, was awarded the Distinguished Flying Cross for extraordinary achievement while participating in aerial flight, in actions against enemy Japanese forces in the Pacific Theater of Operations during World War II.

JAY E. GARDNER

World War II Veteran
Service: U. S. Marine Corps

Jay E. Gardner (MCSN: 0-29687), United States Marine Corps, was awarded the Distinguished Flying Cross for extraordinary achievement while participating in aerial flight, in actions against enemy Japanese forces in the Pacific Theater of Operations during World War II.

GEORGE GARDNER

World War II Veteran
Service: U. S. Navy
Rank: Aviation Radioman Third Class
Action Date: March 18 – June 3, 1945
The President of the United States of America takes pleasure in presenting the Distinguished Flying Cross to Aviation Radioman Third Class George Gardner, Jr. (NSN: 7044248), United States Naval Reserve, for heroism and extraordinary achievement while participating in aerial flights in operations against the enemy in the vicinity of Kyushu, Shukoku and Nansei Shoto. As Radio Operator of a carrier-based torpedo bomber during the period 18 March 1945 to 3 June 1945, he participated in twenty strikes against enemy shipping and shore installations, inflicting extensive damage. His skill and courage were at all times inspiring and were in keeping with the highest traditions of the United States Naval Service.

WARNER FRANKLIN GARDNER

World War II Veteran
Home: Cazenovia, New York
Service: U. S. Army Air Forces, 95th Fighter Squadron, 15th Air Force
Major (Air Corps) Warner Franklin Gardner (ASN: 0-428926), United States Army Air Forces, was awarded the Distinguished Flying Cross for extraordinary achievement while participating in aerial flight as a P-38 Fighter Pilot of the 95th Fighter Squadron, 82d Fighter Group, FIFTEENTH Air Force, in action against the enemy in aerial combat in the Mediterranean Theater of Action during World War II. The skillful and zealous manner in which he has sought out the enemy and destroyed him, his devotion to duty and courage under all conditions serve as an inspiration to his fellow flyers. His actions on all these occasions reflect the highest credit upon himself and the Armed Forces of the United States.
Note: Gardner was an ace who had 5 kills.

WILMER GARDNER

World War II Veteran
Service: U. S. Army Air Force
The President of the United States of America, authorized by Act of Congress, July 2, 1926, takes pleasure in presenting the Distinguished Flying Cross to Staff Sergeant Wilmer L. Gardner (ASN: 33559525), United States Army Air Forces, for extraordinary achievement while participating in aerial flight while serving as a left waist gunner of the 95th Bombardment Group (Heavy), on

numerous bombardment missions against enemy installations over German occupied Continental Europe during World War II. Sergeant Gardner repelled numerous hostile fighter attacks by his excellent marksmanship, thereby assuring the safety of the crew and aircraft. His courage, presence of mind and devotion to duty while engaged in aerial combat on all these occasions are in keeping with the highest traditions of the United States Army Air Force.

JOSEPH T. GARDNER

World War II Veteran
Home: Jacksonville, Florida
Service: U. S. Navy
Lieutenant Commander [then Lieutenant] Joseph T. Gardner, United States Navy, was awarded the Distinguished Flying Cross for extraordinary achievement while participating in aerial flight as Commander of a Catalina aircraft on reconnaissance missions in north and southeast Celebes, from 26 September to 2 October 1944 during World War II.

KEITH GARDNER

World War II Veteran
Home: Spanish Fork, Utah
Service: U. S. Navy
Lieutenant, Junior Grade [then Ensign] Keith Gardner, United States Navy, was awarded the Distinguished Flying Cross for extraordinary achievement while participating in aerial flight as Pilot of a Torpedo Plane in Bombing Squadron FOUR (VB-4), embarked in U.S.S. ESSEX over the Pescadores Islands on 15 January 1945 during World War II.

CHANNING GARDNER

Korean War Veteran (KIA)
Home: Duluth, Minnesota
Service: U. S. Navy
Rank: Lieutenant, Junior Grade, Fighter Squadron 653, U. S. S. Valley Forge
Lieutenant, Junior Grade Channing Gardner (NSN: 0-521458), United States Navy, was awarded the Distinguished Flying Cross (Posthumously) for extraordinary achievement while participating in aerial flight while serving with Fighter Squadron SIX HUNDRED FIFTY-THREE (VF-653), embarked in U.S.S. VALLEY FORGE (CV-45), in action against enemy aggressor forces in Korea on 18 December 1951 during the Korean War.

CLYDE W. GARDNER

Korean War Veteran
Service: U. S. Navy
Company: Fighter Squadron 193 (VF – 193)
Action Date: February 11, 1951

Lieutenant, Junior Grade [then Ensign] Clyde W. Gardner, United States Navy, was awarded the Distinguished Flying Cross for extraordinary achievement while participating in aerial flight while serving with Fighter Squadron ONE HUNDRED NINETY-THREE (VF-193), in action against enemy aggressor forces in Korea on 11 February 1951 during the Korean War.

JOSEPH W. GARDNER

Vietnam War Veteran
Service: U. S. Air Force
Rank: Staff Sergeant
Staff Sergeant Joseph W. Gardner, United States Air Force, was awarded the Distinguished Flying Cross for extraordinary achievement while participating in aerial flight in Southeast Asia on 4 December 1970 during the Vietnam War.

Harold Gardiner, U. S. Marine Corps, awarded the Distinguished Flying Cross for extraordinary heroism during World War II.

Joseph C. Gardiner, U. S. Marine Corps, awarded the Distinguished Flying Cross for extraordinary heroism during the Korean War.

Courtesy to https://valor.militarytimes.com/

NAVY AND MARINE CORPS MEDAL

RALPH GARDNER

World War II Veteran
Home: Iowa
Service: U. S. Navy
Rank: Signalman Third Class

The President of the United States of America takes pleasure in presenting the Navy and Marine Corps Medal to Signalman Third Class Ralph Gardner (NSN: 3216040), United States Navy, for distinguished heroism at the risk of life not involving conflict with an armed enemy, as members of the Armed Guard on board a merchant vessel during its torpedoing and sinking by an enemy submarine. Under extremely difficult conditions, Signalman Third Class Gardner devoted tireless and courageous efforts toward the rescue of survivors, and aided in recovering eight men from floating wreckage and surrounding water and four from a drifting raft.

NELSON C. GARDNER

World War II Veteran
Home: Jamaica, New York
Service: U. S. Navy
Rank: Lieutenant

Lieutenant Nelson C. Gardner, United States Naval Reserve, was awarded the Navy and Marine Corps Medal for heroic conduct in performing rescues after an explosion on 4 May 1943 at Elkton, Maryland.

JOHN N. GARDNER

World War II Veteran
Home: Pennsylvania
Service: U. S. Coast Guard
Rank: Seaman Apprentice

Seaman Apprentice John N. Gardner, United States Coast Guard, was awarded the Navy and Marine Corps Medal for heroic conduct on 3 February 1943 in effecting the rescue of survivors from the torpedoed S.S. DORCHESTER. When the benumbed survivors were unable to make any efforts to climb on board the rescue ship, Seaman Apprentice Gardner volunteered for the dangerous task of going over the side and working in the rough, freezing water to assist the exhausted survivors in reaching safety. He and his fellow volunteers rescued a total of 93 survivors from certain death.
Courtesy to https://valor.militarytimes.com/

Courtesy to Military Times Hall of Valor

References:
https://valor.militarytimes.com/
http://www.homeofheroes.com/verify/recipients_g.html

Gardiner, Charles L., USA - Awarded: SS - World War II
Gardiner, David B., Jr., USA - Awarded: SS - World War II
Gardiner, Douglas L., USA - Awarded: SS - World War II
Gardiner, Henry E., USA - Awarded: DSC - World War II
Gardiner, Jas. W., USA - Awarded: SS - World War II
Gardiner, Jas., USA - Awarded: MOH - Civil War
Gardiner, Kenneth, USA - Awarded: DSC - World War I
Gardiner, Peter L., USA - Awarded: SS - World War II
Gardiner, Peter W., USA - Awarded: MOH - Indian Campaigns
Gardiner, Robert M., USA - Awarded: SS - World War II
Gardler, Harrison M., USA - Awarded: DSC - World War II
Gardnenier, Charles K., USA - Awarded: SS - Korean War
Gardner, Alfred W., (KIA), USA - Awarded: DSC - World War I
Gardner, Alfred, USN(RF) - Awarded: NX - World War I
Gardner, Alonzo J., USA - Awarded: SS - World War II
Gardner, Arthur B., Jr., USMC - Awarded: SS - World War II
Gardner, Augustus Peabody, USA - Awarded: DSM-A - World War I
Gardner, Bruce A., USAAF - Awarded: SS - World War II
Gardner, Burton H., USAAF - Awarded: SS - World War II
Gardner, Carl M., USA - Awarded: SS - World War II
Gardner, Charles (AKA: Simon Suhler), (POW), USA - Awarded: MOH - Indian Campaigns
Gardner, Charles G., USA - Awarded: SS - Korean War
Gardner, Charles L., USN(R) - Awarded: SS - World War II
Gardner, Charles N., USA - Awarded: MOH - Civil War
Gardner, Charles R., USA - Awarded: SS - World War II
Gardner, Claude D., USA - Awarded: SS - Korean War
Gardner, Clyde G, Jr., USN(R) - Awarded: NX - World War II
Gardner, Donald R., USMC - Awarded: SS - Vietnam War
Gardner, Eldon C., USA - Awarded: SS - World War II
Gardner, Elmer W., USA - Awarded: DSC - World War I
Gardner, Elmer, USA - Awarded: SS - World War II
Gardner, Emanuel, USA - Awarded: SS - World War II
Gardner, Eugene M., USA - Awarded: SS - World War II
Gardner, Francis A., USA - Awarded: SS - World War II
Gardner, Frank H., Jr., USA - Awarded: SS - Korean War
Gardner, Frank W., USA - Awarded: SS - World War II
Gardner, Fulton Q. C., USA - Awarded: DSM-A, 1st Award - World War I
Gardner, Fulton Q. C., USA - Awarded: DSM-A, 2d Award - World War II

Gardner, George H., USA - Awarded: SS - World War II
Gardner, George H., USA - Awarded: SS - World War II
Gardner, George L., USA – Awarded: SS - World War II
Gardner, George W., USA - Awarded: DSC - World War I
Gardner, George W., USA - Awarded: SS - Korean War
Gardner, George W., USMC - Awarded: SS - World War I
Gardner, George W., USMC - Awarded: SS - World War II
Gardner, Glen R., USA - Awarded: SS - World War II
Gardner, Grandison, USA - Awarded: DSM-A - World War II
Gardner, Hester N., USA - Awarded: DSC - World War II
Gardner, Howard W., USA - Awarded: SS - World War II
Gardner, Jas. Alton, (KIA), USA(R) - Awarded: MOH - Vietnam War
Gardner, Jas. M., USA - Awarded: SS - World War II
Gardner, Jessie A., USMC - Awarded: SS - World War II
Gardner, John H., USA - Awarded: DSC - World War I
Gardner, John T., USA - Awarded: SS - World War II
Gardner, Koeling B., USA - Awarded: SS - Korean War
Gardner, Lawrence B., USAAF - Awarded: SS - World War II
Gardner, Lawrence N., (KIA), USA - Awarded: DSC - Korean War
Gardner, Leland V., USA - Awarded: SS - World War II
Gardner, Leon P., USA - Awarded: SS - World War II
Gardner, Leonard A., USA - Awarded: SS - World War II
Gardner, Lloyd H., USA - Awarded: SS - World War II
Gardner, Madison D., USA - Awarded: DSC - World War II
Gardner, Martin E., (KIA), USA - Awarded: DSC - World War I
Gardner, Perley H. F., USA - Awarded: SS - World War II
Gardner, Richard C., USA - Awarded: SS - World War II
Gardner, Richard Robert, (KIA), USMC - Awarded: SS - World War II
Gardner, Robert C., USA - Awarded: SS - Korean War
Gardner, Robert J., USA - Awarded: MOH - Civil War
Gardner, Steven J., USA - Awarded: SS - World War II
Gardner, Sylvan, USA - Awarded: SS - World War II
Gardner, Vernon W., USA - Awarded: SS - World War II
Gardner, Vernon W., USA - Awarded: SS - World War II
Gardner, Walter A., USA - Awarded: SS - Korean War
Gardner, Warren F., USA - Awarded: SS - World War II
Gardner, William C., USA - Awarded: SS - World War II
Gardner, William, USN - Awarded: MOH - Civil War

GARDNER FAMILY VETERANS

Daniel Gardner, 5x Great Grandfather, Continental Army
Thomas Gardner, 6x great uncle, Continental Army
George Gardner, 4x Great Grandfather, South Carolina Militia
William Z. Gardner, 3x great uncle, Confederate Army
Wiley J. Gardner, 3x great uncle, Confederate Army
Daniel W. Gardner, 3x great uncle, Confederate Army
Elijah Gardner, cousin, Confederate Army (died of wounds in Mississippi)
Timothy Baxter Gardner, cousin, Confederate Army (died of wounds in Virginia)
William G. Gardner, cousin, Confederate Army
Meredith Thomas Gardner, cousin, Confederate Army
Daniel Jefferson Gardner, cousin, Confederate Army
Joseph Benjamin Gardner, cousin, Confederate Army
John Henry Gardner, cousin, U. S. Army (earned Distinguished Service Cross)
Oscar Wright Gardner, cousin, U. S. Marine Corps
Leroy W. Gardner, cousin, Georgia National Guard
Charles C. Gardner, cousin, U. S. Air Force
Mike Gardner, cousin, U. S. Army (died in Vietnam)
Terrill Gardner, cousin, U. S. Army
Wendell Gardner, cousin, U. S. Navy
Daniel Alexander Gardner, cousin, U. S. Marine Corps
Hugh Gardner, cousin, U. S. Army
Henry Gardner, cousin, U. S. Army
Coy Gardner, cousin, U. S. Navy
William E. Gardner, cousin, U. S. Navy SEAL

GARDNER FAMILY ORIGIN

My Gardner family origin is either from England, Scotland, or Ireland depending on the source.

On January 20th, 1903, Meredith Thomas "Tom" Gardner, grandson of Thomas Gardner (c. 1750 – 1815), my 5th Great Grandfather or 6th Great uncle who lived in South Carolina, had written: **"My Dear Son: I have heard Father say the first ancestor of our family emigrated from England to this country, landing in New York, in the earlier colonial days, perhaps in the latter part of sixteen or beginning of seventeen hundred. He was by occupation a ship carpenter....I have heard your Grand Father often speak of them....The family drifted down the Atlantic coast into South Carolina. From there some members of it went into Tenn., others into Ga., and their lineage and identity lost to us."**

Meredith Thomas "Tom" Gardner had been a Confederate soldier and he printed his Gardner family history, in which he stated: **"The Gardners first came from England to America and sailed down the Atlantic coast. Some landed in the Carolinas and others landed in New York and in Virginia."**

Another note states:
"In the history of Lamar County, Ga. Copies of essay was Thomas Jackson Gardner; He said Gardners (Gardiners) were, Scotch – Irish coming from Northern Ireland in the 1700's. Four brothers Frederick, Samuel, Jas., and John Gardner settled in Upson County, Ga.

In 1850 John Gardner was living in Monroe County, Ga., had 17 slaves and property valued at $13, 250.00. Then the average valuation was about $2, 000.00. The Gardners were very prominent and influential in Monroe County, Ga., before the civil war. The Gardners came from Ireland in 1700's and settled in Virginia. Branches of the family later moved to South Carolina."

According to *A HISTORY OF GREATER DALLAS AND VICINITY Volume II: Selected Biography and Memoirs* Mr. L. B. Hill, Editor, The Lewis Publishing Company, Chicago, 1909, a biography on Wiley Jackson Gardner, my 3rd Great uncle, he stated: **"The paternal grandfather was a Scotchman who first located in South Carolina, after his emigration to the United States, but within a few years changed his residence to Georgia, where he died."**

His paternal grandfather, my 4th Great Grandfather was George Gardner, an American hard case who was most likely born in Virginia Colony, lived in South Carolina, and removed to Georgia.

I give credit to my distant cousins Chris Gardner and Leroy Gardner. They researched the Gardner family history, and I am continuing the tradition. They published a book titled, *GARDNER/BALLARD and ALLIED FAMILIES*.

On Christmas Eve, December 24th, 1952, their eldest brother Ed Gardner and his wife Joann, had been married for only a month, both died in a plane crash in Georgia.

"I was the closet boy to Ed as well as nearest his age. Five years divided us. He became my mentor and my friend. The last flight I had with him was from Truett – McConnell in Cleveland, Ga. He came home one Friday and we flew home together.

I dreampt of him often until ten years ago. He would come to me in my dreams when I had a special need. His counsel did me good and sustained me through rough times.

Once he came to me with two teenage boys who he introduced to me as his sons, in that world.

The last time he came to me from the edge of a woods, I was told this was his last visit. He explained to me his passage and my not having need of him anymore. I had a sense of heaven in those dreams." – Oscar William "Chris" Gardner

"In Genesis 2:24, God institutes the family. The family is the strength of our society. Without a strong sense of family, our strength is diminished. This book is an effort to define our family and thereby give us the strength of unity. Hopefully future generations will be able to look back on this work and appreciate it having been done." – Leroy Gardner

GARDNER FAMILY HISTORY

Daniel Gardner, my 5x Great Grandfather, married Susannah Gholson
George Gardner, my 4x Great Grandfather, married Catherine Beckham
Lewis Gardner, my 3x Great Grandfather, married Martha Sykes
John Joseph Gardner, my 2x Great Grandfather, married Emma Wilson
Thomas Edward Gardner, my Great Grandfather, married Allie Ferguson
Hinton Douglas Gardner, my Grandfather, married Gertrude DeLaCerda

Gardner is a proud surname and it has been passed from father to son. As far back as I knew of my ancestry was my great grandfather, Thomas Edward Gardner, and then courtesy of the internet, I discovered my great – great grandfather all the way to my 5x great grandfather. Hopefully, I can trace it back to the Patriarch of the surname.

My father told me that my Gardner family was from Newton County, Mississippi and that his great – grandfather or great – great grandfather was on the Natchez Trace in Mississippi. This was either Lewis Gardner, my 3x great grandfather, or John Joseph Gardner, my 2x great grandfather. These were the only family stories about the Gardner family that I knew until I began my research.

I was about twelve years old when my father told me he believed we were possibly related to a Confederate general named Gardner who was the Rebel commander at the Battle of Port Hudson, Louisiana. I found out that it was Major General Franklin Gardner who was the "Hero of Port Hudson". After seeing a photograph of him and his strong resemblance to my father, along with the biographical information written about General Gardner, it became a passion to research my family history, along with reading and writing biographies on people with the last name Gardner.

The book was written to tell the stories of warriors named Gardner. My books tell the stories of the war heroes, prize – fighters, and gunfighters named Gardner. It is an ongoing project of researching my Gardner ancestry.

Daniel GARDNER
George GARDNER
Lewis GARDNER
John Joseph GARDNER
Thomas Edward GARDNER
Hinton Douglas GARDNER
Larry GARDNER
Corey GARDNER

DANIEL GARDNER

Born: abt. 1735 Spotsylvania County, VA
Married: Susannah Gholson
Children: Daniel, Thomas, William, George, John, and Isabella
Died: 1796 Kershaw County, SC
Notes: Daniel Gardner served as a Regulator (vigilante) in the Carolinas and it is believed he was granted 100 acres of land for his service in the American Revolution. According to Leroy Gardner, he supplied feed for the animals.
Record lists on May 14th, 1742, Daniel Gardner acknowledged his deed with livery to William Eubank in Caroline County, Virginia Colony.
Daniel Gardner being a Regulator is found at the following:
http://files.usgwarchives.net/sc/colonial/regulatr.txt
South Carolina Department of Archives and History, 1430 Senate St., Columbia, SC 29211-1669;
Daniel Gardner possibly serving in the American Revolution in Pittsylvania County, Virginia Colony:
http://www.rootsweb.ancestry.com/~vapittsy/revolutionary.htm

Daniel Gardner was born around the year 1735 and lived in Caroline, Orange, and Spotsylvania Counties in Virginia Colony. He married Susannah Gholson and they had about six children who survived adulthood. It is believed Daniel Gardner served as a Regulator in the 1760s in the Carolinas, being a vigilante enforcing laws against the outlaw gangs in those regions. It is possible he participated at the Battle of Alamance, between the Regulators and militia. It is also believed he fought in the Revolutionary War and sometime in the 1780s he removed the family to Kershaw County, South Carolina where he was granted 100 acres of land between White Oak and Beaver Creeks. Daniel Gardner died in the fall of 1796 in Kershaw County, South Carolina where he is buried at the Collins – Kilgore Cemetery.

GEORGE GARDNER

Born: abt. 1775 Virginia Colony
Married: Catherine Beckham
Children: George, Daniel, Rebecca, Lewis, John W., and possibly Cornelius Q.
Died: abt. 1835 Monroe County, GA
Notes: George Gardner fought in the War of 1812, serving in either Youngblood's South Carolina Regiment or Tucker's South Carolina Regiment in the South Carolina Militia.
National Archives, Record Group 94, Microfilm ID M652
Index Record to Complied Service Records of Volunteer South Carolina Soldiers
Gardner, George
Private, Youngblood's, 1st Regiment SC Militia
http://sciway3.net/proctor/1812/1812g.html
http://freepages.military.rootsweb.ancestry.com/~york/1812/Tuckers.html

There is a record discovered by Leroy Gardner and Frank Cook which has on September 3rd, 1822, George Gardner being arrested for assault and battery after beating a man with a chair at Beaver Creek, South Carolina.

It is believed his profession was carpenter, he being handed a contract to build his brother, John Gardner's church, the Primitive Baptist Church in Monroe County, Georgia.

George Gardner was born around the year 1775 in Virginia Colony. He lived in Kershaw County, South Carolina where he married Catherine Beckham and they had about five or six children who survived adulthood. Gardner likely served in the South Carolina Militia during the War of 1812, listed in either Youngblood's Regiment or Tucker's Regiment. It is also possible he fought in the First Seminole Indian War as there was someone by his name listed. On September 3rd, 1822, George Gardner was arrested for assault and battery on a man who trespassed onto his property. It was sometime in the 1820s, he and his brother John Gardner removed their families to Monroe County, Georgia. It is believed George Gardner worked as a carpenter and died around the year 1837 in Georgia.

His son Lewis Gardner married Martha Sykes, while his son John W. Gardner married Jane Sykes, and then married Elizabeth Sykes.

The Gardner family migrated from Caroline, Spotsylvania, and Orange Counties in Virginia Colony, then migrated to Kershaw County, South Carolina, then to Monroe and Pike Counties in Georgia, then to Shelby and Jefferson Counties in Alabama, Newton County, Mississippi, and finally to Louisiana and Texas.

LEWIS GARDNER

Lewis Gardner, my great – great – great grandfather, was born in 1810 in South Carolina and lived in Georgia where he owned a farm, married Martha Sykes, and he fathered thirteen children. He removed the family to Mississippi where he owned a plantation. It is rumored he was a bigamist, and in 1863, his wife divorced him. It is said Gardner killed a man on the Natchez Trace and went to Texas where he was a horse trader. Gardner was a gunfighter, being good with a pistol and he died about 1879 in Texas. Mystery surrounds his life, death and reputation.

JOHN JOSEPH GARDNER

John Joseph Gardner, my great – great grandfather, was born on February 26th, 1857 in Pike County, Georgia. He lived in Newton County, Mississippi where he owned a farm and he was a horse trader. Joe Gardner married Emma Wilson on November 20th, 1879 in Decatur, Mississippi. They had six children, five daughters and one son. On December 10th, 1899, he died at age 42 from liver disease because of drinking and he was buried at Crossroads Cemetery in Newton County, Mississippi. John Joseph Gardner was described as a "hard, tough man."

THOMAS EDWARD GARDNER

Thomas Edward Gardner, my great grandfather, was born on March 6th, 1891 in Newton County, Mississippi. He lived in Clarks, Caldwell Parish, Louisiana where he was a cowboy, butcher, and slaughter hand. Gardner was a rancher, he owned a farm, he owned a trucking company, and raised cattle. He married Allie Ferguson in 1914 and they had three children. Thomas Edward Gardner died from an illness on July 18th, 1965 in Pineville, Rapides Parish, Louisiana.

Allie Ferguson Gardner, my great grandmother, was born on February 10th, 1894 in Newton County, Mississippi to Redden "Doc" Ferguson and Clemenzie Jane Everett. Allie Ferguson married Thomas E. Gardner and they had three children, Hinton, Amelia, and Thomas Edward, Jr., in Clarks, Louisiana. She worked on the farm and she knitted quilts as a hobby. Allie Gardner died at age 87 on January 27th, 1982 and was buried at the Welcome Home Cemetery in Grayson, Caldwell Parish, Louisiana.

Thomas Edward Gardner on his horse.

On the left, Hinton Gardner, my grandfather and Thomas E. Gardner

HINTON DOUGLAS GARDNER

Hinton Douglas Gardner, my grandfather, was born on September 28th, 1915 in Clarks, Caldwell Parish, Louisiana. He was deaf and mute, worked on the family farm, and left home. Gardner worked as a cowboy, breaking in horses in Mexico, and then worked at a defense plant during World War II. He worked as a carpenter and was a member of Carpenters' Union No. 1098 in Baton Rouge, Louisiana. On December 28th, 1949, Hinton Gardner married Gertrude DeLaCerda and they had two children. He later retired in 1983 and he died on May 11th, 1991 from heart disease at age 75 in Baton Rouge, Louisiana.

Hinton Gardner and Gertrude Gardner in the 1940s or 50s in Louisiana. Gertrude DeLaCerda was born on October 16th, 1921 in Jackson, Louisiana. She was deaf and attended School for the Deaf in Baton Rouge, marrying Hinton Gardner. They had two children together. Gertrude Gardner died from an illness in 1992 in Baton Rouge, Louisiana.

Hinton Gardner was a tough, strong man, he stood 6 feet tall and weighed about 175 pounds. A story tells that he once lifted a dead cow over his shoulder and carried it across a field to bury it. He had been a cowboy in the LSU Rodeo at one time, he enjoyed fishing, and was an excellent carpenter.

LARRY GARDNER

Larry Gardner, my father, is a native of Baton Rouge, Louisiana. He is tall, handsome, with blue eyes, standing 6' 1, 230 pounds. Larry Gardner works as a heavy equipment operator, truck driver, backhoe operator, and bulldozer operator for various construction companies. My father is a great man.

Larry Gardner is the toughest man I've ever met in my life.

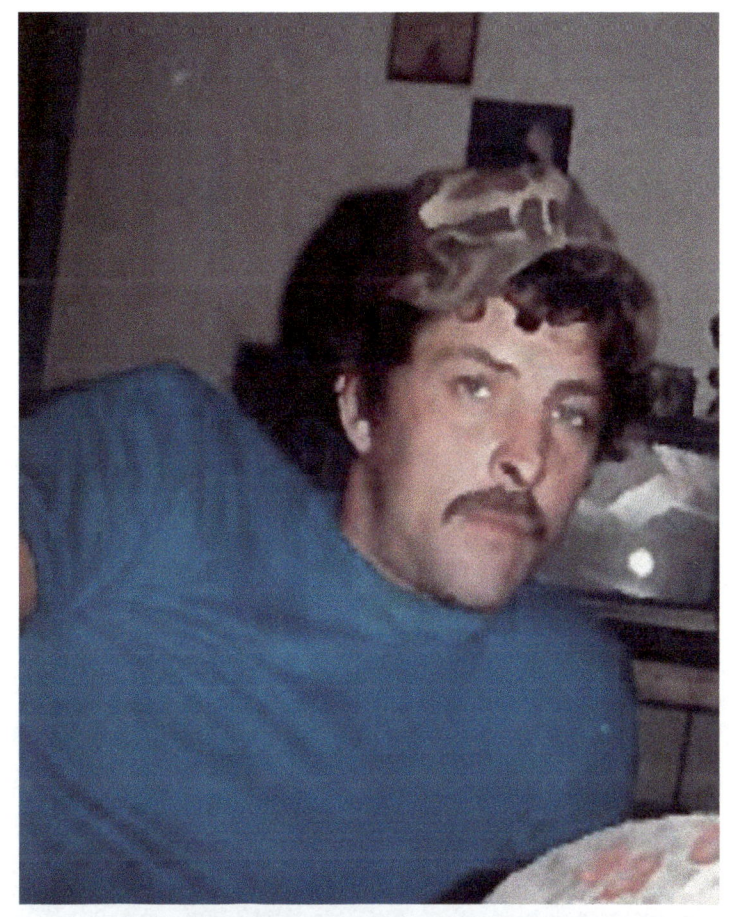

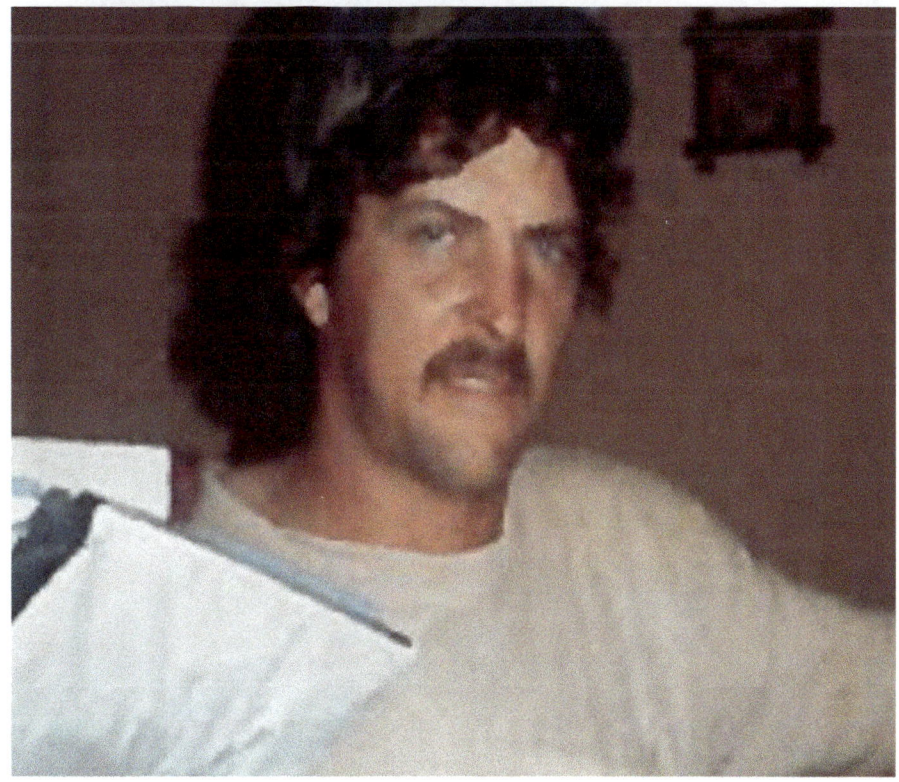

Trent Gardner

Fighting Gardners....Larry Gardner and Trent Gardner

Sons of Trent Gardner

Tyler Gardner

Quintin Gardner

Travis Gardner

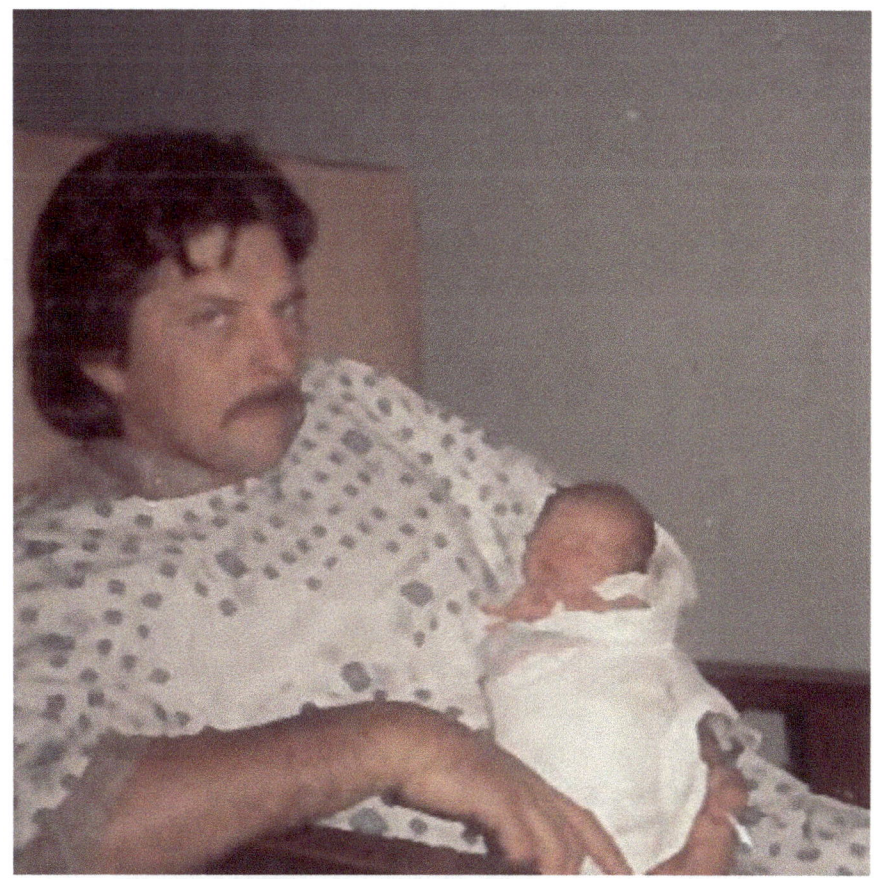

I've heard stories of my father and brother, Trent Gardner getting into barroom fights. A story tells that my father beat two men in a barroom fight, beating one down. Then when the man's friend charged my father with a broken pool stick, my father beat the other man.

My brother has even more stories of his street fights.

Jenny Gardner and Corey Gardner

Jenny Gardner, my mother, is one of the hardest working people that ever lived, a great mother, and a beautiful woman.

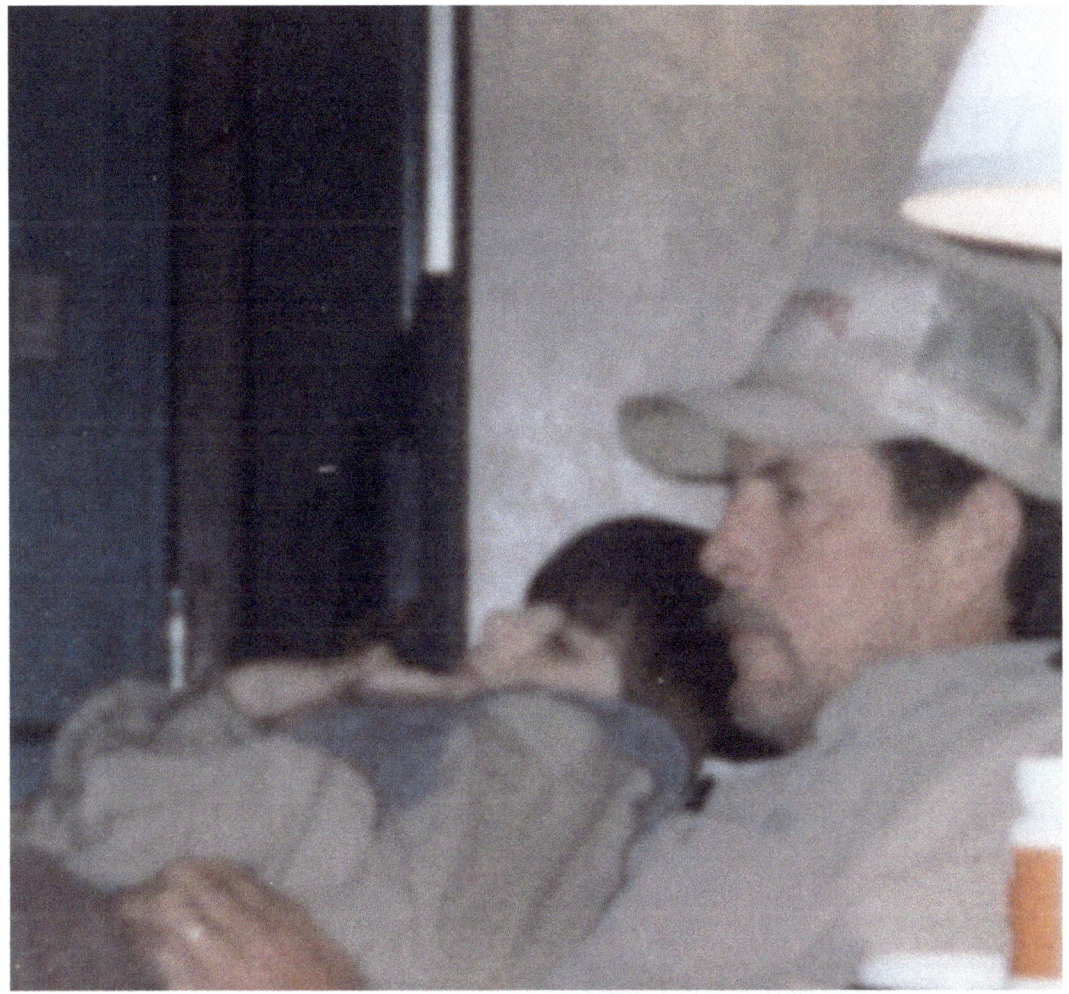

I was about nine or ten years old when I was in 4th grade and a hurricane or tornado was going to touch down in our area. They told everyone in the elementary school to gather in the hallways. I heard my name on the intercom and my parents had arrived to bring me home because of the storm.

As we drove down the street at the intersection, a crash happened right in front of us. One of the cars flipped over. Everyone in the town was frantic driving past them because of the tornado that was going to touch down.

My father pulled the car over in a parking lot and was the only person to check on the people who were in the car that was flipped over to see if they were all right.

Courtesy to Jenny and Larry Gardner

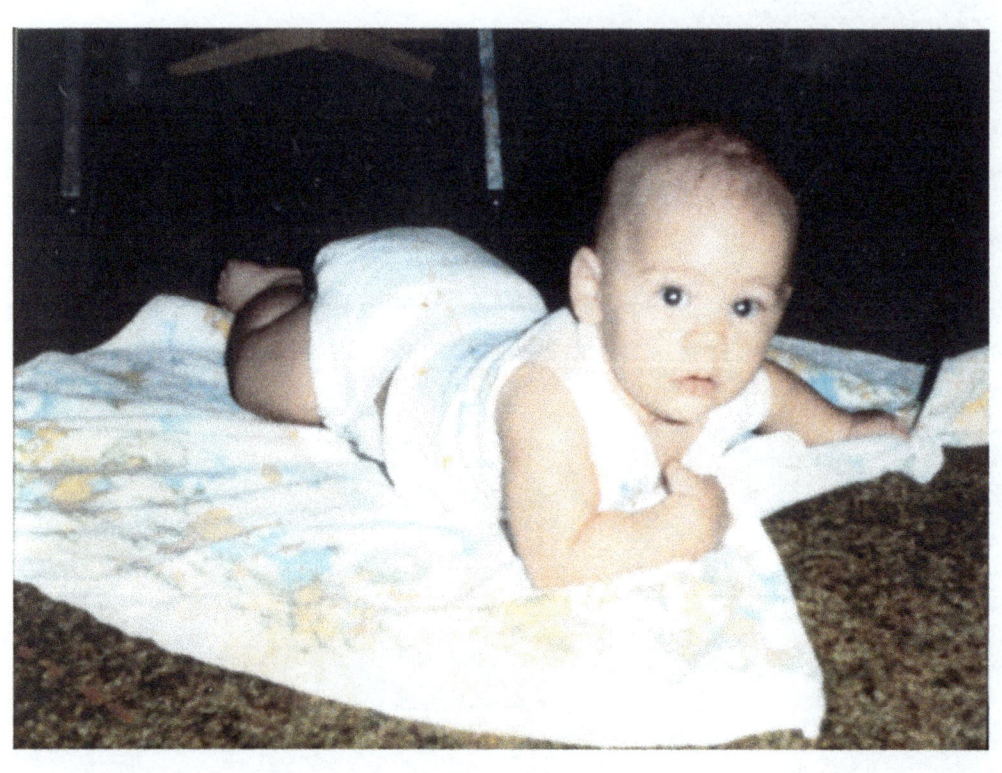

Corey Gardner - 261

COREY GARDNER

JOHN GARDNER

John Gardner, 5x great uncle (sometimes thought to be 4x Great Grandfather) was born in 1778 in Orange County, Virginia Colony to Daniel and Susannah Gholson Gardner. He was known as "Old John" Gardner and he lived in Kershaw County, South Carolina where he married Catherine "Katie" Pringle, the couple producing about fifteen children. John Gardner removed the family to Monroe County, Georgia where he owned a 365 – acre plantation and 14 slaves in 1860 when he died at age 82 from old age. John Gardner was Lewis's uncle. Courtesy to Leroy Gardner

WILLIAM ZEDRICK GARDNER

William Zedrick Gardner, my 3x great uncle, the eldest son of Lewis Gardner, was born on May 9th, 1839 in Monroe County, Georgia. He inherited his father's farm in 1859 and then served as a Confederate soldier in the 53rd Georgia Infantry as a private in the Civil War. Gardner was wounded in 1864 at Richmond, Virginia and came back home.

He fathered ten children, was a farmer, builder, and preacher in Spalding County, Georgia.

Zed Gardner died on June 6th, 1925 at age 87 from old age, described as one of Spalding County's **"oldest, wealthiest, and most influential citizens."**

Courtesy to *GARDNER/BALLARD and ALLIED FAMILIES* by Chris and Leroy Gardner

Courtesy to Darlene Allen for photograph of William Zedrick Gardner

WILEY JACKSON GARDNER

Wiley Jackson Gardner, my 3x great uncle, the second son of Lewis Gardner, was born on October 19th, 1844 in Monroe County, Georgia. He removed to Newton County, Mississippi with his parents in 1859 and enlisted in the 13th Mississippi Infantry during the Civil War, being stationed in Virginia. According to his Veterans' papers, he was 5' 11, with a light complexion, dark hair, and hazel eyes at age 17, being sent back home due to malaria.

According to photographs, he looked to be about six feet tall, over 200 pounds, and dark complexioned.

Gardner enlisted in the 2nd Mississippi Cavalry and earned the rank of corporal, serving under General Johnston while fighting around Atlanta, and later serving under General Hood while at Nashville, and finally at Selma, Alabama.

After the war, he married Quantillia Pullin in 1865 and hauled lumber to Dallas County, Texas, where he was an early pioneer. Gardner served as Master of the Masonic Lodge No. 444 and was later elected as a Dallas County Commissioner in 1888, in the Red District. His eldest son, John A. Gardner was arrested in December of 1892 for murder in Dallas, and his youngest son, Dick Gardner was a noted undercover narcotics detective.

Wiley Jackson Gardner died at age 79 on November 4th, 1924 in Dallas County, Texas.

Courtesy to *GARDNER/BALLARD and ALLIED FAMILIES* by Chris and Leroy Gardner

DANIEL WEBSTER GARDNER

Daniel Webster Gardner, my 3x great uncle, the third son of Lewis Gardner, was born on June 4th, 1846 in Pike County, Georgia. He lived in Newton County, Mississippi and enlisted in the 16th Mississippi Cavalry. Gardner served as a scout and messenger, describing it as a great adventure.

He married Regina Ann Graham in 1866 and removed the family to Van Zandt County, Texas, and later to Coryell County, Texas where he was a farmer.

Dan Gardner died at age 83 from Bright's disease in 1930 and was buried in Bosque County, Texas.

Courtesy to Leroy Gardner

JOHN JOSEPH GARDNER

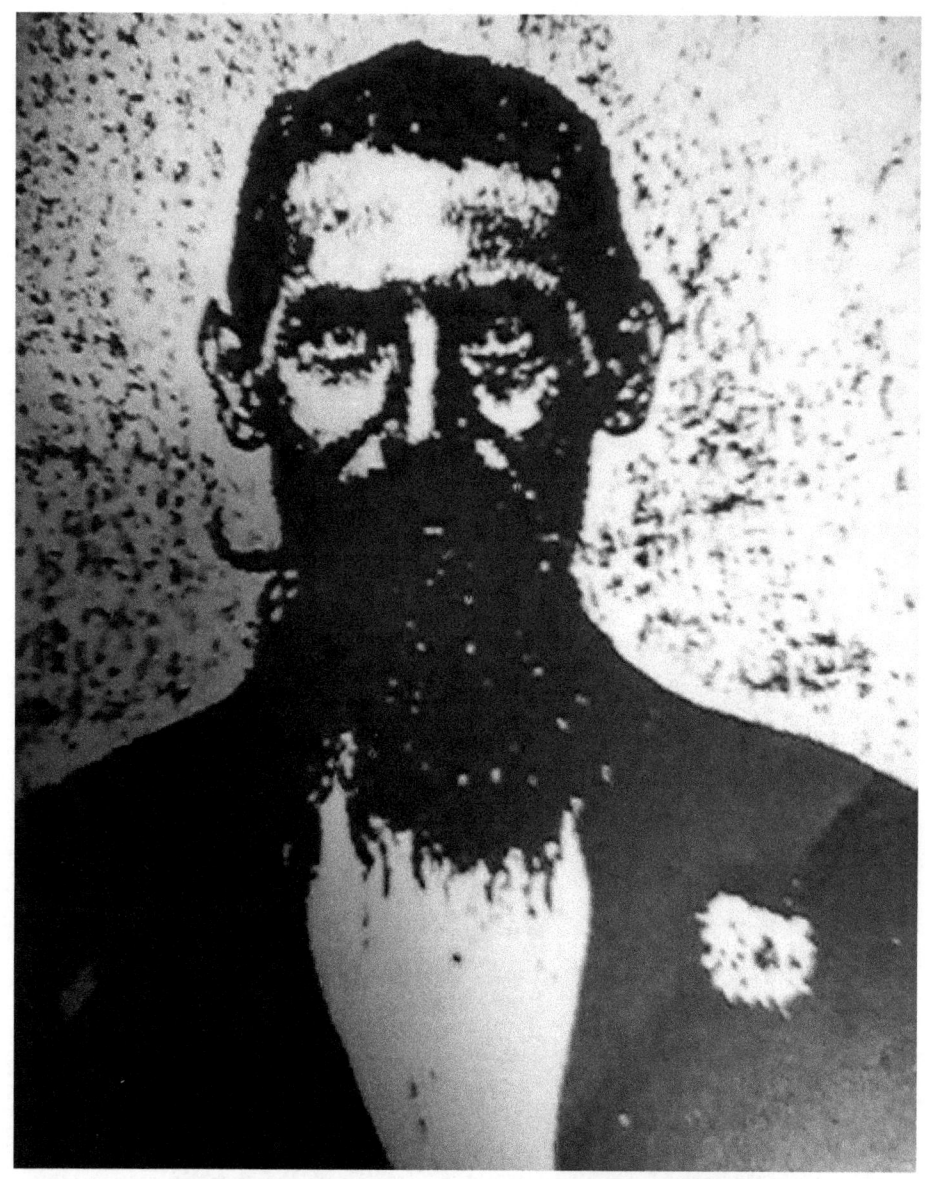

John Joseph Gardner, my great – great grandfather, the fourth son of Lewis Gardner, was born on February 26th, 1857 in Pike County, Georgia. His family removed to Newton County, Mississippi, his parents divorced in 1863, and in 1878 his mother deeded him the family farm. Afterwards, he married Imogene "Emma" Wilson on November 20th, 1879 in Decatur, Mississippi and they had six children.

Gardner was described as a **"hard, tough man"**.

John J. Gardner was a horse trader and he later died at age 42 from liver disease because of drinking on December 10th, 1899 in Hazel, Mississippi.

There is record of a cowboy named Joe Gardner in 1874, being arrested for cattle rustling in 1874 in Mason County, Texas.

There is also record of a man named John Gardner who was arrested for murder in May of 1878 in Houston County, Texas, on February 1st, 1878 according to the *Brenham Daily Banner*.

Lewis Gardner lived in Houston County for a time and it is possible his son John Joseph Gardner lived in Texas.

Courtesy to Elsie Ferguson Broussard for photograph of John Joseph Gardner

DANIEL JEFFERSON GARDNER FAMILY

Front row seated: Daniel Jefferson Gardner, Berry Gardner, Sallie, Aletha, William Frederick Gardner, and Amanda

Back row standing: Emma, Samuel Gardner, Martha, Daniel Jefferson Gardner, Jr., Loula, Thomas Gardner, and Jas. Gardner.

Daniel Jefferson Gardner was born in the 1830s in Georgia, son of Samuel Gardner, grandson of "Old John" Gardner of Monroe County, Georgia. He lived in Scott County, Mississippi where he owned a farm, married four times, and fathered a number of children. Gardner fought in the Civil War as a Confederate soldier. It was said Gardner killed a man in Mississippi and removed to Lincoln Parish, Louisiana where he was the largest land owner for a number of years, one of the first in the region to own a steam cotton gin. Gardner operated a large cattle business and died in 1902 in Ruston, Louisiana.

References:
The Story of John Gardner of Monroe County, Georgia and his descendants by Julia Slemons Harrison Riedel

Courtesy to Leroy Gardner

SAMUEL THOMAS GARDNER

Samuel Thomas Gardner was born in 1855 in Monroe County, Georgia. His father was Jas. Gardner, a gunsmith and farmer. His brother was William G. Gardner, a war hero who had been a Confederate sharpshooter in the War Between the States. They were descendants of "Old" John Gardner of Monroe County, Georgia. Samuel Thomas Gardner married Frances Alice Wilson, who he is pictured with and they lived in Newton County, Mississippi where he owned a farm.

GARDNER FAMILY REUNION, 1913, SPALDING, GA

Left to Right:

Wiley Jackson Gardner, William Zedrick Gardner, Nancy Ann Gardner Graham, and William Zedrick Gardner's sons, William Thomas Gardner and John Davis Gardner.

References:
GARDNER/BALLARD and ALLIED FAMILIES by Chris and Leroy Gardner

WILEY JACKSON GARDNER FAMILY

Wiley Jackson Gardner's sons, left to right:
Standing: Henry Gardner, Hugh Gardner, and Dick Gardner
Sitting: Joe Gardner, John Gardner, and Lewis Wiley Gardner

John A. Gardner was arrested in December of 1892 for killing a man outside of a saloon in Dallas, Texas.
Lewis Wiley Gardner was a farmer in Texas.
Joe Gardner was a farmer in Kaufman County, Texas.
Henry Gardner was a deputy sheriff in Dallas County, Texas.
Hugh Gardner was a farmer and businessman in Dallas County, Texas.
William Daniel "Dick" Gardner was a noted undercover narcotics detective for the Dallas Police Department.

Courtesy to Steve Gardner of Dallas, Texas

JOHN JOSEPH GARDNER FAMILY

John Joseph Gardner's children, left to right:

Josie Gardner Hughes, Thomas Edward Gardner, Beulah Gardner Mabry, and Georgia Ann Gardner Ferguson

Courtesy to Raymond Hicks, son of Irma Amelia Gardner Hicks, daughter of Thomas Edward Gardner

THOMAS E. GARDNER FAMILY

Left to right: Amelia Gardner, Hinton Gardner, Thomas E. Gardner, Sr.,
Thomas E. Gardner, Jr., and Allie Ferguson Gardner

Courtesy to Larry Gardner

COREY GARDNER

9 781733 929806